Feminist and Human Rights Struggles in Peru

DISSIDENT FEMINISMS

Piya Chatterjee, Editor

A list of books in the series appears at the end of this book.

Feminist and Human Rights Struggles in Peru

Decolonizing Transitional Justice

PASCHA BUENO-HANSEN

UNIVERSITY OF ILLINOIS PRESS

Urbana, Chicago, and Springfield

An earlier version of chapter 5 was published as "Finding
Each Other's Hearts: Intercultural Relations and the Drive to
Sexual Violence during the Internal Armed Conflict in Peru,"
International Feminist Journal of Politics 12, no. 3–4 (2010): 319–40.

Library of Congress Cataloging-in-Publication Data
Bueno-Hansen, Pascha.
Feminist and human rights struggles in Peru : decolonizing
transitional justice / Pascha Bueno-Hansen.
    pages cm. — (Dissident feminisms)
Includes bibliographical references and index.
ISBN 978-0-252-03942-3 (hbk. : alk. paper) —
ISBN 978-0-252-08100-2 (pbk. : alk. paper) —
ISBN 978-0-252-09753-9 (e-book)
1. Human rights movements—Peru. 2. Feminism—Peru.
3. Transitional justice—Peru. I. Title.
JC599.P4B845   2015
323.3'40985—dc23   2015003891

A todas las Rosa Cuchillos

y

mi amor, Ana Karina Borja Rodriguez

Contents

Acknowledgments

Dissecting the intricacies of oppression while searching for glimpses of alternative yet always imperfect humanizing gestures and actions demands a source of spiritual and emotional sustenance. I found this source in the creative envisioning held within performance art, specifically the work of *Grupo Cultural Yuyachkani*. I turned to the theater pieces of *Rosa Cuchillo*, *Antígona*, and *Pirca Wasi / Kay Punku*, in times of fatigue and emotional exhaustion, to open spaces oriented by strength, dignity, resilience, healing, and hope. The image of *Rosa Cuchillo* on the cover evokes this connection.

My writing process has always been intimately intertwined with those of friends and colleagues. Rose Cohen, Elisa Diana Huerta, and Gina Velasco, as well as Marco Mojica and Rashad Shabazz, helped to shape and ultimately birth the earlier draft of this book. Those writing-group meetings sustained me, inspired me, and kept it real with the motto, "Get the words on the page." I am also deeply grateful for the guidance I received from Sonia Alvarez, Kent Eaton, Angela Davis, and Rosa Linda Fregoso, who all continue to be great inspirations.

I am ever grateful for the two collaborative projects that started during my time at the University of California, Santa Cruz, the Transloca research cluster, and the Santa Cruz Feminist of Color Collaborative. The Transloca research cluster brought together feminist scholars from throughout the Américas to partake in a sustained, hemispheric dialogue. The principle concern with the feminist politics of translation across the Américas directly informs my approach in this work. The Santa Cruz Feminist of Color Collective rooted me further in the political stakes involved in knowledge production, taught me how to move through conflict productively, and demonstrated the healing power of collective envisioning and intergenerational connection: *gracias hermanas*.

While I wrote this book, the groups who got me through the later drafts shifted to the virtual and reconfigured to include Rashad Shabazz, Kalindi Vora, and Sora Han, who offered excellent advice. Susy Zepeda and Sandra Alvarez have continually given me great insights and comments. Even though we were spread thousands of miles apart, these virtual group meetings nurtured in us the critical interdisciplinary spirit of our UC Santa Cruz graduate training in the early years of this century.

Rashad Shabazz has been my most consistent intellectual *hermano* during the past eight years. We moved through the drafts and final manuscript in lock step. When things would start to feel crazy, I always knew an open-hearted conversation with him would bring perspective to the situation. Thank you, Rashad, for being such an absolutely incredible human being and friend.

At the University of Delaware, the Hemispheric Dialogues research cluster provided important guidance and feedback on the book as well an intellectual home. A special thanks to *mis queridas colegas* Alvina Quintana, Monica Dominguez Torres, Gladys Ilarregui, Rosalie Rolon Dow, and Carla Guerron Montero. Alvina Quintana, thank you for taking me under your wing as an intellectual *sobrina* and demystifying the tenure-track process. I also want to thank my colleagues in the Women and Gender Studies Department, Sue Cherrin, Kathy Turkel, Jennifer Nacarelli, Margaret Stetz, Monika Shafi, Marie Laberge, Alvina Quintana, and Deborah Arnold for all of their encouragement and support over the years.

Having received feedback from so many people, I apologize in advance for any omissions. A few people who stand out significantly include Alvina Quintana, Sonia Alvarez, Gina Dent, Anjali Arondekar, Elizabeth Jay Freeman, Cristina Akalde, Antonia Randolph, Maggie Ussery, Lauren Balasco, Johanna Drzewieniecki, the editors at the University of Illinois Press—Larin McLaughlin, Piya Chaterjee, and Dawn Durante—and the anonymous reviewer. Genevieve Beenen provided editorial support, and at the University of Delaware Nico Carver worked with me on the images, and John Stevenson prepared the maps.

Various grants and fellowships funded the research I conducted to complete this book, which include: the University of Delaware General University Research Program Grant, the UC Chancellor's Writing Fellowship the UC Pacific Rim Program Research Fellowship, the National Women's

Studies Association Fellowship, and the UCSC Feminist Studies Fellowship. I extend a heartfelt thanks to the International Studies Association—Northeast regional governing council and Jennifer Lobasz for honoring me with the Northeast Circle award. The feedback I received from Giovanni Mantilla, Jessica Auchter, Stefanie Fishel, and Dave Benjamin allowed me to re-engage the manuscript at a particularly challenging moment.

In Peru, the book is indebted to the feminist NGO *Estudio por la defensa de los derechos de la mujer* (DEMUS) and specifically the Manta fieldwork team, including Paula Escribens, Diana Portal, Tesania Velázquez, Silvia Ruiz, and Jessenia Casani. María Ysabel Cedano's friendship and enthusiastic support made this book possible. Rossy Salazar, as well as the rest of the DEMUS staff, provided crucial information and insights. Nora Cárdenas and Eloy Neira have been important interlocutors throughout. I am deeply grateful to the community of Manta for welcoming me as a researcher with the DEMUS Manta fieldwork team and all the community members who shared their time and perspectives. Ricardo Ramirez, Johanns Rodriguez, and Ruth Borja of the Centro de Información del Defensoria del Pueblo provided invaluable assistance with the Peruvian Truth and Reconciliation Commission archives. Julissa Mantilla Falcón, Narda Henríquez Ayín, and Mercedes Crisóstomo Meza contributed numerous insights over the years of this research, which benefited this project enormously. Throughout, Marie Manrique always offered a receptive ear and perceptive observations, as well as a treasured friendship. Thank you Marie for helping me through the last part. Maruja Barrig has been a consistent interlocutor over the years, and I am grateful for her generosity at every stage, especially facilitating access to the *Mujeres por la Democracia* (MUDE) archives. Cristina Cornejo, Gonzalo Cornejo, Ricardo Alvarado, Marisol Vega, Viviana Valz Gen, Eduardo Espinoza, Silvia Loli, Gloria Huamani, and Jose Carlos Aguero all contributed to this work.

To my love, Ana Karina Borja Rodriguez. I dedicate this book to you and in recognition of all the sacrifices we have had to withstand to see it in print.

I give thanks to my family for believing in me and encouraging me: Ada Gabriela Bueno and Lloyd Sugasgi, Joe and Angela Hansen, Luz Bueno, Sylvain, Raquel, Paul and Martin Bournhonesque, Theresa Hansen and the whole Greensboro contingent, Vivian and Mario Zelaya, and my cherished daughter, Thais. And in Peru, the Winklemans in Lima and the Buenos in Cusco. And from the other side, I always feel the loving support of Jo Ellen and Alfred Hansen and Elizabeth and Antero Bueno, as well as *mi tía abuela* Hortensia Bueno *y mi tío abuelo* Lucio Bueno, who proudly referred to me as *la dama investigadora*, thereby validating this path I have chosen.

Feminist and Human Rights
Struggles in Peru

Waiting in the Garden of Broken Trees

She pulled out an eight-by-ten photo from one of her bags and explained that her daughter had been taken in the night, and she had not seen her since. Kidnapping and disappearance as well as mass burials of subversives were common during the Peruvian internal armed conflict (1980–2000). She handed me the large photo of a young woman's face with eyes that met me with a strong and clear gaze, her hair pulled back in soft waves. I received the picture, holding it respectfully as I contemplated the image. After some moments of silence, I commented that her daughter was very pretty. She nodded and said that her daughter was only seventeen when she was taken, that she was a very good student and she had not done anything wrong. As she described in more detail the qualities of her daughter and the search she had undertaken over the years, I felt our emotions building in intensity.

Other testimonies tumbled into the foreground of my thoughts—at the Peruvian Truth and Reconciliation Commission's Thematic Public Hearing on Political Violence and Crimes against Women, the woman who testified to having her two daughters, age fifteen and eighteen, taken by soldiers—and who knows what the soldiers did to them. . . . and the Commission's finding that military bases and police stations were spaces wherein officials systematically perpetrated sexual violence. This young woman, her wavy hair softly framing her face, probably had to endure insults, torture, and sexual abuses before her death. I quickly beat back those horrific thoughts, focusing all my attention on the woman before me and the picture that I held in my hands. She continued with her story of time being broken, of not being able to live without knowing where her daughter was and what had happened to her. I asked her when her daughter had been taken, and she said 1985.

More than twenty years had passed since that terrible night. She mentioned the sacrifices involved in traveling to the Andean regional capital of Ayacucho over the years, of the exhausting trip from her rural community and the cost of transportation and work lost. People had told her that her search was in vain, yet she continued. As she slowly came back into herself from telling of her daughter's disappearance and her endless search, she shifted her gaze from the open sky above the buildings to look at me sitting by her side in a garden of broken trees. She asked why I was waiting for the human rights attorney, since we both sat in front of his office that early morning. I said that I was doing research on the effects of the Peruvian internal armed conflict and the work of human rights advocates. A heavy silence invaded the space between us, pregnant with the historic and structural power asymmetries embodied in our differences. She struggled to survive, with much of her time and resources diverted to her search; I travelled in the luxury of interregional buses to conduct a funded research project. She began to ask me about reparations, if there would ever be any, and if so, when? I told her what I knew, that there would be reparations, but individual economic indemnification would probably take a few more years. To that, she responded that she was getting old, that she would not be able to continue coming to check with the human rights attorney about her case, and if it took too long, she would probably no longer be around.

* * *

In the 1980s and 1990s, Peru experienced an internal armed conflict, and for many like the woman I sat with, Rosa Cuchillo,[1] the aftermath continues to direct their lives. Instead of waiting idly for justice, Rosa Cuchillo commits her life to finding her missing daughter. She and the many others like her inspire me to write against impunity, oblivion, and dehumanization.

More than ten years have passed since the Peruvian Truth and Reconciliation Commission (PTRC) (2001–2003) concluded its investigation into the causes and consequences of the internal armed conflict (1980–2000). The political will and public resolve that is necessary for follow-through on the recommendations for institutional, judicial, and policy reform is lacking. Human rights cases continue to backslide in the national legal system.[2] A deepening sense of pessimism and resignation to the workings of inequality and impunity pervade discussions of Peruvian transitional justice. Initiated in the 1980s, transitional justice as a field and practice developed to focus on the political shift away from instability, violence, and repression toward democracy. Approximately two decades into the globalized practice of transitional justice, the PTRC has been lauded as an example of a strong transitional justice process. Yet the PTRC has little to show for itself. The tensions between the goals of justice and deterring future human rights violations and the goals of reconciliation, re-legitimating the state-in-crisis and promoting democracy constitute a central area of concern for scholars and practitioners.

Given the central role that international human rights law plays in the transitional justice processes, this book seeks to underscore its paradoxical character. While well-meaning actors and institutions may mobilize international human rights law to defend rights, such efforts may also lead to further erasure and silencing. Studying the practice of human rights within transitional justice leads to the following questions: Who is visible as a subject under the human rights optic, and how are they rendered visible or invisible? Who is left outside the purview of this human rights optic, and what types of violence remain unaddressed? The goal of expanding transitional justice demands working within the paradox of international human rights law to stretch the framework for thinking about what happened, as well as reframing what can be considered harm.[3]

Gender-based violence serves as the entry point for thinking about how inequality functions within the Peruvian transitional justice process. The gender-based aspect of violence identifies how women are targeted for certain violations because they are women. This examination contributes to the scant literature on the topic of gender-based violence during the Peruvian internal armed conflict.[4] In the process, the book takes stock of the approaches for thinking about the impact of conflict on women and gender-based violence, the limitations of those approaches, and possible alternative paths.

An intersectional analytical sensibility pays attention to how vectors of oppression interact. For example, in the context of the United States, this analytic underscores how gender and race interact to increase the social vulnerability of certain people, particularly women of color. In the context of Peru, an intersectional analytic sensibility reads for the factors, such as ethnicity, language, and gender, that interact to compound the effect of the internal armed conflict on certain people, in this case Andean Quechua-speaking women peasants, *campesinas*. To understand the roots of this violence, decolonial feminisms study the ways that colonial relations of exploitation and domination function and persist to the present day. Decolonial feminisms aim toward full recognition of all by overcoming the "complex interaction of economic, racializing and gendering systems."[5] Combining an intersectional analytic sensibility with decolonial feminisms enables us to theorize more fully the Latin American and specifically Peruvian context. As a result, this examination historically situates gender-based violence, the reasoning that sustains it, and its ongoing impunity as related to the legacy of colonialism in Peru.

Between 2005 and 2012, a total of sixteen months of multi-sited field research in the regional capital city of Ayacucho, the district of Manta in the region of Huancavelica, and the national capital city of Lima provide the basis for this book. Archival research, participant observation, interviews, and discussion groups compose the main elements of this feminist inter-disciplinary approach. Empirical examination, intertextual analysis, and theoretical reflection weave together throughout. Peruvian human rights and feminist movements, the PTRC and a feminist nongovernmental orga-nization (NGO) make up the units of study, with a focus on their negotia-tion between implementing international human rights law and holistically addressing gender-based violence.

In an effort to add breadth to transitional justice discussions, the pres-ent analysis prioritizes the voices and analytical frames of NGO employees, human-rights-activists and feminist-activists, PTRC volunteers and staff, and rural community members in the Andean highlands. Rosa Cuchillo, the woman I sat with in the garden of broken trees, cannot be reduced to a statistic of families of the disappeared. Her struggle, along with that of many others like her, exceeds the category of victim and gives voice to individual and collective understandings of what happened during the internal armed conflict, as well as the demands for justice, reparations, and an end to social inequality. Likewise, the human rights attorney we sat waiting for represents many advocates, practitioners, and activists who dedicate their life energies to the pursuit of justice. In that instance, the human rights attorney could not be found because he was working with forensic anthropologists, repre-sentatives of the district attorneys office, families of those disappeared, and others to exhume a mass grave at a nearby military base.

Productive critique of the limits of human rights and transitional justice balance with consideration of the way the social actors within social move-ments, state institutions, and civil society organizations creatively envision, propose, and enact alternative social relations. This focus falls in line with contemporary efforts to critically assess local practices of transitional justice mechanisms.[6] The practice and theory of transitional justice evolves in rela-tion to the contexts in which it takes form. While grounding this analysis in historical context, practical and theoretical insights suggest ways to move transitional justice processes toward their transformative potential.

Internal Armed Conflict, Social Inequality, and Transitional Justice

The Peruvian internal armed conflict (1980–2000) started when the Shining Path—Communist Party of Peru (Sendero Luminoso) rejected formal incorporation as a political party into the Peruvian political system. During the 1980 elections, the Shining Path burned ballot boxes in the rural Andean community of Chucchi, Ayacucho, and took up arms with the goal of overthrowing the government through a Maoist revolution. Other armed actors included the Tupac Amaru Revolutionary Movement (MRTA) and the armed forces.[7] While initiated in the Andean department of Ayacucho, during the 1980s the violence expanded out, gravely affecting the neighboring Andean departments of Huancavelica, Junín, and Apurimac, and the Amazonian departments of San Martín and Huanuco. Caught in the crossfire, civilians, mostly Quechua-speaking peasants, suffered greatly, losing their lives, families, homes, livestock, agricultural lands, and livelihoods. Many were thrown into the chaos and desperation of forced displacement, as well as the continuous search for disappeared loved ones.

In the late 1980s and early 1990s the violence reached the capital city of Lima: car bombs, assassinations, and power outages became everyday

World locator. (Peru [orthographic projection] adapted under creative commons license [CC BY-SA 3.0] from the original by John A. Stevenson, Addicted04, Connorm.)

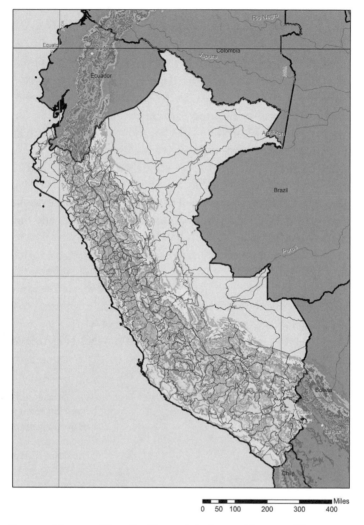

Topographic map of Peru: Pacific coast, Andes, and Amazon. (Map created by John A. Stevenson using ArcGIS.)

news. Then, the conflict dramatically decreased in 1992, when President Alberto Fujimori captured the leader of the Shining Path, Abimael Guzmán, as well as the top cadre of forces. Regional-level political organizing for peace, especially in Ayacucho, grew in strength through the 1980s and early 1990s, contributing significantly to the decline of the conflict. The Shining

Path activities decreased in the 1990s due to lack of leadership and strong national sentiment for ending the violence.

Instead of a national peace accord or formalized halt to aggression through disarmament, the Peruvian armed conflict dwindled to an end, giving way to a national movement against corruption and for democracy and human rights that brought an end to Fujimori's authoritarian regime (1990–2000). In the wake of the conflict and Fujimori's rule, Peru mobilized international human rights law through a transitional justice process to reestablish its legitimacy. Chapter 1 offers an account of this moment of transition with a focus on the role of the human rights and feminist movements.

The field of transitional justice has gained ground over the past several decades in response to the needs of postconflict societies, which have typically fallen beyond the reach of criminal law and formal justice mechanisms.[8] The term *transitional justice* marks a shift in approaching the contexts of political transition and the problems encountered by human rights advocates and activists. Transitional justice signals a response to these problems, "a new sort of human rights activity,"[9] exemplified in transitional president Valentín Paniagua's creation of the Peruvian Truth Commission in 2000. President Alejandro Toledo then mandated the Peruvian Truth and Reconciliation Commission (2001–2003).[10] The PTRC investigated the internal armed conflict with a focus on human rights violations such as torture, extrajudicial execution, kidnapping, assassination, and disappearance.

According to the PTRC final report, a majority of the 69,280 victims who lost their lives in the conflict were Andean Quechua speakers or Amazonians from the Amuesha, Asháninka, or Nomatsiguenga ethnolinguistic groups. Seventy-five percent of those killed were of indigenous origin. The conclusions of the PTRC note that the generalized disregard of this tragedy links back to the historical devaluation of Andean and Amazonian populations since the beginning of the republic. Marisol de la Cadena asserts that the finding puts ethnic discrimination into question for the first time in the history of Peru. "Made public, this truth obliges us to at least begin to interrogate the history of modernity and see how it has legitimated inequality,"[11] an endeavor that requires critical reflection on the legacy of colonialism, which decolonial feminisms facilitates, with a focus on gender, sexuality, and violence.

Ethnic discrimination in Peru has its roots in the colonial encounter with Spain. The colonizers considered themselves as civilized in contrast to the natives. Through the nineteenth and twentieth centuries, the Peruvian nation-state adapted this social hierarchy into an understanding of what it means to be modern. Peruvians' distance from or proximity to the modern ideal determines their access to citizenship.[12] In other words, those who more closely resemble the lighter-skinned, heteronormative, Spanish-speaking, able-bodied, and literate male have more access to citizenship. The resulting ethnicized underclass and the contemporary violence perpetrated against them echoes patterns of domination that shift in shape given the actors and context. Such a critical reflection on the legacy of colonialism historicizes the formation of the nation-state and elucidates how it is implicated in embedded layers of racialized and gender-based violence.

The extreme violence of the internal armed conflict exacerbated historic inequalities, destabilized the state, and drove it to implement transitional justice mechanisms. The contemporary selection of transitional justice mechanisms includes domestic trials, international criminal tribunals, amnesties, truth and reconciliation commissions, and the international criminal court. Truth commissions emerge in response to lack of political will to pursue criminal accountability for human rights violations during armed conflict and the "inflexibility and formality of criminal legal process."[13] Peru decided upon a truth and reconciliation commission and the preparation of cases for domestic trial. The PTRC had the goal of social reconciliation, embodying a peace-oriented restorative approach. In addition, the PTRC collected approximately seventeen thousand testimonies and conducted public hearings to reveal the truth, listen to the victims, and reconcile society. The PTRC also prepared forty-seven legal cases for prosecution in the Peruvian judicial system,[14] exemplifying a justice-oriented retributive approach. This combination balanced the drive for peace and justice while fostering reconciliation. The adoption of these mechanisms demonstrates a rare moment in which the state expressed a disposition to address past human rights violations.

In terms of addressing the effects of the conflict on women, the PTRC belongs to the first wave of commissions since 2000 to incorporate a gender-sensitive approach, along with Liberia, Timor-Leste, Sierra Leone, and Morocco. Prior to that, the Haitian Commission's mandate (1995–1996) was one of the first to include specific language regarding sexual violence committed against women for political ends. Although this precedent had been set, the PTRC's mandate did not include such language, so a gender analysis and documentation of sexual violence were added on later. Newly developing international human rights gender norms,[15] international pressure, and internal PTRC advocacy created the context for this belated inclusion. Chapter 2 explicates the process by which a gender analysis and sexual violence came under the scope of the PTRC.

The PTRC was the first in Latin America to hold public hearings modeled after the South African Truth Commission (1995–2002) and their ground-breaking special hearing for women. Within the scope of the PTRC public hearings, the commissioners developed a thematic hearing on the effects of the conflict on women, which is the focus of chapter 3. The Guatemalan Commission for Historical Clarification (1997–1999) established the precedent of including a chapter in the final report on sexual violence against women. Peru followed suit by building upon the definition of sexual violence in the Rome Statute of the International Criminal Court (ICC) while also taking into consideration the Guatemalan experience, which underscored the likelihood of statistical underrepresentation of sexual violence.[16] The PTRC gender unit, in collaboration with the PTRC juridical team's sexual violence component, used an international human rights framework to expose sexual violence as a human rights violation. Of the acts of sexual violence reported, 83.46 percent were committed against women.[17] Combining this information with the ethnolinguistic profile of the victims reveals that rural Quechua-speaking peasant women, *campesinas*, were the targets of sexual violence.

Sexual Violence and Women as Victims

The opening vignette illustrates the tendency to fixate on sexual violence and my struggle to fully hear Rosa Cuchillo's personal account. Conceptual myopia around sexual violence vexed my early research in Ayacucho, the department in the Andes most heavily affected by the Peruvian internal armed conflict (1980–2000). A number of feminist scholars criticize the exclusive focus on sexual violence in that it tends to erase other aspects of women's experiences of conflict and a more comprehensive gender analysis.[18] This narrow focus hides the complex ways victims understand and manage the consequences of what they live through, which represents the subject of chapter 4. Indeed, in studying what happened to women during the Peruvian internal armed conflict, the intense focus on sexual violence tends to flatten the realities of the subjects, Andean Quechua-speaking rural women. Ní Aoláin, Haynes, and Cahn assert that the political and legal tools used for postconflict accountability do not fully address the range of violations women experience. "A more transformative and structural response will be required at both the domestic and international level."[19] Reaching beyond a focus on the victimization of women, this approach contributes to a transformative and structural response to the harms done to women during conflict.[20]

This critique of conceptual myopia regarding sexual violence simultaneously acknowledges women's rights advocates' and activists' great strides over the past two decades in the recognition of harms against women during armed conflict. The ad hoc tribunals for the former Yugoslavia and Rwanda in the early 1990s mark the beginning of this growing international awareness, building from the nascent efforts to prosecute crimes against women in the International Military Tribunal at Nuremburg and the International Military Tribunal for the Far East (Tokyo Trials).[21] These developments in international law facilitate a paradigmatic shift from defining rape as a violation of family honor to a crime against humanity and a war crime. The development of the legal framework for addressing sexual violence helps to show how women's rights activists and advocates constantly press for revision of the law in order to better facilitate justice.[22] Feminist legal scholars elucidate the gendered dimensions of the law and craft legal tools to address the systematic impunity surrounding sexual violence through criminal accountability.

The Rome Statute embodies one of the most significant contemporary developments in the area of women's rights during armed conflict, shifting the conversation from rape to the more comprehensive legal category of sexual violence. The Rome Statute's article 7.1 defines sexual violence as—"a sexual act realized against one or more people or when these individuals are forced to realize a sexual act among themselves: by force or threat of force or coercion due to fear of violence, intimidation, detention, psychological oppression or abuse of power against these persons or others or taking advantage of an environment of coercion or the incapacity of these persons to give their free consent." Sexual violence includes "rape, sexual slavery, enforced prostitution, forced pregnancy, enforced sterilization, or any other form of sexual violence of comparable gravity are crimes against humanity."[23] These definitions establish an internationally recognized scope of violations that comprise sexual violence. Peru ratified the Rome Statute in November 10, 2001, but has yet to integrate it into the penal system.

Given the tendency to focus on sexual violence in contexts of conflict, international human rights law has had mixed results for women, providing an important yet contradictory site for feminist activism—but nevertheless offering the most effective political discourse to name what happened to women even though the law never fully redresses the scope of harm. As Wendy Brown highlights, we work within the paradox of rights, doing the best we can with the available tools.[24] For example, the PTRC's use of international human rights law made the spectrum of gender-based violence only partially visible. One of the documents discussed by Peruvian commissioners,

"General Suggestions for a Discussion on the Juridical Focus of Human Rights in the TRC," underscores the limitations inherent in addressing sexual violence through law. "The TRC's use of legal categories to document human rights violations, collect information, construct a research design, organize a database, identify consequences, and establish recommendations for reparations, reflects national and international limitations on thinking about sexual violence and gender-based violence more broadly."[25] The PTRC gender analysis, doing the best it could with the available tools, adopted the focus on sexual violence against women into its methodology and overall investigation.

To move beyond conceptual myopia around sexual violence and its inevitable production of women as victims, an intersectional sensibility toward gender-based violence broadens the analytical frame. In addition, analyzing human rights as a discourse assumes that it is constituted in social practice and as a cultural process.[26] A discursive analysis of human rights reveals its underlying logics and default subjects as well as its material effects.[27]

Two threads interweave throughout this book. First, an analysis of the transitional justice process highlights the institutional and legal strategies, based on international human rights law, used to address gender-based violence. An intersectional analytic sensibility exposes how such institutional and legal strategies comply with and/or disrupt historical social hierarchies. Second, rendering visible the broader dimensions of gender-based violence points to alternative epistemological spaces in which Quechua-speaking rural Andean subjectivities emerge.

An Intersectional Sensibility toward Gender-Based Violence

Given the limits of focusing on sexual violence, the UN Declaration on the Elimination of Violence against Women provides an expanded framework for analyzing harm done to women. The concept of gender-based violence identifies any act "that results in, or is likely to result in, physical, sexual or psychological harm or suffering to women, including threats of such acts, coercion or arbitrary deprivation of liberty, whether occurring in public or in private life."[28] In 1979, Peru ratified the Convention for the Elimination of all forms of Discrimination against Women (CEDAW) and then integrated it into the penal system in 1981.[29]

Besides documenting violations of women's rights, Marcela Lagarde suggests an expansive way of understanding gender-based violence that interrupts the dominant way of talking about gender as always implicating bodies, and usually women's bodies. This interruption allows for a closer look at "the gendered nature of practices and behaviors, along with the performance of gender norms."[30] Such an understanding of gender-based violence expands the focus from sexed bodies to include power relationships based on gender norms at the social, institutional, legal, and representational levels. Questions that guide this expanded analytical approach to gender-based violence include: How do gender norms influence what violations the Peruvian human rights movement, and later the PTRC, prioritize? How do gender norms influence dominant representations of women in the PTRC public hearings and sexual violence legal cases? Furthermore, this approach allows for the consideration of the influence of other social factors, such as ethnicity, language, class, and culture, on gender-based violence during the internal armed conflict.

Intersectionality brings light to how gender and race are separate and disconnected categories within legal frameworks, creating analytical blind spots in the law.[31] Cho, Crenshaw, and McCall suggest framing intersectionality as an analytic sensibility, "conceiving of categories not as distinct but as always permeated by other categories, fluid and changing, always in the process of creating and being created by dynamics of power."[32] Rather than assuming social forces to be separate, this analytic sensibility assumes social forces to be interwoven. Intersectionality emerges from U.S. feminist critical-race scholarship and praxis, which traces back through a genealogy of U.S. women-of-color feminisms. Its formulation for the purpose of intervening in the law indicates its applicability for analyzing the utility and limits of international human rights law and transitional justice.[33]

An intersectional sensibility challenges the universal subject of the law and the assumption that the subject exists outside of sociopolitical power relations.[34] The multiplicity of subjects must be situated within their historical contexts, which are fraught with contested power relations. Furthermore, the capacity of human rights to make change by focusing on individual violations obscures structural and institutional inequalities, as well as identities built upon references beyond the individual. Given the central role of human rights in transitional justice, this analysis aligns with McEvoy's call for "a more honest acknowledgement of the limitations of legalism and a greater willingness to give space to other actors and forms of knowledge."[35] Legalism in this case names the focus on legal analysis, or international human rights law, minus attention to sociopolitical context and history.

In the context of Peru, an intersectional sensibility suggests that the success of the state and civil society in addressing the gender-based violence hinges on giving attention to multiple exclusions based on ethnic and linguistic factors,[36] class, and rurality. Ethnic and linguistic factors indicate indigeneity;

yet most of the Andean population does not self-identify as indigenous. The Quechua-speaking peasants affirm their rights as Peruvian citizens, based on an assimilationist model,[37] rather than actively mobilizing around an indigenous identity.[38] Indigeneity is conjugated through culture, class, language, and education.[39]

Given the centralized spatial configuration of Peru, rurality is also an important factor. The coastal capital city of Lima holds the majority of the administrative decision-making power and Spanish-speaking, literate, educated, and wealthy population, while the rural areas get characterized as needing progress and development, given the concentration of poverty, illiteracy, and Quechua-speaking population. Hays-Mitchell's spatial analysis highlights the connection between "geographic isolation, social exclusion, and political marginalization; and the selectivity and intensity of the violence that characterized Peru's internal armed conflict."[40] This spatial configuration, rooted in exclusions based on rurality, language, and ethnicity, is crucial for understanding the embedded layers of violence and their aftermath. Historic social inequality sets the backdrop for transitional justice, manifests as a lack of responsiveness from the judicial system, and results in impunity. Turning back to that early morning with Rosa Cuchillo, a complex emotional terrain surfaces in relation to a lack of resolution and closure.

Embedded Layers of Violence

I turned and gently returned the picture of the young woman. Rosa Cuchillo took it and carefully slipped it back into its place among her things. We sat together quietly, looking at each other, when two women from the neighboring house came out, exclaiming loudly about the broken branch of the small flowering tree in front of their home. "I planted that last year and this year it just started to give flowers! Look mama, that is a bud on the branch that was bent!" The mother and daughter discussed the possibility of tying the branch back into place since it was not completely broken off and not too much time had passed. Indeed the branches of the trees throughout the public garden in which we sat were all bent backwards, hanging limply. We watched as more neighbors came out, some enraged and some in disbelief. "I heard a drunk guy come through here at about four in the morning making noise—he must have broken the branches of all the trees we planted!" After a short while, the city representative in charge of public gardens appeared to hear the complaints of the neighbors and take action. The neighbors deduced that the perpetrator was a man who rented a room in a house that also bordered the public garden. The group of indignant neighbors had grown to about twelve, and they all directed the city representative to the door of the guilty party. A meek, older woman reluctantly answered the door after many repeated knocks. She denied any involvement of her tenants in the broken branch incident and asserted that the person they were looking for was not in. After many accusations, no resolution could be determined, and the woman closed her door. The neighbors stayed convened for a while longer, trying to determine what steps to take next.

Rosa Cuchillo asked, "What kind of person would do that, break the branches of the trees in this nice garden?" She answered her question by concluding that it must be a sick person with lots of anger inside. "Look at all the efforts these neighbors have done to make their living area nice and pretty, and someone comes along and disrespects it all." We discussed what a disgrace this was and how the meek, old woman might have been scared to say anything because her tenant responsible for this act may have threatened her. After elaborating hypothetical scenarios for a while, I realize that a lot of time had passed since I had sat down to wait for the human rights attorney. I mentioned this to Rosa Cuchillo, and we agreed he had probably gone straight to the exhumation. With that, we got up and slowly made our way down the path through the garden of broken trees and out to the street.

* * *

The beauty of human resilience and hope fuels this writing and its contribution to ending the despair produced by social inequality, lack of closure, and embedded layers of violence. The vignettes demonstrate multiple layers of protagonism. Rosa Cuchillo's search for her child, the neighborhood's efforts to strengthen relations through planting a public garden and beautifying their community, and the collective need to recover the bodies of loved ones underscore the quest for justice and the commitment to healing wounds and reconstructing daily life.

In parallel, the broken trees in the public garden of war-torn Ayacucho, Rosa Cuchillo's disappeared daughter, and the mass grave at the military base illustrate the multiple levels of embedded and ongoing injustices and the indignation, frustration, distrust, and desperation they engender. Through a close study of the life stories of poor women in Peru, Cristina Alcalde exposes how violence permeates their lives. One of her most significant contributions proves through empirical study the linkages between intimate violence and broader forms of structural and institutional violence, further reinforcing the significance of embedded layers of violence. Furthermore, the embedded layers of violence evident within the Peruvian internal armed conflict, and society at large, are consistent with the Guatemalan experience and imply a trend worthy of additional comparative research.[41]

The vignette highlights these embedded layers of violence and a continuum of violence, thereby exposing the superficial nature of the break between war and peace that transitional justice purports to create.[42] An intersectional sensibility for understanding gender-based violence comes together with attentiveness to the continuum of violence across peace and war times, and the embedded, multilevel, and historical dimensions of violence. Similar to Alcalde, Jelke Boesten brings attention to three critical issues: the structural and institutional aspects of intersecting inequalities, the role of the patriarchal state as perpetrator, and the continuity of violence against women across times of peace and war times.[43] The Peruvian patriarchal state consistently perpetuates violence against women and reinforces class, race, and gender hierarchies.

Bringing the discussion back to the intimate level, a linear sense of temporality disintegrates under the ongoing trauma of Rosa Cuchillo's missing daughter. The vignettes underscore how the distinctions between past and present lose meaning. Given Rosa Cuchillo's inability to bury the physical remains of her daughter and mourn her loss, she lives suspended outside the linear progression of time, in a "territory between life and death, heaven and hell."[44] The temporally bound nature of transitional justice exists in tension with the continuum of violence, as well as the ways trauma alters the perception of time. Awakened intersectional sensibilities guide a critical assessment of these tensions within transitional justice logic,[45] which contributes to understanding why the Peruvian transitional justice process has run off track.

Transitional Justice and Human Rights

The underlying linear temporal logic of transitional justice alleges the ability to divide a past filled with atrocity from a present based on peace. This temporal logic, anchored in human rights, renders historic and structural injustices as a backdrop beyond the possibility of repair. The present analysis reads across the temporal split between atrocities of the past and the promise of peace in the present to acknowledge histories of legitimated inequality by incorporating social movement and civil society involvement before, during, and after the implementation of the PTRC. Each of these entities works within the international human rights legal framework upon which transitional justice is built. In addition, purposefully blurring the analytical bounds between state and society accounts for the fluid movement of social actors across this alleged divide. Therefore, this book situates the effectiveness of the PTRC within the international, social, political, and historical context of Peruvian society.

This analysis interrogates transitional justice conceptions of time and requires a quick sketch of the temporal coordinates of transitional justice. The field of transitional justice emerged out of the field of human rights in the 1980s through a community of policymakers, donors, activists, scholars, lawyers, and journalists working on political change framed as "transitions to democracy."[46] Transitional justice anchors itself in international human rights as enshrined in the Universal Declaration of Human Rights. The liberal conceptions of human rights, such as the emphasis on individual civil and political (first generation) rights and their universal application, provide the conceptual coordinates for transitional justice. This burgeoning field is part of the "global propagation of liberal norms, practices and institutions."[47] Most significant is the fact that human rights reference points frame the way transitional justice addresses political problems and effects change through legal and institutional reform in the short term.[48]

International human rights law facilitates making a "practical and symbolic break with the past" and offers a foundation for nation-states to claim "a newfound legitimacy and accountability."[49] This break with the past is key to establishing a framework of transitional justice given the concern with "political problems that were legal-institutional and relatively short term in nature."[50] It looks at the past to address wrongs, to the present to construct a new ethical and institutional framework to interpret that past, and to the future in order to fulfill the promise of "never again." Transitional justice mechanisms reckon with the past by constructing a national truth, promising justice, social reconciliation, and reparations for victims.[51]

The break from the past proves over and over to be more rhetoric than reality. When dealing with the colonial past, the history of economic exploitation and legitimated inequality is not foreign to the initial debates around transitional justice. Calls for social justice and economic equality, however, are part of the formation of transitional justice that usually gets ignored.[52] Contemporary critiques demonstrate a continued concern with such issues by clearly identifying the need to address enduring inequalities and structural violence.[53] In other words, the struggle to expand the transitional justice framework persists, and this book contributes to this project of expansion. The reasoning is not just theoretical; it is grounded in the practical results of a transitional justice process. As Ní Aoláin, Haynes, and Cahn contend, ignoring social and economic violations and their links to discrimination has a ripple effect that undermines the postconflict society's chances of future stability.

Recent research on transitional justice typically focuses on the specific mechanisms and their efficacy.[54] Balasco labels this trend toward evaluation of "operationalization and methodology" as the third wave of transitional justice scholarship, following the first wave of normative exploration and the second wave of growth and introspection.[55] As Barria and Roper assert in their comparative study of Argentina, Sierra Leone, East Timor, and Bosnia-Herzegovina, "no transitional justice mechanism, individually or in combination with others, necessarily fulfills all the goals of justice and reconciliation."[56] While the authors point to limitations with policy implementation and difficulties with involving all sectors of society in the process, transitional justice mechanisms must tackle the underlying social hierarchies and logics that create a context wherein authoritarian rule and human rights violations proliferate. Yet to do so would call into question the temporal claim of making a break with the past and press the transitional justice mandate beyond the short term.

The troubling disjunctures held within transitional justice goals and practices fuel the need for this book, which contributes to the developments in transitional justice scholarship that attend to local justice practices as a touchstone for the transformation of state and society.[57] If transitional justice aspires to "redress the legacies of massive human rights abuses,"[58] the mechanisms must reckon with the historic roots of these atrocities. The sociopolitical transformation necessary for true and lasting redress would necessarily touch the lives of women like Rosa Cuchillo and the families of disappeared persons waiting anxiously at the exhumation site to glimpse a tattered piece of their missing loved one's clothing.

Decolonial Feminist Interventions in Transitional Justice

A common quest for justice brought Rosa Cuchillo and me together that early morning in Ayacucho. We are both women, yet we are not the same. The space between us holds histories of privilege and oppression. An intersectional sensibility attunes this analysis to the specificities of social positioning. A feminist-of-color method demands making my political commitments and positioning explicit, breaking from the distant and objective voice. This methodological practice dovetails with the work of Latin American decolonial theorists. Walter Mignolo calls for epistemic disobedience, which involves divesting from the illusion of the knowing subject that floats above the "geopolitical configuration of the world in which people are racially ranked and regions are racially configured."[59] In other words, the who, where, when and why of knowledge production matters. My taste and feel of Peruvian inequality, my preoccupation with social justice, and my desire for cultural belonging as a Peruvian-American shape this study of Peruvian transitional justice processes.

The collectively written essay "Building on 'The Edge of Each Other's Bat-tles'"[60] expresses the ongoing concern with intersectionality that I share with my Santa Cruz feminist-of-color collaborators. We argue that intersectional-ity has become shorthand for the interwoven and coalitional trajectories of action and thought that have produced women-of-color feminist methodolo-gies.[61] Rather, we emphasize the indivisibility of the method of analysis, politi-cal project for radical transformation, and coalitional identity formation. In terms of this study, combining an intersectional sensibility with decolonial feminisms provides a methodological entry point consistent with the ethical and political commitments that guide my writing practice and the intimacy inherent in disclosing my social positioning. This manifold strategy aims to bring the subjects held within this text, the reader, and myself into each other's worlds through a humanizing proximity. My methodological entry point builds from feminist scholars' interventions into transitional justice debates that commonly focus on "under-visibility and under-privileging of women," "the social-discursive constructions of femininity and masculin-ity,"[62] as well as reparations policies and the exclusively legalistic focus on sexual violence, which I refer to as conceptual myopia.

Transitional states struggle with political instability. Their drive for legiti-macy opens a window of opportunity for radical transformation. Therefore, states such as Peru offer "a unique site for feminist intervention" because "assumptions, systems and institutions are up for renegotiation."[63] This period of transition can also result in retrenchment through the consolidation of hierarchal structures, the cooptation of gender, and the reassertion of binary principles such as the private/public divide.[64] Stabilizing the nation-state leads to dependence on established social hierarchies, while changing deep-rooted conditions of injustice requires questioning and further destabilizing the same hierarchies. This tension becomes evident in an examination of the struggles within the PTRC regarding the role and scope of a gender analysis.

The Peruvian nation-state in crisis reconfigures itself through a transi-tional justice process that simultaneously includes historically marginalized populations and entrenches social hierarchies. Gender-essentialist methods that add on "women"[65] provide a perfect example. Gender essentialism is "the notion that a unitary, 'essential' women's experience can be isolated and described independently of race, class, sexual orientation and other realities of experience."[66] The homogenous grouping of "women" assumes a certain type of woman as normative while marginalizing differences among women. The outcome resulted in patchy and piecemeal inclusion, even though the initial proposal of an integrated, transverse axis of gender analysis could have exposed the interlacing heteropatriarchal and colonial roots of injustice. Similarly, studies of gender-based violence during conflict or transitional justice processes tend to nominally identify issues of race/ethnicity and yet forgo an in-depth intersectional analysis, as the PTRC did.[67]

Utilizing an intersectional sensibility sheds light on the limitations of international human rights law and transitional compromises to address the scope of harms experienced during the internal armed conflict.[68] The tension within transitional justice processes of addressing past violence and providing justice for the victims, while at the same time stabilizing the nation-state, manifests from the paradox of rights. Leebaw points out the contradictory role of law in relation to violence simply: "While law can be a tool for regulating violence and exposing abuses of power, law is also utilized to obfuscate and legitimate abuses of power."[69] An intersectional sensibility brings "attention to the violences of legal and administrative systems that articulate themselves as race and gender neutral but are actually sites of the gendered racialization processes that produce the nation-state."[70] This examination of the Peruvian transitional justice processes traces the state's double move of including previously marginalized groups while reinforcing hierarchies, as well as the implications of this double move for meeting the goals of justice, truth, political reconciliation, and nation-state legitimacy.

The transitional justice process of re-legitimating the Peruvian nation-state must be situated within the legacy of colonialism. This book is part of the project of decolonizing "our epistemologies and practices of (transitional) justice."[71] According to Mignolo, the celebratory narrative of modernity, originating in Europe and commonly identified with progress and development, has a hidden flipside. The other side of modernity is coloniality, which encompasses the modes of control Europeans used to manage their American and Caribbean colonies from the 1500s on.[72] These modes of social, political, and economic domination perpetuate injustice, commodification, disregard for human life, and inequality.[73] Therefore, modernity/coloniality refers to the project of colonization of the Américas, the epistemic system entrenched by this process, and its contemporary manifestations within the modern nation-state.[74]

While an intersectional examination of international human rights law and the Peruvian transitional justice process challenges the unity of the political subject, it also demands contextualization and historicization. Language and translation, as well as ethnicity, class, and rurality, surface as important factors for understanding gender-based violence. Christine Ewig emphasizes the care needed when utilizing an intersectional approach to study Peru[75] and uses the idea of internal colonialism to explain how race and sex are tied to geography, in that the coastal elite socially, culturally, and sexually dominate interior territories and peoples. Traveling to Peru with an intersectional sensibility presents significant challenges that take the form of incommensurability—that which cannot be translated across languages, geopolitics, cultures, cosmologies, and histories. Taking this concern with the translation of intersectional sensibility further, Ofelia Schutte suggests that instead of utilizing the U.S.-based race/class/sex categories to understand the Latin American phenomenon, why not explore Latin American–based models of analysis?[76]

Rather than introducing something new, U.S. women-of-color feminist methods—particularly an intersectional analytic sensibility—echo an existing feminist analytic frame exemplified by Peruvian feminist Marfil Francke. Her analysis of gender, class, and ethnicity highlights how gender subordination does not figure into the critical assessment of colonialism, and she asserts that gender is a third strand that gets confused for the other two, ethnicity and class. While ethnicity, class, and gender are related sites of domination, they are not identical. Through her metaphor of "the braid of domination," Francke explains that to dominate and exploit resources, colonial actors exacerbated preexisting differences and fueled conflict among indigenous peoples. She highlights the enduring nature of the sociospatial system of domination, a form of apartheid with a complex system of racial categorization that dictated the spaces inhabited by and the interrelations between Spanish and indigenous peoples. Her analysis dovetails with decolonial theories from the Américas that examine the legacy of Spanish and Portuguese invasion and conquest.

Strengthening previously elaborated insights into the embedded layers of violence, Francke writes that the braid of domination creates "a single structure that runs through all social relations, institutional and personal, public and private, production and reproduction, in the process of daily life and in the historical development of Latin America."[77] In 1990 Francke's work contributed to the project of understanding the full significance of gender within this braid of domination rooted in colonial relations. Her contribution anchors an intersectional analytic sensibility in the colonial roots of legitimated inequalities in Peru. Moreover, Francke's insights harmonize with Maria Lugones's assertion that gender and sexuality are treated superficially within Latin American decolonial theory. While one of the generally recognized modes of domination within modernity/coloniality is the "control of gender and sexuality: nuclear family, binary, normative sexuality, patriarchal superiority,"[78] Lugones builds upon intersectionality and the coloniality of power to explore "the modern/colonial gender system."[79]

The spaces that open at the interface between an intersectional analytic sensibility and a decolonial feminist approach stretch the gaze of human rights law and decolonize transitional justice. Together, an intersectional sensibility and decolonial feminisms gain conceptual traction with the spatial and temporal manifestations of the legacy of colonialism in Peru and their significance for studying how movements, institutions, and organizations address gender-based violence during the internal armed conflict. Decolonial feminisms also highlight the role of binary logics in the reconfiguration of the nation-state and open alternative epistemic spaces for the expansion of human rights and transitional justice logics. This approach builds upon feminist scholars who have begun to shed light on the tension between acknowledging the continuum of violence and the transitional justice goal of establishing a historical break between past and future. The ever-present reality of gender-based violence highlights the contradiction between the goals of democratization and human security and "an exclusively backward looking discourse in transitional justice which is blind to current violations," as well as the historical roots of legitimated inequalities.[80]

Empirical and intertextual analyses draw attention to representational, organizational, intersubjective, historic, and experiential forms of legitimated inequality. Throughout, decolonial feminist analytical tools fold into the chapters, meeting the edge of an intersectional analytical sensibility to stretch the conceptual framework for thinking about transitional justice. An intersectional sensibility underscores how and why feminist and human rights movements' lacked attention to gender based violence. A sketch of the human rights and feminist movements' trajectories contextualizes the emergence of the PTRC and the challenges its investigation faced in addressing gender-based violence through an international human rights framework. The struggle for democratization within the work of the PTRC, the limits of binary logics, and colonial mappings of difference come to the fore in an examination of the PTRC debates surrounding the meaning of gender, its methodological operationalization and incorporation into the final report. Narrative excesses and disruptive moments within the PTRC public hearings offer a way into unraveling the power relations embedded in language translation and temporal frames. Continued attention to colonial mappings of difference sheds light on the limited effect of the PTRC public hearings.

A Southern Andean community-based analysis of sexual violence places a critical light on state responses to cases of sexual violence during the internal armed conflict. This analysis positions sexual exploitation as a manifestation of domination over time, placing a linear sense of history and the goal of modernity into question. Feminist NGO Study and Defense of Women's Rights (DEMUS) initiated a follow-up project on the PTRC's legal investigation into a collective case of sexual violence during the internal armed conflict in Manta, Huancavelica. DEMUS's project implemented a promising interdisciplinary, feminist, community-based method that incorporated the framework of interculturality to address the spectrum of historic social inequalities related to language, culture, indigeneity, rurality, class, and education. This NGO project struggled to negotiate among institutional arrangements, dominant discourses, and affected people's identities, worldviews, demands, and strategies. The practical and conceptual challenges inherent in decolonizing transitional justice become clear through this examination.

Rosa Cuchillo reappears at the midpoint of this book and the conclusion to remind us of the very real quest for justice and underscore the political stakes involved in this project.

1

Parallel Tracks and Fraught Encounters

The Human Rights and Feminist Movements (and Campesina Protagonism) in Peru

The disappearance of family members, as told through Rosa Cuchillo's reflections, traces back to events that occurred in May 1980. The Shining Path—Peruvian Communist Party (Sendero Luminoso) had a very strong presence in the Andean region of Ayacucho. In rejection of the legalization of leftist parties and participation in electoral democracy, the Shining Path burned electoral cards in Chuschi, Ayacucho. This event marked the inception of the armed conflict. Rural communities found themselves caught in the crossfire between the armed forces and the Shining Path. Both sides demanded allegiance from rural communities, which made the communities vulnerable to the constant accusations from both sides of conspiring with the enemy.

From the beginning, rural Andean women, or *campesinas*, struggled for the defense of their disappeared, tortured, and executed family members' human rights[1] and the survival of living family members.[2] They visited police departments and military installations, asking the whereabouts of their family members; they combed through open communal graves where the bodies of disappeared persons were dumped. Campesinas spearheaded local efforts to denounce human rights violations and address the needs of affected people with the help of church groups and human rights advocates. Campesina organizing, especially in Ayacucho, contributed to ending the conflict in the early 1990s. Their collective organizing was unprecedented, creating the context of possibility for the PTRC.[3] However, campesinas were not recognized, and many do not recognize themselves, as full political subjects in their own right.[4] The immediate needs of their loved ones trumped their concern with individual experiences of violence, particularly gender-based violence. Their role as caregivers based on maternal sacrifice, as well as social taboos, tended to bury such violations in silence.

An intersectional sensibility brings attention to the multiple social factors that contribute to marginalizing campesina voices. Although campesina protagonism held a key role in publicizing human rights violations, social exclusions marginalized their voices in the transitional justice process. Campesinas are second-class citizens, especially because their illiteracy rate is high. "The condition of illiteracy is defined in relation to the woman's ability to develop herself in the urban and Spanish literate world, which does not value her knowledge and resources."[5] Their distance from the ideal type of Peruvian modern citizen is determined by a combination of gender, ethnic, linguistic, geographic, and class components.

Besides the important work campesinas did on behalf of their families and themselves, the human rights and feminist movements presented the strongest potential for taking on the defense of campesinas' rights. The human rights movement made a herculean effort to respond to the ever-growing number of victims and survivors of the internal armed conflict. It consistently prioritized the human rights violations of campesinos yet did not place emphasis on gender-based violence. Turning to the feminist movement, while women's rights held a central position in the growing movement, conflict-related gender-based violence was not a top priority. As campesina organizing did not prioritize the gender-based abuses they sustained personally, nor did the human rights or feminist movements.

This analysis explains how and why, despite campesina protagonism and human rights and feminist movements' best intentions, the gender-based violence directed at campesinas during the internal armed conflict slipped through the cracks. Campesina protagonism and the violations of campesina rights are relevant elements of the story that tend to get erased through the workings of legitimated inequalities. My personal affiliations with the feminist movement undermine any claim to objectivity, yet my analytical drive emphasizes understanding the dynamics of legitimated inequalities rather than criticizing the movements.

Utilizing an intersectional sensibility, this analysis reads against the grain of the intersecting progressive discourses of human rights and democracy, as well as the politically regressive discourses of sexism and racism. This approach underscores the workings of legitimated inequalities within the feminist and human rights movements during the conflict (1980–2000) to contextualize the limits of the transitional justice process, especially the work of the PTRC. This sketch of the human rights and feminist movements' trajectories draws upon interviews, field notes, primary documents, and a few women's movement magazines to explain the lack of attention to gender-based violence and the marginalization of campesina voices.[6]

The human rights and feminist movements have similar origins and timing, and both highly value the international realm. Both movements' participation in the second UN Conference on Human Rights, held in Vienna in 1993, illustrates the importance of international law and international political pressure to meet their goals. This event proved to be a lost opportunity for movement collaboration with regard to conflict-related gender-based violence, given the conference's nascent yet promising headway on the issue. The national context of terror and distrust reinforced the distance between the human rights and feminist movements and their development on parallel rather than combined tracks.

Political processes in the mid- to late 1990s, including sectors of the feminist movements' alliance with authoritarian president Alberto Fujimori and the prodemocracy movement to oust Fujimori's regime in 2000, exemplify the limits and possibilities of collaboration between the two movements as well as continued sidelining of campesina rights. Nevertheless, the human rights movement and to a lesser extent the feminist movement play a central role in creating the conditions for a transition to democracy and the establishment of the TRC. The feminist movement advocated for the PTRC to include a gender analysis and the issue of sexual violence. The struggles and gaps this chapter makes evident between campesina protagonism and movement priorities underscore the challenges the PTRC would face in its efforts to incorporate a gender analysis and the issue of sexual violence in its investigation.

Campesina Protagonism and Social Exclusion

The internal armed conflict marked a radical shift in the lives and roles of campesinas.[7] They broke from traditional daily activities to come together in search of their loved ones. Church groups, especially the Evangelical Church, offered support to women's organizing in Ayacucho, the Andean department most heavily affected by the conflict.[8] Through these spaces, women shared experiences, held meetings, and inserted themselves into the public sphere. They lost their fear in the process. In early 1983 in Ayacucho, Angelica Mendoza formed a group, composed primarily of mothers, under the name National Association of Families of the Kidnapped, Detained, and

Disappeared of Peru (ANFASEP). ANFASEP used the Christian cross and religious symbolism to dissociate itself from subversive groups and received support from human rights organizations. Besides religious groups, human rights organizations were the only civil society groups that listened to them.[9]

In November 1984 the Episcopal Church sponsored Angelica Mendoza and Ofelia Antezana, a victim of the conflict from Huancavelica, to participate in an international conference held in Argentina with the Mothers of the Plaza de Mayo. In 1977 a group of mothers who had lost their family members in the Argentine dirty war came together in the Plaza de Mayo in Buenos Aires to protest the military government's brutality against leftist activists and their children's disappearance. Over the years the Mothers of the Plaza de Mayo gained international recognition for their work. The solidarity forged between Argentine and Peruvian women broke the isolation of the Peruvian women's struggle and started a process of sharing strategies with women globally. When Angelica Mendoza and Ofelia Antezana returned to Peru, Ofelia Antezana founded the Committee of Family Members of the Disappeared (COFADER), based in Lima, which focuses on displacement and disappearances. To date, both organizations continue to demand truth and justice.

In addition to ANFASEP and COFADER, organizing for family survival and meeting basic economic needs led to the formation of mothers clubs. "These organizations facilitated negotiating for resources and jobs before offices of the state and developing links of collaboration and support with organizations such as NGOs and human rights groups."[10] The mothers' clubs expanded, and in 1988 they founded the Federation of Mothers Clubs of the Province of Huamanga and participated in a national peace march. The Shining Path attempted to intimidate and disperse this growing movement, but the women would not back down.[11] By 1995, the Departmental Federation of Mothers' Clubs of Ayacucho (FEDECMA) came to include eighty thousand affiliated women.[12] Their main concerns included economic survival and the defense of human rights. A holistic vision encompassed the need to secure employment and income for women, improve nutrition and health, and address displacement and children's mental health.[13] In spite of being constantly stigmatized as proterrorist, *Indias-terrucas,*[14] these women's organizations remained strong as the social fabric frayed under the strain of extreme violence.

While campesinas and campesinos do organize politically, their organizing is not purposefully marked as ethnic. As the campesinas in question do not self-identify as indigenous and in the Andes a significant self-indigenous movement has not been articulated, I do not make reference to indigenous movements. Degregori underscores the fact that that people do not choose to identify themselves as Indian because during the nineteenth century the term became synonymous with poor peasant or servant.[15] To break with this label, people demanded integration into the national culture through access to education, specifically the Spanish language. This assimilationist approach was met with a state willingness to process their demands as peasants, particularly around the recuperation of territories taken from them by powerful regional landowners.

The dominant state discourse on national culture excludes indigenous peoples from the prospect of modernization. Paulo Drinot points out that indigenous people are seen as an obstacle to the nation-state's drive toward progress.[16] Given that progress depends on labor, people marked as indigenous utilize this logic of production to frame themselves as workers and peasants/campesinos to organize and get their demands heard. People who, because of their native language, traditional customs, and connection with territory, might be classified as indigenous, have been on the front lines of class-based organizations like peasant federations and unions. De la Cadena frames the issue from a different angle, arguing that "indigenous social movements *qua* peasant movements, have been on the forefront of social change."[17] Yet in such organizations gender is subordinated to class, and women participants face personal and structural forms of discrimination.[18] Women fight fiercely to gain leadership positions and must constantly prove themselves. Even though the organizing practices of the unions, for example, have become more flexible and have allowed women's participation, they lack awareness of the specific problems women were facing.[19]

From a broad national perspective, campesinas' rights are perceived as add-ons to the main demands of class-based and feminist movements. Campesinas generally do not identify with feminists, since community leaders and members commonly view them as bourgeois, given their urban middle-class focus. Furthermore, the rural women's movements express ostensibly different demands than those of the feminist movement, which in the 1980s was working to establish their autonomy from politically left parties. The feminist movement reflects the same hierarchies seen in the society as a whole, as does class-based organizing and the human rights movement. Therefore, this analysis focuses upon the workings of legitimated inequalities within social-justice-oriented political projects.

Despite campesinas' important role in ending the conflict, they were not integrated substantively into the official transitional justice processes.[20]

Conversely, the human rights movement played an important role in this process. The human rights movement embraces the interpretation of rights as universal, individual, and inherent in each morally equal citizen. While the human rights movement holds this interpretation of rights as a goal to work toward, in practice this set of assumptions offers little traction in addressing the entrenched social hierarchies in question. The dynamics of legitimated inequality through the human rights and feminist movements at both the national and international levels contextualize the marginalization of campesinas during the transitional justice process and situate the challenges the PTRC investigation faced in addressing gender-based violence.

Movement Commonalities: The International Realm

Just as rural women's organizing in Ayacucho in the 1980s benefited from organizing with the Mothers of the Plaza de Mayo in Argentina and the Latin American Federation of Associations for Relatives of the Disappeared and Detained (FEDEFAM), the international realm holds great significance for the human rights and feminist movements. External and internal political pressure on the state to comply with international law presents a formidable force for change. The participation of the human rights and feminist movements in the 1993 second UN Conference on Human Rights in Vienna demonstrates the significance of the international realm. The violent fragmentation of the Socialist Federal Republic of Yugoslavia in the early 1990s brought the issue of conflict-related gender-based violence to the attention of the conference, and the international stage, for the first time. Although the outcome of the conference directly addressed this issue, the potential for the Peruvian delegates to work collaboratively on the matter of gender-based violence did not come to fruition.

As women's issues began to gain international attention, with the 1975 International Year of Women and the first Conference on Women in Mexico City, human rights violations were taking place in the southern cone. The 1973 U.S.-backed coup d'état against Chilean President Salvador Allende ushered in General Agosto Pinochet's military dictatorship and a period of political repression and mass human rights violations. Peruvians plugged into the international human rights network that had its beginnings in the early 1970s with the Chilean coup d'état; for example, aiding in the cross-border escape of Chileans under threat. The human rights movement built off of the Universal Declaration of Human Rights, the Covenant on Civil and Political Rights, and the Covenant on Economic, Social, and Cultural Rights to address the "rights of the person, including the freedom from execution, torture, and arbitrary imprisonment,"[21] with a clear focus on civil and political rights. The Peruvian human rights movement formed with support from regional and international organizations.

The international feminist movement grew within the spaces opened by the United Nations, particularly the UN Decade for Women (1975–1985). In these spaces Peruvian feminists developed strategies, engaged in collective reflection, and worked to transform the national political agenda. In Peru the feminist movement took on the international human rights framework to emphasis sexual and reproductive rights using tools such as the Convention for the Elimination of All Forms of Discrimination against Women (CEDAW). The importance of such conventions lies in ratification: once a state ratifies an international law, it becomes part of its national law through a set of constitutional procedures.

In Peru, feminists advocate for international laws to be recognized nationally through their affirmation by congress and ratification by the president. These changes expand national justice to more effectively address women's rights. Yet in the case of Peru, the implementation of these new national laws "leaves much to be desired because of the antidemocratic, discriminatory, and elitist factors that predominate in Peruvian society."[22] Therefore, rights advocates must struggle not only to pressure the state for ratification but also to fight for every step toward implementation of these new rights. The case of CEDAW, as mentioned in the introduction, illustrates the full incorporation of an international convention into national law. The case of the Rome Statute of the International Criminal Court demonstrates a case of ratification without implementation (as yet).

Similar to the feminist movement, the human rights movement focused its attention on the international community from the beginning. The international community offered critical support and credibility to the human rights movement in its formative years. Control and sanction of state abuse against individuals and groups is "the raison d'être and the principal feature of global and regional intergovernmental organizations that focus on human rights, and of the thousands of NGOs (nongovernmental organizations) that operate from civil society, in every country of the world, to pressure governments to comply."[23] International organizations such as Human Rights Watch (previously Americas Watch) and Amnesty International, in addition to the Washington Office on Latin America (WOLA) in the United States, the Center for Legal and Social Studies in Argentina, and the Pro Human Rights Association in Spain, among others, offered constant support for work in defense of human rights in Peru. These organizations assisted in investigating and documenting human rights abuse cases, placing continuous pressure on the Peruvian government to respect human rights, working within the international legal system, and presenting cases to international and regional commissions and courts. The Peruvian human rights movement learned fast and worked collaboratively, sharing knowledge and skills with their international counterparts.

Although feminists and human rights advocates brought different agendas to the 1993 second UN Human Rights conference in Vienna, the conference serves as an example of collaboration between representatives of the two movements at the international level. While most of the human rights and feminist activists knew each other at the national level, because of their shared background in leftist parties each focused on its own priorities. Human rights advocates were concerned with the issue of torture, forced disappearance, terrorism, and the death penalty.[24] Feminists were interested in sexual and reproductive rights and violence against women.[25] Yet the Latin American Committee for the Defense of Women's Rights (CLADEM) included the issue of armed conflict in its declaration at the conference. "Internal and external armed conflicts have terrible consequences for the population. Women in particular suffer unusual atrocities. The problems encountered by women refugees or displaced women who, besides being forced to flee from their countries, are exposed to suffer further human rights violations, cannot be disregarded."[26] While the issue of gender-based violence during the internal armed conflict may have appeared on the edges of both the feminist and human rights agendas, it did not gain the sustained attention of either group.

The preparation for the conference was divided between human rights and feminist advocates in Peru. The human rights groups had the control of resources and monies for travel, which did not foster collaboration. Nevertheless, the human rights movement had to comply with UN mandates, so they had to share with the feminists. The structure of the conference was set to facilitate national representatives' collective development of a continental platform. The feminists also had separate meetings, but they could not direct all their efforts toward regional-level meetings to forward women's rights because they had to function within the set structure and take part in the dominant national, regional, and international debates. Each country sent a representative to the regional plenary. The Peruvian contingent decided to send a man and a woman; the man was a human rights advocate, and the woman was a feminist.

At the conference the Shining Path had a strong presence and employed intimidation tactics such as taping presentations, taking notes, and creating a sense of fear among the Peruvian participants. The context of the conference forced the human rights and feminist delegates closer together. They developed strategies and mechanisms to protect themselves against the Shining Path's intimidation tactics, building trust, albeit out of necessity. While on the national level the culture of fear and general distrust and suspicion engendered by the conflict divided them further,[27] at the international level the menacing presence of Shining Path pushed them together. According to feminist delegate Silvia Loli, they were in the same space for many days, eating together and sharing informal moments, which facilitated friendships.[28] Vienna created a situation in which the two movements' representatives were more or less obligated to interact throughout the required national, regional, and international meetings.[29]

The second UN Conference on Human Rights broke new ground in 1993 through the recognition of women's and girls' rights as human rights. This recognition specifies the need to eliminate violence against women and girls in both the private and public spheres. The conference provided a space— "to assess the status of women's human rights in particular countries; to explore the human rights framework and critique its inadequacy in addressing violations of women's human rights; to mobilize at the national, regional and international levels to demand that these violations be recognized and responded to by the international community and state governments; and to work with other women's rights and human rights NGOs to promote common action."[30] A statement declaring human rights to be universal, integral, interdependent, and indivisible embodied the call to bring together all the struggles for rights.

The Declaration and the Program of Action both address violence against women in situations of armed conflict.[31] Media and NGO attention to the Japanese "comfort system" of sexual slavery and the violence against women in the former Yugoslavia, particularly against Bosnian women, set the tone in which governments were called to "recognize gender-based violence as a human rights violation, rather than dismiss it as incidental to the horrors of war or as private conduct solely within the realm of domestic law."[32] The Declaration stipulates that violence against women in conflict, including assassination, rape, sexual slavery, and forced pregnancy, constitute violations of human rights and humanitarian norms.[33]

On the national level in Peru, advocates did not take up the international advances regarding violence against women during internal armed conflict because it fell outside the realm of specialization of each group.[34] The human rights advocates stayed on track to defend gender-neutral violations. Human rights advocates put themselves at personal risk in the context of violence, focusing on the documentation of and immediate response to cases of torture, disappearance, and extrajudicial execution. Cases of sexual violence that did crop up fell into the category of torture. Feminists stayed on track to defend cases of domestic violence and rape but did not expand their activities to represent cases of gender-based violence directly in the context of conflict. A de facto division of labor exists between centers that offer legal support and counseling services for the defense of human rights and those that offer similar services for the defense of women's rights.[35]

Although the Peruvian human rights and feminist delegates attempted to build off of the new alliances forged at the international level through their participation in the Andean Commission of Jurists, the effort died for a lack of a collective will.[36] Roxana Vásquez Sotelo, feminist lawyer and former director of CLADEM, asserts that while feminist and human rights movements alike participated actively in the human rights conference, had contact, and made gains, the dialogues have not been valued on the national level, leading one to believe that the two movements have parallel agendas for the most part, with actual points of contact remaining scarce.[37]

Why did this international collaboration fail to translate to the national level? The Shining Path's pressure and other situational circumstances at the conference pushed the delegates together, creating a tenuous collaboration that disintegrated at the national level under the polarizing culture of silence, fear, and distrust.[38] Therefore, the movements fell back into their separate tracks, foreclosing any possibility of prioritizing the effect of the conflict on women. These dynamics inadvertently reinforce the marginalization of the impact of the conflict on campesinas, specifically gender-based violence.

Human Rights and Feminist Movements' Conflicting Alliances

One of the main divisive factors between the two movements is their relationship with religious institutions. While progressive Catholic and Evangelical institutions[39] contribute to the human rights movement, the feminist movement has historically been at odds with religious institutions based on differing views of sexual and reproductive rights. While feminists focus on women's control over their own bodies in the form of the right to abortion and access to family-planning information and methods, religious institutions typically support abstinence until marriage and advocate against contraception and abortion.

A Latin American regional study of the relationship between human rights advocates and feminists conducted since 2000 found that although many feminists consider themselves defenders of human rights, human rights circles are generally unaware of feminist critiques.[40] A women's right to decide her maternity, for example, linked to the right of a person to control what happens to her body, is a "strategic cause for women, which is not understood by human rights groups."[41] From a feminist perspective, one of the most serious problems between the two movements is that human rights advocates lack recognition of feminist contributions.[42] Feminist strategies subvert social norms based on theoretically elaborated interventions in society[43] that question unequal relations of power in intimate to public spaces and resignify varied forms of violence against women as human rights violations. Feminists concern themselves with framing violence against women, domestic violence, and sexual assault as public problems while also accounting for the subjective dimensions of violence, the need for women's self-determination, and a respect for difference.

Liliana Panizo, human rights advocate, explains that those who work on human rights issues have been questioned repeatedly as to why they did not take up the issue of sexual violence. Hinting at sexism and cultural difference, she mentions, "There was something within us that impeded addressing this issue."[44] She explains that in the early 1980s the Pro-Human Rights Association (APRODEH) worked with the case of Georgina Gamboa, a young woman from Ayacucho who was raped and ended up having a baby (this case is analyzed in chapter three). Panizo characterizes her work with Gamboa as an *encuentro*, a meeting or even clash between her cultural references from the coastal capital of Lima and Georgina Gamboa's Andean cultural references. Panizo groups herself in a generation of Limeños who were not educated to appreciate the cultures of the Andes and the Amazon. Upper-class Limeños in general would be more interested in going to Miami than to Cusco, for example. She highlights that the process through which human rights advocates and activists from Lima came to question these issues of cultural difference was from a practical perspective when a project did not work.

With regard to the issue of specifically sexual violence, Panizo mentions that few women wanted to talk, and if it was not a priority issue for them, then APRODEH did not make it a priority. The social taboo around this type of violation was overwhelming. In hindsight Panizo reflects, "We feel responsible for not working on the issue and preparing ourselves more to deal with the processes surrounding the issue. We did not open an institutional space to work with those cases. But we don't feel to blame for not reporting cases of people that did not want to report."[45] Respecting the wishes of the victims was highly sensitive on the part of the human rights movement, yet this approach also left the issue at the margins of their agenda.

Francisco Soberón, human rights advocate, asserts that while the feminist movement had a radical agenda in its inception, it did not have an articulated response to political violence.[46] This general perception contributes to the repeated refrain "the feminists didn't do anything." Returning to the de facto division of labor, feminists focused on the legal defense of women's rights within the national context, specifically rape and domestic violence. Feminists were centrally concerned with violence against women, yet the next section shows how they also ended up leaving campesina rights on the periphery of their agenda.

The Feminist Movement:
"No hicieron nada—They didn't do anything"

In the late 1970s and early 1980s, the three main articulations of the burgeoning women's movement were the popular women's movement, the women leaders in left political parties, and the feminists, all of which shared one goal in common: the struggle for women's rights and against discrimination and oppression. Virginia Vargas asserts that although the three lines of the women's movement express differing life conditions, demands, and strategies, there was significant crossing and sharing.[47] She suggests that the differences "reflect the forms in which women construct movement, manage their realities, and develop identities in relation to gender and other identities such as class, race, age, and geographic location."[48] One example would be that in the 1980s campesinas had to find tools to address their needs; therefore, rural women's rights came about in practice.[49] This examination of the trajectory of the feminist movement and its relationship to the struggles of campesinas focuses on relations of power and privilege.

An intersectional sensibility attunes this analysis to the workings of legitimated inequalities within the feminist movement. While broad strokes provide the general orientation of the feminist movement, it is a grouping that includes activists, advocates, academics, and artists with diverse commitments and modes of action. Generally speaking, feminists started to draw connections between the violation of rural and urban women's rights in the late 1980s after almost a decade of political violence. Ofelia Antezana, founder of the Committee of Family Members of the Disappeared (COFADER), levels the criticism that feminists did not address the issue that mattered most to them: the disappearances.[50] Both the tensions between feminist NGOs and women's popular organizations and the sidelining of campesinas' struggles replicate historical social hierarchies and power asymmetries.[51]

The drive toward feminist autonomy in relation to the leftist political parties from which they emerged spilled over into a general inward-looking focus. When feminists did reach out, it was more toward the international realm. The feminist movement began as unstructured groups made up primarily of urban women engaged in collective reflection, study circles, and activism. Two main feminist centers are Centro del la Mujer Peruana "Flora Tristan," founded in 1979, and Movimiento Manuela Ramos, founded in 1980. The majority of the early participants of both these centers came out of the Left. Maruja Barrig points out that these centers, along with Action for the Liberation of the Peruvian Woman (ALIMUJER), Women in Struggle, and the Women's Socialist Front, joined together to form the Coordinating Committee of Feminist Organizations.[52] In 1980 the Committee outlined their agenda apart from political parties. Their three main points included the right to work and labor stability; the recognition of detained women militants as political prisoners; and the right of women to control their reproduction through sexual education, access to free contraceptives, and abortion.[53] Here, the rights of women affected by the conflict do figure in their agenda in the form of a defense of women political prisoners.

During the political opening in the 1980s in which leftist parties were legalized, the Shining Path took up arms in rejection of incorporation into the formal political process. In contrast, many feminists jumped at the opportunity to take part as political candidates in their own right. Feminists generally prioritized making formal political inroads over building interclass alliances with popular women's organizations or focusing on the impact of the conflict on campesinas. Feminists' emphasis on autonomy and constructing their own spaces made it especially difficult to collaborate with groups engaged in social struggle for basic needs.

Meanwhile, popular organizing of the women's movement in response to structural adjustment and the feminization of poverty grew rapidly in the 1980s. This overlapped with the expansion of the shantytowns on the urban periphery of Lima to accommodate those displaced by the internal armed conflict. Women, including many displaced campesinas (and their families) in very precarious living conditions, created new spaces such as communal kitchens to address their immediate needs. Through that process they came to understand themselves as social and political actors. This phenomenon exploded in the 1980s, with seven hundred communal kitchens in

1986 multiplying to seven thousand by 1989.[54] Popular women's movement participants criticize the feminist movement for their absence in the 1980s. As the following quote from the magazine *Mujer y Sociedad/Women and Society* demonstrates, feminists did not seem to take this movement seriously: "Women's popular organizations are gaining political importance. All the political sectors see women's organizations as their audience and potential base. It seems that everyone is interested in them except the feminists. In the last years we have seen a clear absence of feminists and this absence seems intentional."[55] *Mujer y Sociedad/Women and Society* reflects the concerns of the popular-class women's organizations that were critical of feminists.

Peruvian feminist Roxana Vásquez Sotelo remarks that during the internal armed conflict, the feminists always participated in the marches and public statements.[56] In the early 1980s the feminists took part in political mobilizations against political violence such as the campaign to protest the rape of Georgina Gamboa by the armed forces in Ayacucho and the solidarity campaign with María Antonieta Escobar, who was raped by police when detained under the accusation of terrorism. The women's movement, including the feminist movement, had an awareness of the common practice of sexual violence during the internal armed conflict, perpetrated in its majority by armed forces and the police, as the following testimony in *Mujer y Sociedad/Women and Society* elucidates. "What happened with the women was tragic. When the military did its searches (for terrorists) and captured a girl, they would take her to the barracks. They would tell her that if she didn't do what they wanted, they would accuse her of being a terrorist. Then the higher commanders would call the soldiers and say, 'Make a line, we have brought you a terrorist,' and they would all rape her. After, they would let her go or leave her somewhere."[57] In addition to protesting specific violations against women, another type of activity was the silent vigil, such as the one held on October 4, 1985, in front of the main military installation in Lima (*el Comando Conjunto*), in which feminists participated with miners, housewives, and professionals, protesting recent massacres in Ayacucho.

In 1986 and 1987 small groups of about one hundred feminists staged marches protesting massacres in Andean communities. In response, both the Shining Path and the armed forces started to threaten them. The Shining Path terrorized popular women leaders who were making headway in gaining a response from the state for their basic needs. In general, the Shining Path tried to discredit feminists and popular women leaders and their efforts because they propped up the legitimacy of the state. Under pressure, feminists retreated from staging smaller protests and participated in larger protests with the human rights movement. They also continued to raise the issue in their events such as International Women's Day on March 8 and the Day to End Violence against Women on November 25.[58] All these gestures point to a general and sincere concern, even though feminists did not mount a clear legal initiative to defend cases of human rights violations against campesinas.

In the late 1980s most urban feminists had little knowledge of rural Andean women's lives, priorities, or concerns, as the following excerpt of an article in the *Mujer y Sociedad/Women and Society* illustrates. "The situation of women from Andean communities, be they agricultural or pastoral, is still an unknown reality, just as [with] their daily life, their productive labors, their vision of the world, their ideas and values—what it means to them to be a women."[59] From the perspective of urban feminist academics, although there was interest in researching women in Peru, "studies on rural women were abandoned in the 1980s due to the political violence."[60] Patricia Ruiz Bravo adds that information is limited regarding the gendered aspects of rural life, and this information is also limited by stereotypes about what women do and who they are. This lack of research contrasts with the great quantity of studies that focus on urban women.

A workshop held in February 1988 offers an exceptional case of collective reflection and concern within the women's movement regarding the increasing violence and its effects on Peruvian women. A group of twenty campesinas and leaders from Lima and the regions came together to discuss violence in the daily life of women. The decision to approach thinking about the manifestations of violence through the experience of women was based on the fact that "women are invisible not only in social and political practices but also in sickness, pain and anguish."[61] The workshop opened a space of solidarity and affirmation carved out against the norm of distrust and silence, rejuvenating and renewing the participants. The assassination of two social justice workers, Consuelo Garcia and Saúl Cantoral, preceded the workshop, bringing the weight of the context of violence to bear on their discussions. Building upon the important gains of the human rights movement in investigating and documenting human rights violations, the workshop had the goal of "illustrating the sociocultural, psychological and subjective aspects involved in the current violence on both the individual and collective levels."[62] The report titled "Women, Violence and Human Rights," which came out of the workshop, could not be published in Peru due to security concerns and was first published in Spain by the Commission of Women and Development of the Institution of Political Studies of Latin America and Africa (IEPALA).

The Human Rights Movement:
"Ensuciando los zapatos/Getting your shoes dirty"

The human rights movement started in the early 1980s in response to the escalating violence of the Shining Path and armed forces. With the armed forces' incursion into Ayacucho in 1983 to rout out the Shining Path and the systematic disappearances and detentions under General Noel, activists and advocates founded the Pro-Human Rights Association (APRODEH) in 1983 and one year later the Legal Defense Institute (IDL). Preceding these organizations, the Commission on Human Rights (COMISEDH) established itself in 1979.

The struggles for labor and land rights in the 1970s form the roots of the human rights movement. The origins of the human rights movement grow out of a long history of denouncing injustice in Peru. Joanna Drzewieniecki dates the precursors of the human rights movement to the end of the nineteenth century at the time of the introduction of leftist ideologies in Peru and the leftist lawyers use of the legal system to defend indigenous people and poor urban populations against abuses.[63] Colleta Youngers[64] dates the inception of the human rights movement to 1977 after the national strike against President Morales Bermudez's conservative military regime[65] and the subsequent repression of unions and their leadership. The organizations that came about in this moment were not long lasting but did allow the participants to develop organizational skills and sowed the seeds of the human rights movement. These precursors were rooted in progressive churches and leftist political activism, which shared a commitment to social justice.[66] These earlier formations did not use the term *human rights*; rather, they framed their struggle in terms of social and economic rights and the end to military dictatorship.

Two significant precursors to the human rights movement during the late 1970s include the National Commission on Human Rights (CONADEH) and the committees for human rights (CODEH). In 1979, CONADEH formed between progressive Catholic and evangelical churches and the leftist parties to create an organization with national presence.[67] Yet it was unsuccessful and collapsed as a result of leftist party divisions and power struggles, and it was later transformed into an NGO, the Human Rights Commission (COMISEDH), still active to date. Another important development was that of the CODEH on the departmental level bringing together diverse sectors of society, including leftist political activists and religious activists also in response to the political repression after the 1977 national strike and to struggles for socioeconomic rights.

The Catholic-based Episcopal Commission of Social Action (CEAS) was founded in 1976 in response to growing economic crises, national strikes, and massive layoffs in industrial and state labor sectors. CEAS worked with unions to resolve labor disputes, search for detained leaders, and assist with job training. When the internal armed conflict started, CEAS mounted a broad and intense response, working with people affected by the conflict, especially the displaced. CEAS searched for detained persons, educated affected populations about their human rights, spoke out against the violations, and created a network to protect those whose lives were threatened. Their work utilized civil and political rights to investigate, document, and address cases of torture, disappearance, massacres, and extrajudicial executions. CEAS defended the right to life, liberty, personal integrity, and due process. Yet access to these services varied regionally, as CEAS and other religious groups could not provide a uniform presence in all affected areas. CEAS's work highlights the role of religious groups within the broader human rights movement.

From the beginning these nascent human rights groups were in contact with international human rights organizations. On the domestic level the human rights movement responded to the unwavering demands of the families of the victims for justice. "Getting their shoes dirty" is but a euphemism for consistently risking their lives to defend victims' human rights. Rosa Cuchillo's case illustrates one life struggle, among tens of thousands, that human rights advocates represent to this day. In those first years, human rights advocates focused on influencing public opinion, advocacy in the defense of human rights, acquiring material resources from the state for affected communities, and legal reform.

The budding human rights movement was vulnerable to attacks from the state under the assumption that they were supportive of terrorists because of their leftist party affiliations. The radical Left in Peru before the Shining Path declared armed struggle in 1980 could be understood as a "'family' of political projects inspired in Marxism that competed among themselves, each seeking to impose its own revolutionary ideology."[68] Certain groups, including Revolutionary Vanguard and the Leftist Revolutionary Movement (MIR), were more involved in developing a human rights focus.[69] It is of note that in the early 1980s it was leftist parliament leadership from the Unified Mariateguista Party (PUM) and the Union of Revolutionary Left (UNIR) that spearheaded investigations into human rights violations. Human rights advocates began to challenge President Fernando Belaúnde's counterinsurgency strategies that resulted in rampant human rights violations and complete impunity in the 1980s. In response, the government labeled the human rights movement proterrorist.

From a conservative political perspective all groups within the radical left were comrades in arms and in solidarity with the Shining Path. This framing tactic served to discredit politically the leftist parties. In addition, the state saw the issue of human rights as an obstacle to winning the war against subversives by any means necessary.[70] As part of the war against subversive groups, the state launched campaigns to discredit human rights organizations, in addition to threats and direct actions against them. In the 1990s Fujimori "made the denigration of human rights groups into a personal crusade"[71] and "accused them of being 'apologists' of terrorism."[72] Fujimori's vilification of human rights groups was a small piece of a larger strategy that included new legislation that broadened the definition of terrorism, imposed draconian punishment, and did away with due process.

Hostile attitudes toward human rights organizations on the part of both the state and the Shining Path created a precarious context for their work. After the armed struggle started and the human rights violations began, the more traditional Marxist Leninist or Maoist camp, including *Patria Roja* and *Bandera Roja*, felt that human rights were a bourgeois issue. Human rights advocates called upon the Shining Path to honor international humanitarian law. The Shining Path attacked the human rights advocates as defenders of the state and as part of an imperialist tactic that combines repression with the supposed respect for democratic formalities such as human rights.

Besides the different leftist and religious groups, the newly born human rights movement also included youth who were not formally connected to leftist parties, as well as union activists, intellectuals, and lawyers committed to democratic principles.[73] The discourse and ideas of the most progressive sectors of the Catholic Church strongly influenced the movement. The exception to this would be APRODEH, which evolved out of a strongly secular leftist party.[74] In the early stages the human rights movement navigated between subordination to leftist political parties and religious institutions, grounding itself in an organizational culture that privileged consensus.

The magnitude of the human rights violations and the lack of state response overwhelmed the fledgling movement. Quickly, they united under the umbrella group the National Coordinator of Human Rights (Coordinadora) in response to the escalation of the internal armed conflict and the attacks and threats they suffered from both the Shining Path and the armed forces. Participants in the first National Human Rights Conference, which took place in January 1985, founded the Coordinadora. Civil society organizations, including APRODEH, IDL, the Commission of Andean Jurists, the Peruvian section of Amnesty International, and the Commission of Rights and the Construction of Peace (Codepp), as well as the families of victims (ANFASEP and COFADER), formed the Coordinadora.

The first order of business was to deliver a forceful message of full rejection of the use of violence by subversive groups and the armed forces alike. This was the only way to distance themselves fully from the Shining Path and establish their own credibility. The Coordinadora facilitated power sharing and consensus decision making under the extremely tense and dangerous conditions of the internal armed conflict. Although the roots of the human rights movement came out of labor and land struggles, this new articulation narrowed its agenda to respond to the staggering human rights violations and did not include peasant groups or unions—with whom it would have been political suicide to align because this would imply party affiliation.

The human rights movement's relationships to the Catholic and Evangelical churches contribute to its enduring legitimacy. Religious groups lend moral authority to the movement and the Coordinadora specifically. In particular, the Episcopal Commission of Social Action (CEAS) contributes "a moral and ethical value to human rights work, credibility; a national reference point for parochial human rights groups and unified progressive groups of the Catholic church, which makes up the backbone of the human rights movement; and the support of religious leaders who promoted human rights and offered more legitimacy."[75] Indeed, the Coordinadora's first executive secretary (1987–1992), Pilar Coll, came from the ranks of CEAS, exemplifying the central role of religious organizations in the formulation of a human rights response to the conflict. Her religious affiliation and distance from leftist militancy afforded her more legitimacy. Also, as a Spanish expatriate living in Peru, she was less likely to be labeled proterrorist by conservative sectors.

The Coordinadora demanded that the state respect international human rights law and that both the armed forces and subversive groups respect international humanitarian law as applied to internal armed conflict. The Coordinadora's four membership principles include "repudiation of all forms of violence and condemnation of terrorist groups, revindication of democracy as the best political system, independence in relation to the state and political parties, and opposition to the death penalty."[76] The PTRC's final report highlights the main juridical contributions of human rights groups, which include the nullification of general amnesties for perpetrators of human rights violations; the right of victims to truth, justice and reparations; and the responsibility of the state to prevent the repetition of the conflict through effective reforms of security forces. In addition, the Coordinadora advocated for the legislation that recognized torture within the Peruvian penal code.

One of the critiques of the Coordinadora during the 1980s and 1990s was that people from the Andean departments, where the majority of the human rights violations were occurring, did not have proportional representation. Although some campesinos affected by the conflict were included in the Coordinadora through ANFASEP and COFADER, they did not have equal decision-making power in relation to their counterparts in Lima. Yet on a practical level, highly trained attorneys were an indispensable component to the defense of human rights. The exigencies of professional training to defend human rights cases compounded with regional hierarchies and social fragmentation. The extreme violence produced a generalized fear within society that inhibited solidarity toward the victims of human rights violations. "The victims were not equal, they did not form part of 'us.'"[77] This social polarization only exacerbated historic social hierarchies as experienced within the movements.

Little by little, awareness among people within the human rights movement increased, and they began to work on women's human rights issues. In the 1990s, human rights organizations such as Americas Watch and the Women's Right Project (1992) as well as the Pro-Human Rights Association APRODEH (1994) in Peru began to give more attention to the violations women suffered, including detention and torture. Sexual violence fell into the legal category of torture.[78] Even though human rights advocates were defending cases of sexual violence, the overall social context of distrust and polarization made collaboration with feminists unlikely. The social context eroded the possibility of drawing conceptual and practical linkages across different subsections of society and social movements. In the late 1990s the social fragmentation gave way to groups that began to express opposition to Fujimori's corruption and abuse of authority. During this period of civil society awakening, human rights and feminist movement forged a collaborative relationship.

Fraught Encounters in the 1990s

The 1990s presented moments of both conflict and collaboration between the human rights and feminist movements. Francisco Soberón, veteran human rights activist, alludes to how sectors of the weakened feminist movement allied with the Fujimori regime, raising great suspicions within the human rights movement. However, the work of Women for Democracy, *Mujeres por la Democracia* (MUDE), reanimated the relationship between the two movements in the late 1990s through their collaboration in the prodemocracy movement that contributed to the ousting of Fujimori's authoritarian regime in 2000. This moment of collaboration and generalized civil society engagement created the unique political context for transitional justice and the implementation of a Peruvian Reconciliation Commission. Throughout this period, however, legitimated inequalities continued to define the default position of these movements towards campesinas' rights.

Fujimori's authoritarian rule was epitomized by his military-backed self-coup in 1992, which included the suspension of the constitution, dismissal of congress, and declaration of a state of emergency. That same year Fujimori captured the Shining Path leader Abimael Guzman along with the top cadre of leaders. While Fujimori enjoyed spectacular public approval, he needed to bolster his image on the international stage. Fujimori used the banner of women's issues to blanket himself with legitimacy under the cloak of modernity, a classic "gender-washing" strategy. He appeared at the 1995 UN Conference on Women in Beijing, the only president in attendance. His speech received a warm reception from some of the Peruvian feminist participants.

Through the 1990s a sector of feminists worked with Fujimori instrumentally because of the new political opening he facilitated. Fujimori created a Ministry of Women and Human Development, a Public Defender for Women, and a Congressional Committee on Women. Schmidt claims that since "professionals recruited from feminist NGOs staffed the committee . . . , there was a direct link between a cohesive female congressional caucus and the feminist movement."[79] The Fujimori regime also incorporated women and women's issues through passage of a law against domestic violence and a quota law "that obliged political parties to present women candidates in at least 30% of the races for local and Congressional office."[80] All of these developments strongly appealed to feminist activists and political advocates and increased feminist strategies centered on the state. These high-profile links created the impression of a generalized alliance with the feminist movement in the eyes of the public, while sectors of the feminist movement strongly opposed Fujimori throughout.

The main tension that dominated the feminist movement in the 1990s emanated from frictions between those who chose to pursue negotiations with Fujimori and those who were alarmed with the democratic closure and swing toward authoritarianism under his administration. In hindsight, feminist negotiation strategies failed, in that they "did not allow for a long-term vision that could translate collective demands into democratic gains."[81]

As human rights advocate Liliana Panizo explains, there was a high level of pragmatism in the Peruvian feminist movement that led certain individuals to collaborate with Fujimori because he was making structural changes that favored women's rights, even though he was a dictator.[82]

During this period, feminists prioritized sexual and reproductive rights and gains in formal politics over the effects of the conflict on women or the economic demands of the popular women's movement that was suffering from Fujimori's neoliberal economic policies. Women struggling to meet their families' basic needs continued to organize communal kitchens. Fujimori's populist engagement with women's organizations did not open channels for real participation or economic relief from extreme poverty. Meanwhile, elements of the upper-class sector of the women's movement, the feminists, found entry into governmental circles.[83]

Fujimori's family-planning policy, which put him at odds with powerful religious institutions, made him a natural ally for feminists. He included voluntary sterilization as an acceptable contraceptive method, to the approval of the feminist movement. When the feminist organization CLADEM's 1999 investigation *Nada Personal/Nothing Personal* exposed how 243 women from nineteen departments were sterilized without informed consent, some feminists found themselves on the wrong side of the issue.[84] One group, including the NGO *Movimiento Manuela Ramos*, wanted to reform from within using their connections to foster dialogue. The other group wanted to publicly denounce and protest but found it difficult to craft a message that stood apart from the Catholic Church's public denunciation. The feminists' inability to present a strong and clear response to the issue undermined the movement's credibility and exposed its weakness in defending campesinas' rights. Overall, this messy debacle further tarnished the feminist movement's reputation in the eyes of the human rights movement.

Javier Ciurlizza, human rights advocate and ex-PTRC executive secretary, highlights the conflicting issues, how the human rights movement strongly criticized the feminists for allying with the authoritarian regime.[85] How can you dissociate women's human rights from a regime that is increasingly authoritarian? From the perspective of human rights advocates, how could the feminists overlook the two massacres by the national secret service death squad "*Grupo Colina*" that had recently taken place in *Barrios Altos* (1991) and *La Cantuta* (1992), or the 1995 amnesty laws that formalized impunity as a state policy? As Chiurlizza explains, this issue caused a rift, although it was never explicit. He also explains that later the feminists regained a much broader and integrated vision, which was made clear through their leadership during the prodemocracy movement,[86] which in the late 1990s highlighted a shared legacy of the Peruvian left, the culture of dissent. In addition, this example further illustrates the circumstantial quality of their collaborations.

The Prodemocracy Movement and "Women for Democracy"

In the mid-1990s with the capture of Shining Path leaders, the violence in the Andean and Amazonian regions declined, as did the car bombs and general power outages in Lima. In response, the human rights movement opened and shifted their focus. "As the political violence lessened and the political parties weakened, human rights work stopped being understood in ideological terms, and the equation of human rights with terrorism began to fade in the minds of the people."[87] The constant accusation of terrorist affiliation decreased, allowing the human rights movement to move out of a defensive positioning. In 1997 the human rights national meeting formally adopted the struggle for democracy and citizenship promotion in response to Fujimori's growing authoritarianism. According to Sofia Macher, human rights advocate and ex-Coordinadora executive secretary, instead of solely prioritizing individual cases of human rights violations, the Coordinadora shifted to a more political agenda and framed the struggle for democracy as inseparable from the struggle for human rights.[88]

The human rights and feminist movements shared the underlying culture of dissent, a legacy of the Peruvian Left, which helped them overcome the culture of fear that dominated during the internal armed conflict and authoritarian regime. Sofia Macher reflects on the human rights and feminist movements: "Here you see the similarities and the possibility of the two movements working together to advance rights within an international context. We both belong to large networks and share visions for the future. We have democratic standards that we have won in international spaces. I think that our formation in legal and democratic standards made it easy to understand the struggle for democracy in that moment."[89] In the struggle for democracy, a broad coalition drew upon its international networks to bring attention to the Peruvian government, questioning its credibility.

Fujimori's decision to run for a third term in 2000 took his corruption and disregard for the constitution to new heights. His public support had severely declined, driving him to rely further on intimidation tactics and bribery. He forced a law through congress that would allow him to run as a candidate in 2000. Fujimori won the presidency in 1990, which was at that time in Peru a one-term position. In 1993, shortly after his self-coup, he introduced a new constitution that would allow him to run for a second term, which he did in 1995 and won. The Law of Authentic Interpretation of the Constitution that he forced through congress in the late 1990s claimed that his 1990 election did not count because it occurred under a previous constitution. Therefore, running in 2000 would technically only count as his second term.

Fujimori's blatant manipulation of the political process alarmed his political opposition and civil society. The authoritarian repression was so strong, silence reigned, and there was an overall terror about voicing an opinion. As Jo-Marie Burt writes, "Key groups in civil society devised ways of framing their opposition to the regime as something positive and proactive: a struggle to recuperate democracy."[90] The Coordinadora took a central role in crafting this message. In the buildup to the 2000 elections, middle-class rejection of authoritarianism fused with popular-class discontent regarding Fujimori's economic policies.

In 1997 a dozen women came together to form Women for Democracy, *Mujeres por la Democracia* (MUDE). Liliana Panizo, human rights advocate and MUDE member, explains that it was a diverse and intense space in which the women who participated held a common position with regard to Fujimori and his dictatorship, yet they had very distinct trajectories.[91] The coalitional space included women from leftist political parties, the human rights movement, the feminist movement, academia, progressive Christian organizations, and popular education initiatives. Each person participated on her individual behalf as a citizen exercising her own rights in support of democratic practice.[92] While the diversity of backgrounds could signal major differences, they all held similar anticapitalist and antineoliberal principles that stem from participation in leftist political parties. These professional women all moved within similar progressive middle- and upper-class spaces in Lima.

MUDE's organizing during 1997–2000 channeled women's demands of, support for, and participation in the prodemocracy movement, and it contributed to the groundswell that eventually stripped Fujimori of his legitimacy. MUDE participated with the broad alliance of groups to denounce Fujimori's authoritarianism. This alliance included Transparencia, a nonprofit civil association dedicated to election monitoring; the Democratic Forum, a grouping of high-profile Peruvians in support of democratic processes and human rights; as well as housewives, political-party militants, and students. In the initial stages MUDE worked closely with the Democratic Forum and the General Confederation of Peruvian Workers (CGTP). Their immediate goal was to gather the necessary signatures for a referendum regarding the constitutionality of Fujimori's third term in office. In the process of gathering signatures in the various departments of Peru, the dynamic they developed led them to create their own space focused on women's political commitment to democracy. The MUDE participants did not want to institutionalize themselves in the form of an NGO. Instead, they each chipped in and passed the hat around to supportive organizations in order to meet their financial needs.

As MUDE, they began to organize marches dressed in black,[93] influenced by the global Women in Black movement committed to peace, which began in Israel/Palestine. These performative acts contributed to the newly developing civil society assertions into public space and received immediate support. This experience led MUDE to believe that taking to the streets was just as important as writing articles and signing statements.[94] In addition to public mobilizations, MUDE also held large public forums to discuss and reflect on pertinent issues such as poverty and the position of the government toward women, drawing popular attention. At one such forum the feminists from both factions—those working with the Fujimori regime to advance women's issues and those taking a strong position against the authoritarian regime—explained and justified their political strategies. The debate created a clear division, and at that moment the MUDE slogan emerged, "What is not good for democracy is not good for women," signaling a shift in articulation of women's struggles toward a broader prodemocratic vision.[95]

The MUDE slogan criticized the factions of the feminist movement who continued to negotiate with the authoritarian regime. Those factions forsook democratic principles for specific political gains. As Barrig asserts, "Celebrating victories such as the creation of government institutions to serve women and quota laws to increase political participation have become frayed at the edges by the persistent reality of inequality among women."[96] The slogan turns the previous feminist assumption, "What is not good for women is not good for democracy," on its head. Indeed, the Fujimori regime demonstrated that women expanding their rights and practice of citizenship did not go hand in hand with democratic practices.[97]

The issues of popular women's economic concerns and violence against campesinas during the conflict do present themselves on the MUDE agenda. With regard to campesinas and the effect of the internal armed conflict, MUDE included it as a top priority in its list of key points for democratic transition. In 1998 the Democratic Forum developed a list of thirty points for democratic transition. MUDE organized seventy-three women to dedicate a day to debate the thirty points and come up with their contribution from a women's perspective. In relation to the first point, "Democratic government, transparent electoral process," they conclude: "It is not possible to construct a democratic government upon a base of impunity. Therefore, a Truth Commission should be established. The struggle against impunity is not limited to the crime of illicit appropriation [corruption] but also includes the sanctioning of those responsible for human rights violations and the reparations of victims, with special attention to women who have suffered sexual violence."[98] The combination of perspectives present in MUDE produced remarkable foresight into the future transitional justice process.

In June 2000, soon after Fujimori started his controversial second/third term, the Organization of American States (OAS) responded to the political crisis in Peru by sending a mission. The OAS established the *Mesa de Diálogo*, a roundtable for dialogue with chosen political elites from the Fujimori administration, the political opposition, and representatives from civil society to develop an agenda for reform.[99] Human rights advocates Sofia Macher and Jorge Santistevan were invited to participate along with sixteen others. As corruption scandals and massive popular discontent unleashed overwhelming pressure on his administration, the *Mesa de Diálogo* became a central space for political negotiation.

Although MUDE did not have a seat at the *Mesa de Diálogo*, the group felt very strongly that the OAS mission should stay neutral and autonomous, that its agenda should not get coopted by powerful national interest groups, and corruption could not continue to be the status quo. To this end, MUDE organized a march of about three hundred people to the OAS office in the high-class residential neighborhood of San Isidro in Lima. The symbolic and performative elements of dressing in black, carrying flowers and a coffin, and having many people walk in costume on stilts through the residential neighborhood captured the attention of everyone around. This novel approach to making a public political statement caught the OAS security off guard. This was not the typical angry crowd in an unruly street protest. Although the OAS did not open their doors to receive the MUDE-led group, the march contributed to introducing a new mode of communicating political demands that broke down the overwhelming silence, polarization, and fear of the previous years.[100]

In November 2000, Fujimori took the presidential jet to Brunei to participate in an economic summit and then went to in Japan, abandoning his position.[101] Fujimori's political opposition gained control of the congress and voted him morally unfit to serve as president.[102] The congress picked Valentín Paniagua, another participant in the *Mesa de Diálogo* and President of Congress, to succeed Fujimori and facilitate a clean and transparent election process, initiating the period of transitional justice. Among the highlights Rebecca Root points out, the fact that human rights advocates participated in the *Mesa de Diálogo* positioned them as highly influential actors in the transition period.[103]

In light of the new elections to come, MUDE made it a priority to address the manipulation of popular women's vote that was so blatantly demonstrated in the 2000 election. Fujimori created a perversely clientalistic relationship with popular women through a mix of favors and threats. The favors included food for their communal kitchens and presents in exchange, of course, for political support. As long as they expressed support, they did not have to worry about the underlying threat of the favors, stipends, and presents drying up. To ensure that this type of manipulation did not continue with the future administration, MUDE developed a campaign of "Commitment to Citizenship" for the presidential candidates to sign, committing themselves to the following: "Not to use either state resources or the power of their position to exercise pressure over women who participate in popular organizations by offering them current or future support conditioned to their vote; not to offer one-time funds to women's popular organizations that do not have a serious commitment to their continuity; not to damage the dignity of poor women with gifts that undermine their citizenship."[104] On February 27, 2001, MUDE organized a public signing event in which all the presidential candidates, including frontrunner Alejandro Toledo, appeared and signed the "Commitment to Citizenship" with the full attention of the national press. Transparencia and the Special Defender of Women's Rights of the National Ombudsman's office observed the electoral process to assure that all candidates fulfilled their commitment.[105] Again, this demonstrates MUDE's clarity around the need to respect popular women's rights.

While the prodemocracy struggle demanded deep collaboration across civil society, and particularly between human rights advocates and feminists, the relationships did not last. After Fujimori's regime imploded and the transition to democracy began, civil-society unity frayed. Once Valentín Paniagua established the transitional administration, the movements went back to their parallel tracks—not even meeting to conduct a final debrief or evaluation. Much of this has to do with the fact that only some of the groups were invited to the table to be part of the transition process. In line with legitimated inequalities, campesinas were not on the list of invitees, and feminists also found themselves on the outside looking in.

Transitional president Paniagua convened a working group that included the Ministries of the Interior, of Defense, of Justice, and of Women. In addition, representatives of the Evangelical and Catholic Churches, the Ombudsman's office, and the Coordinadora took part. The transitional government under Paniagua excluded popular-movement representation, to which regional movements and labor groups immediately responded with petitions and demands. Yet in a transition to democracy that facilitates governability and goes hand in hand with neoliberalism, "professional politicians and political analysts" guide the process.[106] Human rights advocates of the more professionalized ilk were included in planning the transition, and many were eager to effect change from within through public service. The human rights movement took advantage of a window of opportunity given the weakness of political parties.

Four key factors positioned human rights groups to take a primary position in the transition: "the high level of coordination among domestic NGOs, their ability to position themselves as critics of both the state and the insurgents in the conflict, their effective networking with international NGOs, and the strategy of 'forum shopping' to exert pressure on the state from multiple sources."[107] Although groups like ANFASEP, comprised mostly of campesinas, were "the backbone of the movement,"[108] their voices were not heard at the table. Socially legitimated inequalities were reinforced by the normal order of things regarding who gets to sit at the table.

Before the fall of the Fujimori regime, the human rights movement prioritized the need to establish a truth and reconciliation commission, as echoed in MUDE's first point for democratic transition. Since inclusion of a truth and reconciliation commission was not part of the initial transition agenda, human rights advocates who had been invited to the table made it one of their top agenda items.[109] Although Paniagua did not initially support the idea, the pressure of two groups tipped the balance. Fujimori's political opponents in congress saw the opportunity to establish themselves as ethical leaders by supporting an investigation of Fujimori's abuses with a focus on corruption. This group's influence combined with the human rights movement advocacy efforts, represented by Susana Villarán (MUDE) and Diego García Sayán. These two high-profile human rights advocates were key figures in getting human rights violations included into a broader TRC investigation.[110]

The PTRC was folded into the transition to democracy as the key transitional justice mechanism along with the preparation of legal cases to be tried at the domestic level. The struggle for democracy and inclusion continued in the work of the PTRC and the civil society follow-up efforts. General excitement about the transition and the opportunity to build a more inclusionary state marked an important moment in Peruvian history. The PTRC embodied this hopeful and visionary moment.

Conclusion

Peru follows the international trend toward embracing the transitional justice paradigm. Paige Arthur highlights four factors that brought transition to democracy into vogue. "In most of the countries undergoing political change, democracy was a desirable goal for many people; the delegitimization of modernization theory; the transformation of the transitions concept from a tool of socioeconomic transformation to one of legal-institutional reform; and the global decline of the radical Left."[111] Three of these factors feature prominently in Peru. The exigencies of responding to massive human rights violations transformed demands on the state from socioeconomic terms of class domination common in the 1970s to civil political terms from the 1980s on. The decline of the radical Left in Peru weakened the popular voices demanding socioeconomic justice. Historic and legitimated inequalities became the backdrop to the urgent focus on addressing massacres, torture, disappearances, and extrajudicial executions.

As the conflict declined, the problem of Fujimori's authoritarianism took center stage. A generalized popular demand for democracy was the most effective frame through which to combat his regime. Democracy was indeed the desirable goal, as the prodemocracy movement of the late 1990s illustrates. Overall, the internal armed conflict redirected the energies and focus of the human rights movement away from broader social and economic inequalities toward individual violations, as well as the demand for democracy.

Introducing an intersectional sensibility to the analysis contextualizes how campesinas' second-class citizenship translated into exclusion from formal transitional justice processes. During the conflict their demands ended up on the edges of the peasant, feminist, and human rights movements. While the movements held the potential to take up gender-based violence during internal armed conflict, they placed little value on the issue. Although gender-based violence during internal armed conflict had come to light on the international stage and through the 1993 UN Conference on Human Rights, neither the Peruvian feminist movement nor the human rights movement took up the banner. Awareness of and attention to this issue was in its nascent stages, and both movements had more pressing issues.

The dynamics of legitimated inequality as played out through the feminist and human rights movements highlight the forces of erasure against which campesinas struggle. The second half of the 1990s presented moments of both collaboration and conflict among the two movements, further situating the struggles for inclusion that were to play out in the PTRC. Given the separation between human rights and feminist agendas, the PTRC and various NGOs break new ground by conceptually and practically bridging the concerns of the two movements in the ongoing struggle for justice. Returning to Arthur's factors, the struggle for socioeconomic justice gave way to the transitions concept of legal-institutional reform, which fit with the focus on human rights violations in Peru, the justice-seeking aspects of the TRC mandate, and the decision to prepare domestic legal cases. As the next chapter demonstrates, within this legal-institutional reform focus, the PTRC made a concerted effort to include a gender analysis and to address gender-based violence, specifically sexual violence.

2

Gender Implementation in the Peruvian Truth and Reconciliation Commission

When the Peruvian Truth and Reconciliation Commission (PTRC) initiated its investigation in August 2001, a gender analysis was not included. The twelve commissioners felt pressure to address the issue of gender, which functioned largely as a placeholder for "what happened to women." Developments since the early 1990s brought gender-based violence, specifically rape, to light on the international stage. In 2000 the UN Security Council's landmark resolution 1325 recognized that women are the most affected in armed conflicts and called for the full implementation of human rights and international humanitarian law.[1] International pressure coupled with funding sources that required a gender component, and women's and feminist movements' advocacy compelled the commissioners to integrate the issue of gender into their investigation.[2]

Studying the debate around the meaning of gender, its methodological operationalization and incorporation into the final report allows for a reflection on the struggle for inclusion within the PTRC. Human rights law provides the most salient political discourse to address gender-based violence, yet this discourse can never capture the full scope of harm. This paradox of rights sets the backdrop for analyzing how the PTRC reinforces a logic that upholds social hierarchies while also opening new spaces to consider a gender analysis. The PTRC illustrates the double-edged sword of feminist strategies of inclusion.

PTRC archival materials and interviews with PTRC staff, volunteers, and consultants illustrate how incorporating gender hinged on constant negotiation between a legalistic approach and a gendered social interpretive approach. The push to document direct human rights violations against women led the PTRC staff to conform to a simplified definition of gender as conflated with biological sex difference and thus the word was made interchangeable with "woman." Therefore, a victim-centered investigation placed emphasis on documenting sexual violence against women, rape in particular.[3] Jose Burneo, an expert in international law, headed the Juridical Unit. Given his familiarity with sexual violence as a human rights violation, there was more initial support for including such cases in the scope of the PTRC investigation than incorporating a gender analysis.[4] Indeed, the PTRC broke new ground in Peru by addressing gender-based violence, specifically the sexual violence that fell outside the main focus of the feminist and human rights movements. Yet the problem of conceptual myopia around sexual violence reappeared, reducing the potential of a gendered social interpretive approach.

Simultaneously, feminist academics advocated for a gender analysis that not only accounts for the gender-based differential of human rights violations but also an analysis of historic power relations and the gendered symbolic, cultural, social, political, and economic aspects of the conflict. Narda Henríquez, feminist sociologist and PTRC gender consultant, writes:

> The gender perspective is not only an optic from or about women, the gender perspective has an interpretive value to explain how differences are constructed, how discriminatory practices are institutionalized in organizations, public entities, and political culture. All of society requires this analytical perspective to achieve not only a better life, but also a better government. This is not only about gender equity, it is a perspective central to the understanding of our reality, ourselves and what we hope to achieve through our interpretation of our recent past.[5]

The underlying premise of the gendered social interpretive approach is that gender is socially constructed.

A small number of advocates internal and external to the PTRC, including Narda Henríquez, favored a gendered social interpretive approach, suggesting gender be implemented as a transversal axis of investigation and woven through the whole report. This approach is typically called gender mainstreaming. The vast majority of the PTRC relied on the universal (gender-neutral) human rights approach, including religious perspectives ideologically invested in the concept of gender based on biological sex difference. The legalistic orientation within the PTRC methodology, in addition to the time pressures and space limitations in the final report, curtailed the potential contribution of a gendered social interpretive approach. A careful review of the PTRC methodology exposes how feminist advocates eventually had to take a conceptual step back to accept the subordinated integration of gender into the PTRC.

In my interviews and personal exchanges with feminist-minded PTRC staff and volunteers, their reflections on the personal impact of the PTRC open a space to consider the embodied connections between gender, language, ethnicity, and culture, as related to the Peruvian geographic imaginary, colonial mappings of difference and identity formation. One person's reflections, whose identity I leave anonymous, stands out to me. She remembered how after participating in a workshop in Ayacucho, a young man approached her and asked her about her last name. He mentioned that it was also his last name, a family name from his community. She confirmed that her family was from the same community and he replied that all his family had been killed in the conflict.

The realization that much of her family must also have been killed changed her. She remarked that she is no longer the same person: "*Me marcó, ya no soy la misma persona.*" This personal connection to the atrocities of the conflict jarred her out of a position of social distance. Growing up in Lima, her family purposefully did not teach her Quechua so that she would not suffer discrimination. She went on to identify as, and live the life of, a Limeña with a commitment to fighting for women's rights. The encounter in Ayacucho collapsed the sociospatial divides that had defined her identity up until that moment.

Assimilation demands the repression of one's indigenous language and culture. Peruvian geographic imaginary posits the coastal capital of Lima in opposition to the Andean and Amazonian regions—social divides Peru inherited from its colonial past. She asserted that working for the PTRC gave her the unexpected opportunity to reconcile with her heritage and history. Her emotionally painful catharsis allowed her to holistically reconstruct her identity. Many commissioners, staff, and volunteers experienced similar moments that bridged socially constructed divides. These cathartic moments elucidate the PTRC's decolonial undercurrent, the intimate and humanizing transformation of the relationship between the colonial "self" and the indigenous "other."

While analyzing the PTRC's incorporation of a gender analysis seems a singular task, an intersectional sensibility suggests that language, ethnicity, and culture, as related to the Peruvian geographic imaginary and colonial mappings of difference, matter in the analysis of gender. As discussed in the previous chapters, an intersectional sensibility highlights the limits of compartmentalizing gender and race as separate within the law and works to make visible gender-based violence against campesinas, as well as campesina protagonism.

An intersectional sensibility dovetails with decolonial feminist thought through the deconstruction of binary logics. Decolonial thinker Freya Schiwy explains that gender and race interact through Spanish and Portuguese colonialism. "They coalesce into gender specific forms of oppression and mesh long-standing imaginaries in order to justify economic, political, ethnic, and epistemic hierarchies."[6] Decolonial feminist analyses deepen the critique of separate social categories such as gender and race, highlighting how binaries are instruments of colonial relations both in the past and in the present because they establish frameworks of superiority and inferiority. Besides reading for the intersections of separate categories, decolonial feminist analyses emphasize that the bodies that inhabit such categories cannot be separated into parts. Those bodies and collectivities form an integral whole before the imposition of such categories.

Documenting human rights violations and ending impunity are paramount tasks. Analyzing the PTRC methodology highlights the challenges of defining and operationalizing a gender perspective, as well as documenting sexual violence within data gathering and testimony processing. Yet a critical examination of the PTRC's conceptual limits sheds light on possible alternative formulations of transitional justice. The conceptual limits explored here include the separation of social categories such as gender and ethnicity, the dominance of binary logic inherent in the private/public sphere, political/criminal violence and extraordinary/ordinary violence, and the colonial mappings of difference within the Peruvian geopolitical imaginary.

An intersectional sensibility and decolonial feminist analysis interlace with an awareness of the continuum of violence against women to show how binaries such as the public/private spheres obfuscate gender-based violence during the internal armed conflict. A close reading of PTRC materials and interviews exposes how the logics that lead to subordinated integration of gender also reinforce colonial mappings of difference. In other words, who produces knowledge where and what people and places provide data overlap with racialized mappings of Peru. The PTRC's conceptual limitations, as well intense time pressures, circumscribe the possibility of addressing historic social hierarchies and threaten the promise of a transition to democracy.

Engendering the PTRC Investigation

The PTRC held a neutral, independent, and autonomous relationship with the state.[7] This mandate included investigating the crimes and violations of human rights that occurred between 1980 and 2000, analyzing the causes of the violence, and interpreting these events with a perspective toward preventing repetition. The PTRC main office where the commissioners met was located in Lima. The commissioners' guiding questions included: What happened to whom? Who were the perpetrators? Why did it occur? What were the consequences? How do we respond to what happened in terms of justice and reparations? What do we do so it doesn't happen again?[8] Answering these key questions in the final report was an important step toward the transition to democracy: a staff of five hundred and total budget of $13 million was put to the task.[9]

Peru strove to establish the legitimacy of a new democratic regime through a transitional process that included justice and accountability mechanisms combined with truth-seeking, reconciliation, and peacemaking mechanisms. As Chandra Lekha Sriram asserts, "Most transitional justice processes include both accountability mechanisms along with peacebuilding and peacemaking efforts."[10] The PTRC drew heavily from a reconciliation/truth-seeking model. The commissioners' discussions favored this type of communicative model to meet the fundamental rights of the most gravely impacted victims—which included the right to know the context, causes, circumstances and authorship of the crimes, the right to legal process, the right to reparations, and the guarantee from the state that the crimes will not happen again.[11] Through a model that honors these four rights, the PTRC is "more than a sum of its investigations, contribution to justice and proposals for reparations, because it is a public, participative process based on dialogue."[12] As one commissioner states, "The product we want to create will help toward reconciliation, reparation, healing, not a product for the judicial system or human rights organizations."[13]

The PTRC balanced the drive toward truth seeking/reconciliation with support for justice in legal terms in order to strengthen the democratic regime. Therefore, the PTRC combined the truth-seeking and justice goals by utilizing truth-seeking language and conceptual components while denying amnesty for perpetrators[14] and mounting a juridical unit that prepared cases to be passed to the state prosecutor for trial. One of the main ways the PTRC proved its efficacy toward the end of its mandated period was by presenting forty-seven cases ready for prosecution.

The juridical dimension of the PTRC investigation included "in-depth case studies," "emblematic cases," and the work of the Anthropological Forensic Team in investigating mass graves.[15] In-depth cases included collecting historical and contextual information regarding the community and a detailed analysis of the impact of the conflict, key players, and events. The emblematic cases were a select set of legal cases that represented specific types of violations. The emblematic Manta and Vilca case highlights cases of sexual violence in rural communities occupied by military bases (the focus of chapters four and five).

The PTRC documented human rights violations, developed a methodology, collected information, organized the database, identified consequences, and made recommendations for reparations and institutional reform. National laws and international human rights and humanitarian law offer categories to document harms committed during the conflict, yet the method of analysis to construct a national historical truth differs from the method of analysis for legal procedures.[16] The combination of justice and truth seeking/reconciliation set the stage for the underlying tension between legalistic and social interpretive approaches to incorporating a gender perspective. Empirical evidence documented through legal categories is critical for proving the impact of the conflict. Simultaneously, such a focus "can under-specify the power relations maintaining gender inequalities, and in the process de-links the investigation of gender issues from a feminist transformatory project."[17]

The legalistic approach to addressing gender and socially conservative religious values ended up reinforcing each other and closing down the conceptual space to pursue a gender-interpretive approach. The religious presence on the commission included three commissioners, Monsignor José Antúnez de Mayolo, La Salle priest; Father Gastón Garatea Yori, Sacred Heart priest; and Minister Humberto Lay Sun, Evangelical leader.[18] The underlying social conservatism of these religious actors supports a sex and gender binary, the "natural" complementarity of men and women, heterosexuality, the traditional family, and uncontrolled fertility. These assumptions reinforce the private and public sphere divide and the subordination of women. Women's sexuality (or violation thereof) falls squarely within the private sphere. In contrast, a gender-interpretive approach understands gender to be a social construct, opening the door to the acknowledgement of gender inequalities, fluid expression of gender and sexuality, and the defense of women's reproductive and sexual rights, along with sex education, including birth control and pro-choice positions.[19]

The ongoing tensions between the feminist and human rights movement due to their conflicting relationship to religious actors and institutions, specifically regarding sexual and reproductive rights, continued to play out in the PTRC. Feminists such as Maruja Barrig tirelessly advocated including abortion rights in the PTRC recommendations, especially in cases of rape. The struggle to legalize abortion has been a top priority for feminists. In Peru, abortion can be performed legally only if the health or life of the woman is in danger. Abortion is illegal even in cases of incest and rape. Adolescent girls comprise 78 percent of rape victims forced into unwanted maternity by the state.[20] Another conflict involved whether to include Fujimori's policy of forced sterilizations within the PTRC investigation: feminists advocated for inclusion since those policies were part of Fujimori's social policy. As Commissioner Sofia Macher explains, the commissioners did not include this because the forced sterilizations did not have any logical connection to the conflict or terrorism.[21]

Taking a stand regarding the need for a gender analysis, one of the two women commissioners, Sofia Macher—sociologist and previous executive secretary of the National Coordinator for Human Rights (Coordinadora)—advocated for the gender program.[22] The commissioners drew from international precedents, including the South African commission's three special public hearings for women,[23] its office of public relations for women,[24] and the Guatemalan commission's recognition of gender-based violence as a tool of terror within its counterinsurgency strategy.

The Gender Unit

In 2001 representatives from the PTRC met with the *Defensora de la Mujer,* feminist NGOs, and the faculty from the Gender Diploma of the *Pontifícia Universidad Católica de Perú* (PUCP) to discuss the incorporation of a gender perspective. The institutional relations functioned most smoothly with the PUCP Gender Diploma faculty, especially since the PTRC president, Salomon Lerner, was also the president of the university. In January 2002 the PTRC brought Julissa Mantilla Falcón onboard as a gender consultant.[25] The young attorney with strong credentials and an affiliation with the PUCP Gender Diploma, and loose ties to the feminist movement, fit the role. While the feminists were of the first to engage in the struggle for democracy, they did not have significant involvement in the PTRC. In the postconflict period, feminist efforts to collaborate with the PTRC emphasized the international and national levels over the subregional and community levels, building on their strength in the international realm yet echoing the general marginalization of rural Andean women.[26]

In May 2002 Julissa Mantilla became the head of the Gender Unit, all the while working on sexual violence cases within the juridical team. The three goals of the Gender Unit included incorporating a gender perspective in the investigation and synthesizing information;[27] developing a set of operational definitions, including human rights violations against women; and conducting a special training for PTRC high-level professionals.[28] The initial gender-mainstreaming strategy of integrating gender as a transversal axis of the investigation combined with the strategy of creating a Gender Unit.[29] The Gender Unit included a small staff in the Lima office that worked to adjust the methodological instruments, run gender-sensitivity workshops for PTRC staff and interviewers, build an awareness campaign regarding violence against women (specifically sexual violence), develop alliances with civil society organizations,[30] and collaborate in the preparation of the thematic public hearings on women.

During the first months of work the Gender Unit had no budget, so its strategy was to build alliances with other units that had budgets and attach activities.[31] The dynamic of having to ask for help exemplified the fragile sense of institutional commitment to a gender analysis. Mantilla built alliances with the Methodology Unit and also the Juridical Unit, as well as with the PTRC psychologists.[32] Since the general disposition regarding gender ranged from ambivalence or indifference to resistance, Mantilla struggled hard to make headway, and the issue became personalized: she was equated with the issue of gender. The alliances she made offered crucial support, given the occasionally combative environment.[33]

As the Gender Unit's presence became known, PTRC women staff with concerns regarding sexual harassment approached it for support. The de facto job description of the Gender Unit included addressing gender inequalities in the workplace. Mantilla explained that "there were a series of needs and the Gender Unit had to respond to all of them."[34] For example, the man who managed the digital database engaged in sexual harassment against one of the female staff by making inappropriate comments about her body and clothes, as well as requiring a kiss in order to release the data she needed. Mantilla posted sexual harassment informational sheets all over the office using the man's exact quotes. Everyone in the office made the connection, and the harasser became the focus of public mockery. This creative strategy not only stopped the sexual harassment but also educated the staff.[35] Nevertheless, the sexist tendencies within the organizational culture posed an obstacle to implementing a gender analysis.[36]

DEFINING GENDER

The process of defining and implementing a gender perspective consisted of a continuous negotiation between the legalistic use of gender to facilitate the documentation of sexual violence and a gendered social interpretive analysis of the internal armed conflict. Time pressures and late incorporation rushed the process. Besides the ambivalence, indifference, and sometimes outright resistance to gender analysis, the PTRC found itself navigating through generalized international confusion regarding the term "gender" and its conflation with "woman."[37]

The Gender Unit synthesized academic-based social constructivist explanations of gender for implementation. Gender is defined as "classification of human beings according to their socially and culturally significant characteristics (masculine and feminine)."[38] Mantilla summarizes the social interpretive framework that she strove to incorporate in the following quote. The TRC "adopted the idea of gender as a social construction that, based in the physical differences between men and women, permits an analysis of different socially assigned roles, identities and stereotypes." As presented in the gender training, "the concept of gender is constructed through symbols and representations, normative concepts, institutions and subjective identities."[39]

The gender consultants drawn from the PUCP Gender Diploma reinforced the social interpretive approach. Henríquez asserts that sexual violence is part of a social and cultural context with institutionalized and gendered codes of power expressed through the treatment of bodies.[40] Ruiz Bravo, through her consultancy and volunteer work, consistently pointed out that the political violence was founded upon a gender system that produces and reproduces social exclusion and domination that affect both men and women. Pushing back against the trend to conflate gender and women, she asserts: "gender is not a 'woman problem,' rather it highlights power relations and the injustice of the social order."[41] Ruiz Bravo also sees the study of masculinity as central to a gender analysis.

The Gender Unit worked to implement a social interpretive approach yet had to focus on the requirements for a successful project proposal and realistic implementation timeframes and goals. Given that "not everyone realizes the utility of the concept of gender as a category to locate social actors in their social context and analyze how that context influences the roles that those actors fulfill in the day to day,"[42] the Gender Unit had to work toward a more punctuated intervention. To implement a gender perspective some general strategies included "attending to the gender differential of the impact of the conflict, recognizing women's voices as historically ignored, recognizing how traditional gender roles may influence research, disaggregating gender in statistical work, and developing mechanisms to make women visible and their voices heard and the human rights violations against them registered."[43] To support these strategies, the Gender Unit produced a guide to the use of nonsexist language,[44] created a bibliography of relevant materials on gender, and conducted trainings on gender sensitivity.

The Gender Unit found itself constantly clarifying misrepresentations of the gender perspective. Mantilla writes in a typical memo, "I want to express my concern regarding the text that under the title 'Gender Perspective' presents information that presents gender as equivalent to women, which is incorrect."[45] An example that illustrates some of the most severe miscommunication can be seen in the memo written by commissioner Alberto Morote Sánchez, engineer and former president of *Universidad San Cristóbal de Huamanga*. Mantilla circulated a proposal to the commissioners that suggested a single, uniform notion of gender. In Morote's memo, he questions Mantilla's assertion of women's moral superiority over men, with much bold indignation. He writes, "I would appreciate if you could illustrate for me the evidence that serves as the basis for your example regarding subjective identities, *the moral superiority of women over men.*" In a long response, Mantilla explaining that she in no way meant to assert women's moral superiority over men; rather, she was referring to a gender stereotype that informs the subjective construction of men's and women's identities. Indeed, the idea of women's moral superiority over men is a gender stereotype that circulates in Peru, especially with regard to female police officers who are assumed to be less corrupt than their male counterparts. Commissioner Alberto Morote Sánchez mistook the mention of a stereotype for the affirmation of the stereotype. This highlights the general lack of exposure to an analysis of gendered social norms.[46]

Stereotypes, especially the assumption that women's traditional role in the domestic sphere sheltered them from the effects of the conflict, prohibits the full investigation into the gendered consequence of the conflict. A gender perspective assists in examining the assumed masculinity of public space and femininity of private space, which recognizes men as direct actors and victims while rendering women's experiences invisible. This gendered public/private sphere divide exemplifies one of the main reasons women historically fall out of TRCs. Crimes committed against women traditionally fall within the private sphere and do not require due diligence.[47] To maintain the public/ private divide, sexual acts in the private sphere must be categorized as non-political.[48] Resistance to extending the concept of human rights to private behavior is linked to a fear of reducing "the status of the human rights canon as a whole."[49] Yet the status of the human rights canon is mounded upon the backs of women relegated to the private sphere.

Similarly, the basis for claiming extraordinary violence assumes the political nature of violence during conflict. Some violations present themselves in concentration only during conflict, such as massacres. These violations of political and civil rights are therefore framed as extraordinary violence as opposed to ordinary violence. The binary of extraordinary/ordinary violence assumes that violence during conflict only happens in the public sphere. Violence that occurs in the private sphere is assumed to be criminal, not political, and therefore not related to conflict. This logic is based on the assumption of a dichotomous relationship between political and criminal violence. The political/criminal violence binary finds its logical buttress in the public/private divide.

There are many violations, particularly those in which women are targets, such as gender-based violence that happens in both the private and public spheres before, during, and after conflict. To acknowledge and address the full spectrum of gender-based violence, the public/private divide, which supports the "false barrier between political and criminal violence," must be fundamentally rethought, as transitional justice addresses only political violence.[50] The binary framework of extraordinary/ordinary, political/ criminal, and public/private accepts "the existing terrain as legitimate—that is, enduring levels of violence against women in post-conflict contexts are no longer a regional or international peace and security issue, but rather one of individual security and domestic legislation and, as such, fall outside the ambit of the gains that have been made in the international legal framework."[51] In the effort to frame sexual violence as a human rights violation, advances in international law place emphasis on the systematic and generalized nature of the violations, thereby occluding the overwhelming numbers of day-to-day individual cases.[52] This current approach used by transitional justice mechanisms obfuscates the continuity of gender-based violence and risks entrenching social marginalization through binary logic.[53]

The overarching goal of doing away with the distinction of private/public spheres, political/criminal violence, and extraordinary/ordinary violence would strike a deathblow to the heart of male supremacy.[54] If this obstacle could be surmounted, serious cases of domestic violence could qualify as torture.[55] International legal advances in recognizing women's rights chip away at the heteropatriarchal values that undergird the public/private divide, reducing the conceptual stumbling blocks to adequately addressing gender-based violence. Although challenges to the private/public distinction grow, the division nevertheless dominates. Such is in the case of the PTRC—which drew from international law for its legitimacy.

THE PTRC METHODOLOGY

When the PTRC incorporated the Gender Unit, the Lima-based Methodology Unit had already completed the research design.[56] The objectives were to document the causes and consequences of the conflict with a focus on the historical truth. The four axes of work include processing existing work, collecting testimonies, reconstructing local contexts (including consequences of the conflict), and conducting in-depth studies. Testimonies were at the center of the investigation, and hundreds of staff and volunteers conducted seventeen thousand interviews. Once gathered, the testimonies were classified using legal operational definitions and then linked to the consequences. As mentioned earlier, the PTRC combined a justice model with a truth-seeking model. The justice model would be able to get at only a small percentage of the number of cases, so the commissioners blended it with a truth-seeking model to reflect the truth of the testimonial interviews.

The interviews enacted reconciliation through effective listening, recognition of the interviewee's truth, and an expression of solidarity. The interviewers received instructions to emphasize that the testimonial interview contributed to constructing the national historical narrative. The interviews also served to document human rights violations. At the individual level, the goal was to collect details of the violation(s) and specifics of location, time, and condition of victim. At the collective level, the goal was to document the fraying of the social fabric through massacres and other collective violations, while also gathering the specifics of location, time, and other details.[57] The golden rule: Never promise anything to the testimony giver, especially legal follow-up on their case.[58] Through interpretive analysis, the PTRC wove together the moral, factual, and political aspects to construct a historical truth.

One main complication to testimony gathering was the testimony giver's expectation that justice would be achieved for the individual's particular case. As Lisa Magarrell from the International Center for Transitional Justice notes in a memo regarding the public hearings in Huamanga and Huanta, Ayacucho, frustrated expectations can have a potentially negative effect on the PTRC process. Given the massive number of cases, it would be impossible for the PTRC to address each one and guarantee justice. Magarrell suggested reframing justice in more general terms to include recommendations for reparations and institutional reforms; indication/admission of state responsibilities; offering information to identify victims and perpetrators of cases; identifying patterns of violations and their causes.[59]

The organizational structure included investigation teams reporting to the central investigation group and passing data to the methodological information systems team. Within the methodological information systems team, there were three units: the Training and Supervision Unit that oversaw the data collection in the regional branch offices and communications with the central office; the Processing and Classification Unit, which classified data and entered it into the database; and the Database Unit, which designed and maintained the database. Together they produced a qualitative analysis, statistical reports, and summaries of cases that all supported the development of the final report.

The Gender Unit proposed a methodological intervention based on the social interpretive framework elaborated by the PUCP consultants. "The proposal for including a gender perspective in the methodology is to understand how unequal relations between men and women are generated and maintained. These unequal relations are at the core of the internal armed conflict, which the country suffered, [affecting] the subversive groups and the state alike. The gender focus allows us to highlight and understand the link between societal power relations, differentiated impact of human rights violations, and the consequences on the men and women of Peru."[60] The objectives included: discovering the issues relevant to women in the context of the political violence and their causes, processes, and consequences; placing human rights violations against women within the scope of the internal armed conflict; illuminating the role of women in subversive organizations; incorporating women leaders and women victims in the PTRC's investigation process; and raising the consciousness of the population regarding equality between men and women and the guarantee of rights.[61] These objectives reflect the conflation of gender and women rather than a social interpretive framework explicated in the proposal. This demonstrates the growing distance between intentions and implementation. Besides the organizational culture of resistance to gender analysis, a close look at the attempts to incorporate a gender analysis into the methodology exposes the conflation of gender and sexual violence.

The gender analysis ended up focusing on women and a few issues related to women, such as sexual violence and more specifically rape,[62] rather than the gendered aspects of human rights violations and consequences of the conflict.[63] This happened because of conceptual myopia around sexual violence and the reduction of gender to biological sex difference. The last-minute approach that attempted to go from historical invisibility of women buried in the private sphere to full inclusion in the public sphere led to the overemphasis on sexual violence.

Since women were the majority of testimony givers regarding the violations against others, it was critical to publicly reach out to women testimony givers and make an intervention in the testimony-gathering process. The Gender Unit developed "flyers, posters and radio programs to explain that sexual violence is a human rights violation that should be denounced, creating support for women."[64] The first draft of the "Proposal for Operational Definitions of Human Rights Violations, Crimes, and Other Juridical Situations," prepared by the Juridical Unit in May 2002, included a section on violence against women. The operational definition of violence against women draws directly from the 1993 Declaration for the Elimination of Violence against Women: "All acts of violence directed against women due to their condition as women, with the capacity to produce physical, psychological or sexual harm, including threats, coercion or denial of liberty."[65] This is an example of the implementation of the legalistic approach that highlights sexual violence.

A gender social interpretive analysis of sexual violence helped to contexutalize the crime. As Mabel González Bustelo writes in a short paper circulated by Mantilla, "considered an issue of a sexual nature, those acts are depoliticized and part of the private sphere, a completely erroneous conception since the objectives are not sexual but military, strategic and political."[66] Mantilla also mobilized the wording in the Declaration and Program of Action from the 1993 UN Conference on Human Rights held in Vienna (paragraph 38), sentences from the war tribunals of Rwanda and the former Yugoslavia, and article 7 of the Rome Statute to establish legal precedent regarding sexual violence as a crime against humanity.[67] These international precedents assisted in confronting the unspoken assumptions of sexual violence being a private affair.

After much work, the thematic guide to gathering testimonies came to include sexual violence among the questions regarding human rights violations. Questions on human rights violations fit into a series of questions that started with a general exploration of what happened and when, access to judicial process, context and antecedents, identification of perpetrators, identification of victims, the long-term effects of violations, hopes for the future and possible legal action. The particular framing of questions on sexual violence did not benefit from the gender interpretive approach: "How many people participated in the rape and how many times? And were other people raped?" The questions reduce the gender perspective to rape, rather than altering the methodology.[68]

The gender-sensitive methodology did not only overlap with a methodology to document sexual violence, but in many cases they were implemented as one and the same. Given the lack of organizational support for gender analysis, the Gender Unit staff joined with the staff working on sexual violence legal analysis and cases.[69] Diana Portal, staff of the sexual violence team of the Juridical Unit, reflects on their collaborative work.

> Working with the team was a great experience; Julissa Mantilla was responsible for both the Gender Unit and the work on sexual violence within the juridical team. But we considered ourselves all one team; we would have meetings and share information between the five of us.[70]
>
> Although there was an institutional space for the Gender Unit and it was part of the work plan, there was no operationalized gender-sensitive methodology. This problem affected both the study of gender and also the study of sexual violence. Julissa pushed to have this methodology happen. The testimony-gathering process did not consider sexual violence; the database did not include sexual violence either. Therefore, they had to adapt the database to include it and also do a campaign to convince women to tell their stories, since they usually tell the stories of what happened to others.
>
> We read through and categorized the testimonies that had to do with sexual violence, which total about 540, the transcriptions of the regional public hearings and conducted an ATLAS-Ti–based analysis of the materials gathered and produced by the unit on in-depth studies.[71]

As a followup, Mantilla suggested that additions to the database include human rights violations against women other than sexual violence, which had been reduced to rape. The main categories were assassination, violations of due process, forced disappearance, displacement, arbitrary detention, slavery, and kidnapping. Mantilla suggested adding gender-based violence such as vaginal perforations under the category of torture and forced abortion and sexual slavery under sexual violence. With regard to consequences, she specified the impact of the human rights violations on sexual and reproductive health of the victims.[72]

The memo Julissa Mantilla sent to the Juridical Unit on November 18, 2002, more than a year into the two-year mandate, exemplifies the lack of gender mainstreaming. "Unfortunately, the research done on human rights in Peru has not used a gendered perspective that collects information differentiating between men and women."[73] In a last-ditch effort against the seemingly inevitable subordination of a gender social interpretive approach, late in 2002 two consultants from PUCP, Patricia Ruiz Bravo and Tesania Velázquez, wrote a methodological proposal for the gender analysis of testimonies, including suggestions for the best use of existing data. Highlighting the continuum of violence, physical and psychological violence against women, and the way it is experienced on a daily level stretches the framework for thinking about the impact of the conflict. They assert that the political violence was based on an unequal gendered social order that produces and reproduces systems of exclusion and domination. "To introduce a gender focus implies observing the way this axis of differentiation and social inequality defines identities, roles, spaces, positions, and power relations, and also how it articulates with other systems of exclusion."[74] Therefore, political violence must be understood in its long-term context, marked by structural social and gender violence.

Given that a transversal axis of gender analysis had slipped out of reach, the consultants argue that the gendered perspective must concentrate specifically on what happened to the women, given that the other areas take a gender-neutral view, which favors documenting what happened to the men. This was a conceptual step back to accepting gender as a "women problem," and it truncated the understanding of gender to biological sex difference, yet there was no other choice, given the circumstances. The gender-mainstreaming efforts to maintain a transversal axis in the report gave way to the "Violence and Gender Inequality" chapter because of the small size of the Gender Unit, its conflation with sexual violence legal work, the resistant organizational culture, time pressures, and the limits of binary logic. This outcome is consistent with other cases. Similarly, the South African TRC did not respond to women's organizations' call for an integrated "understanding of the gendered nature of struggles and the need for a more nuanced gendered methodology in its research and reporting," and so a chapter was devoted to women.[75]

Nevertheless, the consultants critiqued the group's data-gathering methods for not collecting both objective and subjective elements of each interview. By leaving out the affective components of the testimonies, the data tends to objectify the victims rather than recognize their subjectivity. They suggested utilizing an analysis that "makes visible the feminine subject and the existing representations in relation to her actions in the unfolding political violence, considering the relations between feminine identities, cultural matrix and social positioning as central axes of investigation."[76] One of their main suggestions was to work with the regional branch gender coordinators to address these problems.

Colonial Mappings of Difference: The South Central Andean Branch Office/*La Sede Sur Central Andino-Ayacucho*

While the central office in Lima elaborated the methodological design, it depended on the regional branches for implementation. The branch offices were charged with collecting testimony, translating and transcribing, investigating cases, implementing educational campaigns, holding regional public hearings, and collaborating with local organizations. The work of the branch offices in advancing the goals of the Gender Unit exposes the cultural, conceptual, and linguistic gaps between the central and branch offices and the division of labor internal to the PTRC. Entrenched legacies of colonialism manifested themselves through the division of knowledge production in the capital (Lima) and data gathering in the branch offices.

In the PTRC archival documents many general statements recognize the need to include intercultural and gender components in the regional work. The term "intercultural" is used to address cultural, linguistic, racial, and ethnic differences. Yet the communications between the Gender Unit in Lima and regional branches do not include references to intercultural issues. Although there were forward thinking social actors that pushed for such an integrated approach,[77] the methodology conceptualized gender and ethnolinguistic factors as separate. An intersectional sensibility highlights how this conceptual separation fragments the full picture of campesinas' lives.

On May 28, 2002, the Gender Unit contacted the branch offices with the goal of identifying one person with whom to coordinate. Naming branch-office gender coordinators consolidated the incorporation of the gender perspective. Gender coordinators were charged with integrating a gender perspective into the testimony gathering and outreach, selecting testimonies to support a gender analysis, and coordinating with local organizations.[78] Furthermore, they developed communication mechanisms to make visible this issue in the PTRC products, formulated a proposal for the thematic hearing on crimes against women,[79] contributed to the PTRC recommendations, and defined the inclusion of gender in their final report.

The central office called upon the branch offices to develop a proposal of how to incorporate a gender perspective into their work. The Gender Unit suggested that such proposals could include: working with the questions used to gather testimonies to make sure that they include gender differential and sexual violence, coordinating with local organizations to motivate women's testimonies about what happened to them (with an emphasis on sexual violence), and conducting a publicity campaign regarding the gender perspective and sexual violence. There were no additional funds made available for this work. The late start date of the regional gender coordinators inhibited full incorporation of the gender perspective as an integral part of the overall PTRC strategy.

The Gender Unit depended on branch-office gender coordinators to assist in the enormous task of sensitizing PTRC staff, with a focus on testimony gatherers. The Gender Unit, coordinating with the Training and Supervision Unit, made huge efforts to train interviewers on a gender perspective and sexual violence, as well as to provide gender-sensitive questions to prompt testimony givers.[80] Besides the actual interviews, another critical link was the team of people who listened to the one- to two-hour testimonial interviews in Quechua and translated and transcribed them to Spanish within the chronological format. This position was one of mediating meaning and conceptions of time, and the team received limited training to sensitize them to the importance of getting all the information down, whether they thought it was relevant or not. This led to concerns about the full representation of sexual violence within these transcriptions.[81] Then they were to enter the material into the database, yet another level of mediation.

The gender-sensitivity trainings happened after the majority of testimonies had been gathered. Until that point, the interview questions did not include the issue of gender, so such questions were incorporated through the individual interpretation and will of the interviewer.[82] The belated inclusion of the gender perspective caused much confusion. As one mobile interview team coordinator in Ayacucho highlights, "each time we came back from the communities, there was a new form to use and new questions."[83] In the training workshops for the interviewers, the regional gender coordinators discussed how to ask women about the impact of the conflict, and then the coordinators followed up with interviewers regarding their techniques and what they were finding in relation to gender issues. The trainings had many obstacles, such as lack of coordination with other PTRC-required activities and the lack of funds for interviewer per diem. In some cases the regional director did not oblige the interviewers to go to the trainings. Indifference toward gender trainings echoes Mantilla's experience of resistance within the organizational culture.

While most were able to understand and work with a gender perspective in the abstract, it was not implemented in practice. The interviewers forgot to ask women if they were also victims, and in many cases there were not enough women to interview women. In the communities, Kimberly Theidon points out that the men in leadership did not always condone the practice of women giving testimony. "*A ellas se les va la lengua*"—the women say too much. The women could easily say something to undermine the community's carefully constructed and rehearsed narrative of innocence ready to be delivered to the representatives of the state—with hopes of receiving compensation for suffering.[84]

In Ayacucho, the branch office named a contact person, Gubercinda Reynaga Farfán, and she developed a twofold work plan. First, follow up on the incorporation of the gender perspective with the testimony-gathering teams through additional bibliographical materials and discussion spaces for reflection on gender issues as related to their work. Second, establish collaborations with women's organizations, networks, and institutions to deepen a gender perspective and promote testimonies from women about human rights violations they experienced.

In an interview, Reynaga made the point that the regional office had already been working with women's organizations regarding gender issues and women's testimonies at the request of the local organizations. For example, on International Women's Day (March 8) they delivered a workshop on gender and human rights in the neighboring department of Apurimac in the town of Chincheros to sixty of the principal public authorities. This reflects the influence of decades of work by women's organizations for survival and the defense of human rights. Women's leadership development took root in response to the internal armed conflict and the economic crisis of the late 1980s (see chapter 1). Therefore, Reynaga asserts that any successes of the regional office with regard to integrating a gender perspective or documenting human rights violations against women must be understood within this context.

Women's organizations largely supported the PTRC's efforts to mobilize women, under the logic that if women's voices are not heard, then the truth will be incomplete. Yet these same campesina protagonists are placed in the "homogenous victim" category. Sheila Meintjes highlights similar dynamics in South Africa. "The way in which such organizations of survivors were treated as the subjects of gross human rights violations as opposed to actors in the struggle against apartheid, tended to define them as 'victims.'"[85] Both Meintjes and Reynaga underscore that women in contexts of conflict are not just victims.

Besides reinforcing the central role of campesina protagonism, Reynaga challenged the dominant geopolitical imaginary about who produces knowledge and who provides data.

> In November of 2001 they started working in the TRC branch office and I joined in January 2002. One of the main problems was that the research instruments were all designed in Lima. They did not take into consideration the people here who could have collaborated in the methodological preparation. I don't mean this to be a harsh critique; maybe it was the rush to get started. And as a self-critique, maybe we didn't push for our involvement in the design . . .

Here she changed the subject to the weather voicing her discomfort,

> Excuse me, I think some little leaves got into my clothes, I have a terrible itch . . . When I was walking through the plaza to get here, the wind picked up the dust, dirt and leaves . . .

Breaking from her perfect composure, she paused to scratch her upper back, reaching into her shirt collar. Her ill ease made me curious about physical and emotional discomforts and how they sometimes mirror each other. Reynaga's discomfort communicated to me the vulnerability she felt in having been so forthcoming in her critique.

Reynaga's comments illustrated how colonial mappings of difference embedded in the geopolitical imaginary undermined the inclusive goals of the PTRC. Decolonizing the geographic imaginary demands a spatialized analysis of the colonial-self and indigenous-other binary at the root of colonial racialization. The Andean region, constructed as the geopolitical "other," provides the resources in the form of data to be elaborated by the knowledge-producing coastal "self." As feminist geographer Maureen Hays-Mitchell explains, thinking through the spatiality of power relations helps us understand how inequality functions across scales and in particular places.[86] Campesina protagonism and ways of knowing exceed the data they provide as victims. Reynaga's comments underscore how an intersectional sensibility must be adjusted to spatialized inequalities.

After her powerful critique of the gendered geopolitics of knowledge production, Reynaga quickly resumed her composure, moving onto a safer topic . . .

> Anyway, in the branch office, we were few women. I worked with a woman lawyer and I had a woman assistant. We had previously worked with a gender perspective and in relevant circumstances; we were including gender in our work.

Then later, the Lima office sent the gender program director, Julissa Mantilla, to do the trainings with the fieldwork team and the organizations of women affected by the conflict. But, as an urban person, she struggled to translate the concepts to the context of Ayacucho. My director said to me, "Look, you know this material, make it more simple." Her presentation did give us some ideas but I had to translate it to this reality in addition to coordinating with women's networks and federations such as COTMA[87] and FEDECMA[88] to motivate the women to give their testimonies. The simplified trainings were for the fieldwork team, and some of them had never worked from a gender perspective and were very sexist. But little by little they began to understand as the testimony gathering demanded it of them, and they discussed the issues and cases among themselves. I did two training blocks, one with the people who missed the first training and another with new people, as they became part of the team. . . . So we did achieve some impact. Also I worked with the interviewers from COMISEDH.[89] The resistance was strong at the beginning, even to the idea of discussing the topic, but by the end they were able to have a useful discussion.

The resistant organizational culture resurfaces in Reynaga's comments, as does spatialized difference. The social distance and power asymmetries between Lima and Ayacucho limited the PTRC's ability to fulfill its goal of implementing gender sensitivity trainings.

Reynaga jumped directly to the issue of sexual violence.

So, we did gather emblematic cases of rape of women. But if this had been incorporated from the beginning with a general call to all staff, it would have been better. The main problem was that the incorporation of the gender perspective took place after the initiation of testimony gathering and had to be incorporated in a partial way under the circumstances. Also the outreach materials to motivate women to give their testimonies about what happened to them arrived after the investigation process ended.

Geographical distances and the lag time reinforce regional imbalances.

Reynaga's written materials do not reflect these overarching concerns with the gendered geopolitics of knowledge production that were so pronounced in the interview. Rather, the written materials stick to the same language and framing presented by the Gender Unit. In her capacity of branch-office gender coordinator, Reynaga developed a set of suggestions for incorporating the gender perspective into the testimony-gathering process.[90] "The gender perspective will allow us to: establish gender-differentiated statistics regarding the impact of political violence, recognize the gendered violation of human rights during the political violence, recuperate all the voices to construct a whole truth of what happened, including the direct impact on women, and the need to break the silence." This opening statement directly echoes the key points of the gender perspective as established in the Lima office.

The next section of this same document authored by Reynaga explains how to incorporate the gender perspective in the process of gathering testimonies by highlighting how to create the best context in which women would be able to give a testimony that included sexual violence. This reflects the goal of the Juridical Unit's efforts to document more sexual violence cases by collecting testimonies from women about sexual violence that occurred to them or other women they know. All of the following suggestions in the document echo informed consent principles and have to do with ways of being sensitive to women testimony givers. For example—

> Make efforts to develop trust, to express empathy and solidarity, and to guarantee privacy and discretion. Have women take women's interviews as desired, and use the idiomatic expressions of the zone to formulate questions. Start with general questions and then go to specifics. One suggestion is to formulate indirect questions about sexual violence that occurred in the community or neighboring communities. Be attentive to the testimony giver's attitude, and it may be necessary to stop taping if she wants to speak about sexual violence. Interviews that deal with sexual violence demand special attention at the end, and the testimony gatherer must remind the testimony giver of their positive qualities, her courage in facing the impact of the violence and the importance of raising her self-esteem.

Gathering women's testimonies of direct human rights violations seemed to be the primary operational concern of the branch office's gender perspective. The gendered investigation of the causes and consequences of the conflict and gendered methodological reflections were of secondary importance. Yet broader gender-sensitive aspects were not totally omitted. For example a suggested workshop with interviewers had the goal of reflecting upon the gendered perceptions of the interviewers in their gathering of testimonies and the extent to which social stereotypes were reinforced. The three main questions were: How did the testimony giver's gender influence your work? What stereotypes of men's and women's roles does the interviewer have? What human rights violations did men and women most commonly identify? Therefore, at every level and stage, the Gender Unit made efforts to include a gendered social interpretive approach, yet the time constraints, communication barriers, dominant geopolitical imaginary, and binary logic precluded its full development.

In hindsight, Mantilla remarks that incorporating a gender approach was an impossible task given that it was not included from the beginning. The gender program was never fully institutionalized. It was always seen as a side issue that got addressed out of the good will and volunteerism of TRC employees.[91] In an interview, she stated that "in practice, the gender mainstreaming approach didn't work—it ended up making the issue of gender invisible because it got lost among everything else. Therefore, it was critical to have a chapter on gender [in the Final Report] for the sake of recognition. In the future, people will notice the chapter, and it sets a precedent."[92]

PTRC Chapter: "Violence and Gender Inequality"

Following the debate about the design of the methodology, the adjustment of the methodology to include gender, and the gender-sensitivity trainings, the discussion regarding how to write the final report also took up the question of gender as a transversal axis of analysis.[93] In determining the components of the national historical narrative in the final report, the PTRC followed the Guatemalan model of naming historical inequalities as directly linked to the causes and consequences of the conflict.[94]

Commissioner and anthropologist Carlos Iván Degregori stands out as a strong proponent for a serious analysis of historical inequalities. Gender consultants, Narda Henríquez, and a handful of others took part in these visionary conversations. Degregori's outline for the final report included historic-structural factors such as ethnic-cultural dynamics, regional idiosyncrasies, class, generational differences, and gender.[95] His early hypothesis was that the "most important factors that determined the form of violence in the country were ethno-cultural and regional differences."[96] Degregori advocated for highlighting gender, ethnicity, race, and intercultural relations as transversal axes that should be present in the final report's sections and subsections.[97] He made early statements to recognize and work with collective frameworks instead of assuming individual frameworks for interpreting the causes and consequences of the violence. "The final product should contribute to changing the geographic imaginary of Peru that makes us feel so distant from and indifferent towards the suffering of our compatriots."[98] Degregori's decolonial vision informed the PTRC's radical potential for transformation, exemplified by the carthartic personal encounters of many staff and volunteers.

All Gender Unit staff and consultants repeatedly asserted the need to address the intersectional aspects of inequality. "This issue [gender] needs to be crossed directly with the issue of racial discrimination: How many affected women were indigenous? How does this phenomenon relate to urban women?" Consultant Narda Henríquez produces an important thread of analysis. "I suggest that in addition to the role of women as social actors, the issue of social and imaginary representations must also be considered as elements of memory in which gender codes are registered and articulated with other codes related to ethnicity and power."[99] Peruvian anthropologist Elisabeth Acha also makes a gesture toward analyzing inequalities. "The revision of recent history is a reiteration of the tendency to make invisible and undervalue the feminine and the indigenous. During the internal armed conflict, indigenous women continued to be the lowest ranking on the social hierarchy. Neither women nor campesino communities were passive. In many cases they have gained symbolic recognition; however, they run the risk of being marginalized through the construction of democracy and the reproduction of the usual routes of subordinated integration."[100] Although these quotes illustrate a clear interest in an analysis of inequalities, which is integral to a gender-interpretive approach, such comments were hard to operationalize and implement.[101]

While the final report directly identifies the cemented social inequalities and ethnic discrimination, a gender analysis is tucked into the "Violence and Gender Inequality" chapter. Gender appears in a few additional spots—in a section on subjectivity written by psychologists, in the discussion of social movements,[102] and in the section on testimonies. The production of the "Violence and Gender Inequality" chapter further elucidates the underlying tensions between the legalistic and the social interpretive approaches that came to a head under intense pressure to produce a final draft in three months. The authors of the first draft emphasized the juridical and quantitative perspective. The next draft incorporated an extensive sociopolitical analysis; this 150-page document can be found under the title "*Contra Viento y Marea: Cuestiones de Género y Poder en la Memoria Colectiva*." The editorial committee considered it too long for the final report, however. The next draft incorporated an anthropological perspective. A sociologist and psycologist finalized the chapter, cutting it down to the present length.[103]

Throughout the strained revision process, the editorial committee pressured to cut and condense while insisting that the analysis be based on empirical evidence. Since the database did not reflect a gendered methodology, such an analysis of empirical evidence was a challenge to construct.

Although there were great intentions, innovative research on sexual abuse of men, for example, fell out because of the immensity of the task. External actors also pressured to make the chapter only about violations of women's human rights, further aggravating the situation.[104] In retrospect, Mantilla bemoans how, after so much work on sexual violence, the "Violence and Gender Inequality" chapter addresses only rape instead of the more inclusive category of sexual violence.[105] Mantilla felt forced to approve the report, or nothing would have been included at all.

Although the conditions for the production of the "Violence and Gender Inequality" chapter were far from optimal, the chapter did analyze the gendered impact of the conflict, with attention to historic inequalities. Echoing one of the PTRC's main conclusions, the "Violence and Gender Inequality" chapter opens arguing that "differences were not born by the conflict, rather the conflict developed through previously established ethnic, social, and gender inequalities."[106] This assertion connects violence to inequalities that reproduce systems of exclusion and domination.[107] The chapter couches general data regarding the demographic of affected women in a historic understanding of social hierarchies. The majority of affected women are from poor, rural, Andean communities, precisely the communities that experience political, social, and economic exclusion from the state and are targeted for mistreatment and humiliation because of their indigeneity.[108] With little access to formal education, young Quechua-speaking campesinas find themselves "vulnerable, with [fewer] resources to demand their rights, interface with governmental bodies, and read documents that could negatively compromise them upon signing."[109] The chapter underscores the "fundamental problems of our society: the rejection of the 'other,' the exclusion of indigenous people, authoritarianism and the abuse of power from above."[110] The PTRC final report acknowledges the historical continuity of violence, from colonization (with the establishment of the Spanish Viceroyalty of Peru in 1542) to the war that won Peruvian independence in 1821, to the internal armed conflict. Furthermore, this recognition of the continuity of violence questions the assumed linear temporal shift from atrocities of the past to a democratic future.

A subsection titled "An analysis of violence: gender, racism and machismo" starts with the assertion that an analysis of masculinity associated with war and racism allows for an interpretation of the specific characteristics of human rights violations of women. "The fact that the majority of affected women are Andean and Quechua-speaking makes evident their position in the last rungs of the social and power hierarchy. What happened to them was not part of the national preoccupation. Those women were high in the mountains, far from progress and civilization. Peruvian society did not find itself interpolated by those crimes."[111] According to this analysis, the majority of affected women fall outside of the frame of Peruvian progress and civilization. Quechua speaking campesinas are forced to blend into the subordinate backdrop of backwardness, from which civilized Peruvian society establishes itself in binary opposition. Thus, this chapter asserts that structural violence must be fundamentally addressed to realize any chance of national reconciliation.

Besides acknowledging inequality, the chapter points to the complexity of women's roles. A long section describes all the roles women took, from popular women's organizations and organizations of families of the disappeared to participation in self-defense committees (Rondas) and the Shining Path. This effectively shifts the frame away from the reductive view of women as victims. The chapter analyzes how women came out of their traditional spaces to find their dead and their disappeared, and to demand justice. "It was from 'traditional' role of mothers, sisters and daughters that they searched for justice and entered public institutional spaces."[112] Rejecting narrow representational practices, the conclusion argues that women were not only passive victims but also social actors, organizing for survival. "Given the image of suffering, poor and incapable women, we want to reveal their capacity to act and respond."[113] One of the most significant lines follows: "These multiple images and feminine representations are alive in many parts of the country, and they are not exclusionary but can coexist in one person."[114] This assertion honors the multidimensional subjectivities of women affected by the conflict and the complexity of their experiences.

Within the context of the whole final report, "Violence and Gender Inequality" shows how inequalities interact within the internal armed conflict. It vindicates the complex and sometimes contradictory roles women played during and after the conflict. By underscoring the roles women played, the chapter destabilizes the assumption that women are always and only victims and opens a space to acknowledge, hear, and learn about women's multiple subjectivities.

Conclusion

Given all the difficulties, the PTRC made significant advances within the international context of TRCs by organizing a public event staged on International Women's Day, March 8, 2002, to present its gender perspective, conducting a women's thematic public hearing, producing chapters on gender and sexual violence in the final report, investigating cases of sexual violence, and suggesting gender-sensitive recommendations for reparations and institutional reform. Peru advances the recognition of gendered transitional justice norms on an international level. As Mantilla points out, "the question has changed from 'why include gender?' to 'how are we going to implement it?'"[115] Several lessons can be gleaned from this reflection on the methodology implemented by the PTRC.

An analysis of gender inequality must be included in the mandate, and the relevance and implementation must be clarified from the start. This can be done by analyzing relevant vectors of oppression, such as gender and race/ethnicity relationally as transversal axes throughout the research design, data analysis, public hearings, recommendations, and final report. While the PTRC took strides toward inclusion by adding the Gender Unit and conducting a legal investigation into sexual violence, the efforts to address social inequalities were limited because gender and race/ethnicity issues were separated. When taken together and operationalized in the methodology, the cathartic interpersonal encounters that demonstrate the decolonizing undercurrent of this transitional justice mechanism would manifest at the macro level—thereby facilitating social reconciliation.

An exploration of the process of defining, operationalizing, and incorporating gender exposes how the PTRC placed more emphasis on international and national law to develop its methodology and gave less attention to the communities affected by violence. An intersectional sensibility and decolonial feminist approach bring to light how the underlying public/private divide makes inevitable the subordinated integration, or "add-on" strategy. The legalistic approach tends to collapse gender with biological sex and reduces the broad scope of relevant issues to sexual violence, specifically rape. As Fionnuala Ní Aoláin asserts, "The discursive frame of transitional justice as rooted in legal discourse may bolster rather than challenge dominant hierarchies given the field's patriarchal roots."[116] The binary logic manifest in political/criminal violence and extraordinary/ordinary violence illustrates this bolstering effect. To move past this, prioritizing a relational analysis of violence in private and public spaces exposes both the multiple manifestations and temporal continuum of gender-based violence.

The proposal to include economic, social, and cultural rights violations in transitional justice analyses[117] gets at the "underlying practices of social injustice, marginalization and exploitation"[118] as related to inequalities. Lisa Laplante asserts the need to shift from framing socioeconomic causes of conflict as historical context to rights violations. She explains that the historical framing "leaves policy change to the discretion of political leaders," while the violations framing "makes redress and reform a political imperative."[119] Such a shift would "initiate a long-term reform process" and create a lobbying tool for civil society follow-up and would include local actors.[120] To ensure that recommendations are implemented, accountability and enforcement mechanisms such as timelines and benchmarks must be put in place to measure and evaluate progress.[121]

Much must still be done to reconfigure the conceptual parameters of the TRC model and fully integrate an analysis of the historical inequalities at the root of conflict. Such a reconfiguration, as suggested by Degregori, would offer a solid foundation for inclusive citizenship and robust democratic practice. A key piece of this reconfiguration consists of dismantling the geopolitical imaginary that reinforces colonial mappings of difference. Naming commissioners who are culturally and linguistically competent, given the affected communities, would represent an important first step. A second step could be to create a collaborative research design for investigation that centers input from affected communities. Last, reassessing potential products could improve outcomes. The report fulfills the expectations of the literate, but what other products may be more meaningful and useful for the goals of justice and reconciliation, taking into consideration affected communities?

These transitional justice suggestions are far reaching and demand commitment, vision, and long-term political will.[122] Broadening the transitional justice mandate by taking on these policy suggestions depends on a conceptual and methodological approach that can manage anxiety regarding the increasingly unstable terrain upon which transitional justice is based. In turning from policy suggestions to the symbolic realm of public hearings in the next chapter, commissioners made great efforts to construct and implement a new space of horizontal communication to facilitate the national reconciliation process.

3

National Reconciliation through Public Hearings

Representative Repertoire, Choreography, and Politics of Reception

The PTRC public hearings[1] marks the first time that the state listened to the voices of historically marginalized Peruvians. Those most deeply affected by the conflict were invited to speak on a national stage. The hearings aimed to build a new national narrative by giving voice to the victims/*testimoniantes*[2] and educating the public on lesser-known aspects of the internal armed conflict utilizing a human rights framework. One of the public hearings' eight principles, "to contribute to national reconciliation, understood as the re-establishment of social harmony and the overcoming of forms of discrimination that exclude and victimize certain social sectors and impede the affirmation of democracy,"[3] offers an entry point for this analysis.[4] While great efforts were made to fulfill this principle, an examination of the thematic public hearing on Political Violence and Political Crimes against Women (thematic hearing on women), and a few other testimonies by women in other hearings, demonstrates how procedural and representational issues hindered the hearings' full potential. This analysis highlights how careful attention to the workings of language, temporality, and gender representation could aid in overcoming discrimination.

Those who gave testimony wished to be recognized as members of a national community that historically denies and resists such recognition.[5] *Testimoniantes* carry the responsibility of speaking as representatives of their community and delivering a piece of a fragile history.[6] Participation in the public hearings offered a way to inscribe one's testimony onto the national imaginary.[7] The singular subject position of victim, however, circumscribes the revelatory force of the testimonies. The legal category, essential for determining injury, is "imbued with negative social and cultural value."[8] Moreover, the focus on individual suffering and victimization renders structural violence as an unfortunate backdrop.

Many testimoniantes reported feeling a sense of relief after testifying. However, expectations of justice and reparations have been frustrated. According to a PTRC assessment titled "The Impact of the Public Hearings on Participants,"

> Although the experience of the public hearing signified a step forward in the restoration of victims' dignity, it is important to remember that the majority of the victims continue to live poor and marginalized lives. Public opinion is not receptive to their voices and their impact on the national political agenda is still very limited.

This analysis scrutinizes the power relations embedded within the public hearings. Impervious public opinion reveals the colonial foundations of the national emotional terrain.

The representational repertoire and choreography of the public hearings undergird the construction of a national historical truth and determine the hearings' capacity to sway public opinion. The production of state discourse happens in the realm of representation. As anthropologists Arandhana Sharma and Akhil Gupta assert, "public cultural representations and performance of statehood crucially shape people's perceptions about the nature of the state."[9] An analysis of the prevalent representations of women reveals the reconstitution of the racialized and heteropatriarchal nation in a moment of state instability. In the case of Peru, Nelson Manrique explains that national history functions to legitimate the existing social order, its representatives, and its beneficiaries. The PTRC focus on women's suffering serves the new national narrative by reifying women's normative role.

Interviews I conducted, videos of hearings, cultural activities surrounding the hearings, archival interviews with *testimoniantes*, transcriptions of testimonies, archival materials (such as polls and surveys, memos, meeting minutes), and internal reports contribute to this intertextual analysis. Reading for disruptive moments and narrative excess expose the parameters of the new national history. I did not attend the live hearings and therefore utilize the videos of the hearings, which were edited by Sofia Macher (commissioner in charge of the public hearings) and an assistant. They produced a one-hour segment of each hearing following two main criteria, to highlight the moments of greatest import and to create a balance between the different types of testimonies.[10] Multiple levels of mediation took place in the production of these audio/visual texts.

The cacophony of voices and parallel realities present within the PTRC public hearings trespass choreographed interactions and representational categories. Careful analysis of the testimonies exposes disruptive moments related to lack of adequate language translation and cultural insensitivity, in addition to temporal misalignments. Campesina protagonists delivered their testimonies, yet dominant linguistic and temporal frames, as well as gendered representations, obstructed the full meaning of what they wished to convey.

The testimonies that exhibit ambivalent emotions toward pregnancy due to rape and mothering children of rape demonstrate the gendered logics upon which the national historical narrative is built. The Peruvian urban and educated population's general sense of pity for and lack of identification with rural Quechua-speaking victims highlights the fragility of Peruvian reconciliation. Enduring colonial mappings of difference within the national geographic imaginary emerge in the public-opinion response to the hearings, reinforcing the discrimination that impedes democracy and social harmony.

Setting the Stage for the Public Hearings

The PTRC framed the hearings as a healing ritual focused on the recognition of the victims.[11] Through the commissioners' active listening, the victims could deliver their testimony and feel heard, thereby reestablishing the relationship between the victimized individual and society. Those running the hearings made a concerted effort to create a horizontal space of social relations that included the victims and the commissioners as representatives of the state. In this carefully constructed space, reconciliatory acts could take place. This revolutionary effort was meant to be a corrective to popular attitudes of either suspicion or commiseration toward victims and the state's historic stance of confrontation or clientalism toward marginalized social groups.[12] The challenge of such a proposal was to somehow suspend the history of vertical social relations.

The design of the public hearings endeavored to maximize the healing potential for the *testimoniantes*/survivors, the educational capacity for the Peruvian population, and the reconciliatory and reparatory possibilities for the nation. The public hearings' choreography intended to fulfill three main goals: "to validate the victim's truth as part of national reconciliation, reaffirming the dignity of the victims; to convert the testimonies into a peda-gogical instrument for society to know the truth and assume the need to defend human rights; and . . . to enrich the PTRC investigation by incor-porating the direct experiences of the victims."[13] The PTRC document that spells out the normative and operating principles of the public hearings places emphasis on the commissioners' first visits to rural areas and the deep impression direct contact with affected communities had on them. "Contact with this *truth* has allowed the PTRC to discover the enormous potential of public audiences as a tool for education and reparation."[14] Among the twelve commissioners, Commissioner Beatriz Alva Hart, a conservative politician, Fujimori supporter, and member of the Lima elite, found herself deeply questioning the values of her social class and publicly apologizing for their indifference.[15] This intimate transformation of Commissioner Hart's emotional relationship with the "others" of Peru illustrates the root goal of reconciliation: overcoming discrimination. Similar to many PTRC staff and volunteer experiences, such life-changing moments make up the PTRC's decolonial undercurrent. Although public opinion as a whole may have been unreceptive, many people's lives were forever changed as a result of working for the PTRC.

With the goal of creating a horizontal relationship between the victims and the representatives of the state, the commissioners opted to build one level on the stage, in contrast to the South African hearings, where the com-missioners where seated at a higher level than the victims in a courtroom setting. The Peruvian commissioners had a semicircular table custom made, and they invited the testimoniantes to sit with them there.

According to Commissioner Macher, an informal meeting with repre-sentatives of the popular theater collective *Grupo Cultural Yuyachkani* and other human rights and cultural workers, such as Javier Torres from the NGO Rural Education Services, centrally informed her decisions concerning the configuration of the space for the hearings; the appropriate tone, clothing, and attitude of the commissioners; the quality of interactions between com-missioners and *testimoniantes*; and the locations where the hearings would be held.[16]

If the priority of the space was to facilitate communication based on demo-cratic principles, then the design had to make the *testimoniantes* feel com-fortable. Such a national space had never existed, and in order for it to hold a new narrative of the nation, it had to be free of meaning, thereby giving the *testimoniante* the power to tell their story without narrative interference.[17] The space reflected the most formal instance of the state. Commissioners

Thematic public hearing for auto-defense committees in Junín. Testimony of Guillermo Flores Jorge, representative from the auto-defense committees (CADS) of Vinchos. (Peruvian Ombudsman's Office Information Center for Collective Memory and Human Rights photographic archive 0102190202009.)

dressed in suit and tie—their highest official embodiment of the "listening" state—offered their full attention to the *testimoniante*. Commissioners did not ask questions or lead the *testimoniante*; they just listened. The locations where the hearings were held, such as a university auditorium, were entirely covered with cloth to further create the feeling of a new and clean space. Gigantic pictures and graphic designs were hung as a backdrop to the stage to create a unique and consistent setting. A bronze plaque placed on the building memorialized the ritual of national healing.

The Thematic Public Hearing on Women

In contrast to the historical regional hearings, individual case hearings, and hearings with institutional authorities, the thematic public hearing on women placed an emphasis on gender-based human rights violations, such as sexual violence, and held value as a tool for national education on the issue. The hearing had the goal of initiating a national dialogue about the issue, emphasizing that violence against women is a result of the systematic exclusion of women from decision-making power and the maintenance of patriarchal formations of the private and public spheres.[18] The other objectives included symbolic reparation through the recognition of the victims' dignity and their civic values demonstrated by their struggle against impunity and assumption of new roles in the public sphere.

One of the initial formats proposed for the thematic hearing on women included attention to women active in armed groups, women as part of the civilian population, sexual violence, conditions of detention, social reinsertion, widows and families of the disappeared, displacement, and women as defenders of human rights.[19] As the program gained shape, the PTRC Gender Unit grouped testimonies into three issue areas: specific crimes against women, gender roles during violence, and women constructing peace. The Public Hearing and Victim Protection Unit, the Gender Unit, and civil society representatives engaged in heated discussion about ranking priority issues.[20] The Gender Unit proposed that sexual violence should be placed as central to the thematic hearing and framed as a crime against humanity, in contrast to the initial proposal to construct a more panoramic vision.

The PTRC presented its interest in women's rights, its gender analysis, and the importance of women in reconstructing a national truth on International Women's Day, March 8, 2002, at the event "Breaking the Silence." In this event Sofia Macher, director of the Public Hearings and Victim Protection Unit, publicized the public hearings, specifically the women's hearing, spelling out the frame for women's testimonies:[21] "We will present the specific way women lived through the political violence. Women will not only explain the violations they suffered but also explain their courageous participation in combating the violence and taking care of their families."[22] The reduced grouping of themes made room for other types of presentations, such as a panel on the Impact and Experiences of Political Violence on Women, in which local leaders and specialists took part. The Public Hearing and Victim Protection Unit organized an international seminar on Political Violence and Crimes against Women, to contextualize Peru globally. In addition, they organized a Citizen Dialogue the day after the hearings, where groups from civil society would discuss the issues presented in the hearing and present concrete recommendations to the PTRC.[23]

In turning to the testimonies, narrative excesses and disruptive moments evidence both the procedural and representational limits of the public hearings and the reassertion of the existing social order within the new national history. The testimonies by Dorisa Ccellccascca Llesca and Maria Cecilia Malpartida illustrate these procedural limits related to language, narrative style, and temporal frames, as well as the forced completion of the ritualized choreography.

PROCEDURAL LIMITS

The PTRC mediated the testimonies through case selection, testimony preparation, and (in several cases) translation from Quechua to Spanish. Eight women offered testimonies. There were to be nine, but as Gubercinda Reynaga Farfán, the gender coordinator for the PTRC's south central office in Ayacucho, explained to me, one of the women she interviewed and suggested be included in the hearing became immobilized on the national stage: "The Chungi case, I interviewed her and it was a very rich interview but in Lima she froze. That case didn't even get included in the summaries."[24] Another case from Chungi, the testimony of Dorisa Ccellccascca Llesca, was also troubled.

* * *

When Dorisa Ccellccascca Llesca initially stood to be sworn in, she appeared distraught when spoken to in Spanish. After an awkward pause, Commissioner Morote, the only commissioner who spoke Quechua, addressed her, at which point she looked to the PTRC staff around her for guidance. Ccellccascca sat and began to explain in Quechua the details of the violence she and her family experienced caught in the crossfire between the armed forces and the subversive group. A Quechua-Spanish interpreter seemed to struggle as she left long gaps of silence. Ccellccascca spoke with such detail that her testimony stretched on and on. At a certain point the same commissioner interrupted her, saying something in Quechua that was not translated into Spanish. Soon after, she abruptly announced that she finished her testimony, saying that it would take days to tell the whole story. The time allotted by the PTRC to recognizing the violations suffered by Dorisa Ccellccascca Llesca had elapsed.

* * *

This moment of incommensurability highlights the burden placed on Dorisa Ccellccascca Llesca to translate herself into the PTRC timeframe, style of narration, and language. Reynaga commented that Ccellccascca's case was very painful yet emblematic: "But she did not have contact [with Spanish-speaking urban culture], and language limited her power to explain the richness of everything that she lived in a way that the public could understand."[25] The superimposition of the PTRC's sense of temporality upon Ccellccascca's narrative timeframe highlights the heterogeneous and disjunctive temporalities at play and the conflicts among them. She had not internalized the instructions regarding her delivery and explained her experience from her own referent, which did not coincide with the PTRC's sense of temporality. The PTRC's underlying temporal frame makes some speaking positions possible and others impossible.[26] Much like the national geographic imaginary described in chapter 2, the dominant temporality reinforces a colonial sense of cultural difference, naturalizing a vertical power relationship.

The unidirectional interpretation served the Spanish-speaking commissioners and audience, leaving the Quechua-speaking audience to grasp whatever they could. While they were invited to voice their suffering and receive state recognition, it was of secondary importance for them to be able to understand the proceedings. This lack of equal interpretation in Quechua and Spanish contradicts the desire to create horizontal relations between victims and PTRC commissioners. Unidirectional translation finds its roots in Spanish colonialism, for it was an important tool in cultural conversion and assimilation of indigenous languages. Observe the "geopolitical directionality of translation"[27] and the inequalities among languages and ways of knowing.

The problems surrounding interpretation undermined the care given to setting the stage and designing the ritual, illustrating the PTRC's edge of cultural and linguistic capacity. In addition, the fact that various interpreters were replaced before one with adequate skills stepped in speaks volumes regarding the commitment to making sure historically marginalized victims could be understood.[28] Reasserting Spanish over indigenous languages reinforces the marginalization of Quechua speakers in the construction of the new national history and intertwines with the dominant geographic imaginary and temporality to effectively alienate certain speaking positions such as that of Dorisa Ccellccascca Llesca.

Compulsory completion of the ritual in the case of Maria Cecilia Malpartida further elucidates the procedural parameters of the hearings. Malpartida's unintended break with the choreography of reconciliation exposes the limits of empathetic listening.

* * *

It was September 10, 2002 and in a solemn voice a commissioner spoke, "We call forth Mrs. Maria Cecilia Malpartida." All stood to receive her pledge to make her declaration with honesty and good faith and narrate only the truth.[29]

When the subversive group [Peruvian Communist Party—Shining Path] arrived, my husband always resisted them. . . . My husband stood up to them and as a warning they took him and strangled him but left him with life. But he didn't stop. . . . One day my husband went to Pucallpa and when he came back, they took us both out of our house at 5 A.M., took us to the school and separated us. I could hear him screaming and then they came to tell me that he had confessed to having gone to the military in Pucallpa, he was a traitor. When they let me go at 3 P.M. I saw him bleeding from the ears and hands. He had begged them to free me. . . . Then when I was home, the whole community started to go to the school and someone told me that I had to go to, it was a fiesta dedicated to me. They took me and made me sit. Then they brought him out all bloody and made him kneel while they insulted him "traitor, snitch, you went to the military to denounce us!" . . . They brought me to my husband and told me to stab him with their weapon. I didn't want to, this is the man I love, my husband and the father of my child! Instead I armed myself with courage and stabbed the subversive leader that had been stabbing and beating him. How I wish they had killed me along with him! (Crying.)

When he died I was three months pregnant. At that time, I became a useless person: I became crazy. They took me home and tied me up. . . . Then after a while they let me go but watched me closely. I tried to escape but they captured me. . . . They took my shoes and tied me to a motorcycle and made me run all the way back to town. If I had fallen they would have dragged me.

Then they took me again, hands tied and blindfolded, in a car to the subversive camp. I was made to cook, sew flags, and wash, no one talked to me, only orders. . . . They beat me naked with ishanga (a bush with lots of thorns) when I tried to escape. I got sick with a high fever. . . . (Crying.) *Then they took me back home but always watched me.*

A friend offered to help me escape in the truck full of plantains they were taking to sell in Tingo Maria. But the subversives came to look for me there too. . . . I gave birth to my son but the sister of my husband took him at three months. I don't know where my son is, he will be thirteen the fourteenth of October. I want to know him! I want my son back! (Crying.)

My mother made me move all the time so I wouldn't get caught. I didn't tell anyone what had happened. My brothers and sisters hid me. . . . My mother took me to Iquitos. After a while I got involved with someone and had a baby. . . . Mother brought me back to Tingo Maria and I went home. A few days later, the police detained me for terrorism and took me to prison. . . . They hung me from my hands and feet and did not care that I had my six-month-old baby with me. . . . They also drowned me. . . . They kept me five months in Tingo Maria, then to Huanuco. . . . So much time passed. . . . I said to myself that if they sentence me, I will kill myself and my daughter too so she wouldn't have to suffer. . . . During this time my family rejected me, I no longer had the support of my family, they doubted me. (Crying.)

Then I was to have my day in court but I did not have a lawyer. A police officer came to me and said he would be my lawyer because he had just finished his legal studies. I didn't believe him, I thought he was making fun of me. But he came on the court day in a suit and represented me.

Since all that happened, I suffer from loss of consciousness, I pass out all the time. I just fall. Last time I almost broke my arm.

The lawyer never showed up again and my court dates were postponed two more times. Then they asked me if I accepted my defense as it stood and since I didn't understand anything that was happening I just said yes. Then they read the sentence: due to lack of evidence I was acquitted. How easy it is to say that I am absolved after so much time passed and all the things I had lived through!! So many years to just say so easily, you are absolved! (Fury and Violent Sobbing.)

Mister Commissioner, I ask that the body of my husband be moved to a cemetery. . . . And please find my son. . . . My daughter is sick from so much time in prison, she has intestinal tuberculosis. . . . I have cancer. . . . I don't ask anything for myself but for my daughter.

That is all I have to say.

One of the commissioners said the closing words:

In the name of the Peruvian Truth and Reconciliation Commission, I express our solidarity with the horrible suffering that you have lived through. I extend to you our recognition for having shared your experiences with us and of your personal strength to continue on. We will do everything to meet your requests.

Malpartida could not stop crying and her breathing was shallow. The four PTRC staff around her urged her to stand and pass in front of the table of commissioners to shake hands with them. This was the last obligatory step of reconciliation. Everyone in the auditorium, the commissioners and the audience, were already standing waiting for her. With a PTRC staff person holding her by the arm, she managed to get up, and she slowly moved toward the center of the stage. She shuffled along carrying the weight of brutal injustices with an extended hand as she mumbled "thank you for listening, thank you professor, thank you. . . ." Her shallow breathing turned into hyperventilation and just as she was engaged in the last hand shake, she lost consciousness, her hand slipped out of the commissioner's grasp and she fell backward onto the floor. The moment of impact, when Malpartida's unconscious form hit the floor, burst the seams of the carefully woven act. Her body lay in the form of a cross, reordered the logic of the public hearing; body as evidence, testimony as truth, and empathetic listening as reconciliation.[30] Some commissioners came around the table toward her while others leaned over the table and peered down at her, dumbfounded. Malpartida had just finished giving her testimony: she was case number five.

After a short recess, the commissioners reconvened on the stage absent Maria Cecilia Malpartida. Before moving on, a commissioner addressed the disappearance

through a closing statement, bridging the physical void with the audience by sutur-
ing the narrative of reconciliation.

> *Mrs. Maria Cecilia Malpartida is better. It is important to reflect upon how dif-*
> *ficult these experiences have been that our country has lived through during*
> *the twenty years of horror. Mrs. Maria Cecilia Malpartida wanted to give her*
> *testimony. For her and surely for many other people, to give testimony here in*
> *a public hearing is very important because it means that the state can com-*
> *prehend and understand what they have suffered. To remember is very dif-*
> *ficult, to return to those scenes that we who have not lived them directly have*
> *a hard time hearing. Mrs. Maria Cecilia Malpartida reached a point where she*
> *needed to break from her memory and her loss of consciousness was probably*
> *the way she could break from those horrible memories she was reliving. As I*
> *said, she is better. She feels relieved and feels that it was important to receive*
> *our solidarity and above all our attention to what happened to her, as these*
> *things also probably happened to many other women.*

* * *

While the commissioner's closing statement asserts the state's ability to
comprehend and understand victims' suffering, Malpartida's body offers evidence to the contrary. Her absence of consciousness and physical presence
confronts the commissioners and audience with the coercive aspect of reconciliation, the unwillingness to hear her warning or believe she would have
the audacity to improvise on her role as *testimoniante*. Her body, through its
inert silence, spoke truths about irreconcilable trauma that cut to the heart
of injustice. Her testimony was but a prelude.

The incomprehensible excess of Malpartida's collapse, the space between
her testimony and her lived reality, reveals the naturalized way the procedural
exigencies of the public hearing reinstate social hierarchies in the name of
nation reconciliation. Malpartida's full humanity, held in the balance between
death and survival, overwhelms the PTRC choreography and shatters the
nation's image of itself as passing through a transition to democracy based
upon a new national narrative. She is not dead, yet the shadow of death is
upon her. Instead of her body as a site of forensic evidence, it simultaneously
represents death—her testimony replete with death, the death of almost
seventy thousand people during the internal armed conflict—and survival.
She survives against her will, wishing to have been assassinated alongside
her husband and then plotting the murder of her baby girl and her own suicide to escape endless torture and unjust imprisonment. Her ambivalence
toward life undermines the PTRC narrative that celebrates her "struggle to

continue on." Malpartida's inanimate body frustrates the proper closure of the act of reconciliation. Similarly, Ccellccascca's temporal frame, language, and style of truth-telling exceed the design of the reconciliatory act. These two testimonies demonstrate the procedural limitations of the hearings that align with the exclusionary logics of the existing social order. To further explicate the power relations embedded in the public hearings, an analysis of the representational categories exposes the gendered dimensions of the new national narrative.

REPRESENTATIONAL LIMITS

Inclusion for women in the new national narrative hinged on a convincing enactment of maternal commitment and self-sacrifice. The family metaphor serves as an organizing figure for national history within a heteropatriarchal framework wherein the dominant representations of women fit with and sustain the representation of men as protectors.[31] The focus on women's suffering reifies women's normative role, thereby remasculinizing the state. The public hearings allow the state to reconcile the national family symbolically by positioning itself as a savior to women and children.[32]

As Juan Millán summarizes in his PTRC report on gender violence, the roles women took in the places where the violations occurred include "protecting their children and husbands, impeding the recruitment of their sons into the Shining Path, maintaining "familial tranquility" by staying silent about the violations they experienced, and, finally, taking on the role of head of household when their husbands were absent." Yet, this description of women's roles minimizes the empowering force and tenacity of women's collectives that struggled against indifferent institutions and gained recognition in public spaces. The multifaceted and sometimes contradictory life experiences of most women, including witness, direct and indirect victim, community organizer, perpetrator, subversive, and human rights advocate, exceed the dominant categories. Narrative erasure of the violations committed against imprisoned subversive women and the framing of the issue of rape and the children of rape elucidate the representational limits of motherhood and victimhood.

Who is considered a victim, according to the PTRC?

> Victims are those that have had a violation of their rights as recognized nationally or internationally. This also implies that victims are non-combatants, understood as civilians or military or political personnel, members of auto-defense groups or subversive groups outside of armed confrontations.[33]

During the PTRC event "Breaking the Silence" in 2002, Pilar Coll of the PTRC[34] pointed out systematic sexual violence in prisons against subversive women. Not only are doctors abusing women sexually, but women are also denied conjugal visits, thereby denying them any [hetero]sexual sex life.[35] Through my PTRC archival research I found the issue of gender-based violence against subversive women in prison mentioned in a few memoranda and reports. One of the memos, written by Jose Burneo, coordinator of Clarification of Events (*Esclarecimiento de Hechos*), addresses the gendered aspects of prison conditions, torture, and cruel, inhuman, and degrading treatment: "Incorporating the gender perspective implies registering the cases as differentiated between men and women, understanding that the consequences and impact are different in each case and, above all, that both sectors should be considered equally important."[36] This is one of the most explicit directives regarding the gendered aspects of human rights violations in prison, followed by a detailed breakdown of questions and issues to explore under each aforementioned violation. Such an investigation would make obvious the human rights violations of subversive women in prison. However, neither the public hearings nor the legal cases, nor the final report took up this issue.

The southern Andes regional branch gender coordinator's final report describes the many aspects of gender-based violence against women, including violations against imprisoned subversive women.[37] The PTRC branch-office gender coordinators interviewed women in jail and compiled their findings. Indeed, the PTRC holds about one thousand interviews with detained people documenting human rights violations. Discussions among the regional gender coordinators gave life to the idea of having a public hearing for women in prison. Why was that public hearing never realized? As Commissioner Macher points out, the Law 28592 excludes the legal recognition of these violations.[38]

Violations against subversives were understood to be committed against the guilty. Through their political transgression, imprisoned subversive women lose the ideological innocence associated with being female. By breaking out of traditional gender roles, they forfeit the protection given to women as subordinates within a masculinist social order. Subversive women gave up their families and children to dedicate themselves to the revolution, thereby shutting the door to any claim of motherhood. Claiming victimhood under these circumstances while simultaneously recognizing women's protagonism beyond motherhood becomes an impossibility, given the heteropatriarchal logic of the national narrative. The PTRC, based on a human rights framework, is structured on a gender hierarchy, combined with national ideological and political biases and historic racial, ethnocultural, class, and regional exclusions.[39] Therefore, the imprisoned subversive woman must stay conceptually locked away because acknowledging her victimhood AND her rejection of motherhood AND her betrayal of the nation cannot all happen together. She embodies an impossible combination. Acknowledgement would unravel the logics that undergird the new national history.[40]

Two testimonies, that of Magdalena Monteza Benavides during the hearing on Lima and Georgina Gamboa Garcia during the hearing on Ayacucho,[41] shine a stark light on the PTRC's gendered logic. These two hearings present the issue of children of rape. Magdalena Monteza Benavides called her then-nine-year-old daughter to the stage after her testimony, and Georgina Gamboa Garcia's twenty-year-old daughter accompanied her during her testimony. Through a legal gaze, these children embody the physical evidence of rape. Simultaneously, the children of rape signify the failure of the state to take responsibility, in that state actors, national police, and armed forces all father children and neglect their paternal obligations. Similar to the imprisoned subversive woman, the possibility of reconciliation with raped women depends on the extent to which they fulfill their motherhood role.

The efforts to incorporate the children of rape into the national historical narrative function as a symbolic gesture of reconciliation with race and class overtones. Silva Santiesteban argues that the children-of-rape issue triggers "*la bastardia originaria*/the original bastard" historical paradigm of Peru.[42] From a historical perspective *Peruanidad*/Peruvianess is rooted in the phenomenon of children born out of wedlock, typically to a man of privileged social positioning and a woman of lesser social status. This phenomenon, in which the father denies filiation, finds its roots in the colonial encounter with indigenous women. Silva Santiesteban highlights the iconic figure of the first Peruvian, Garcilaso de la Vega, son of a colonist and indigenous royalty. The racial, class, gender, and heterosexual stratifications of contemporary Peruvian society echo the historical paradigm of the "original bastard." This structural violence engenders an emotional world filled with hate and the desire for revenge.

Systematic sexual violence during the internal armed conflict and the children born from these acts reactivate the pattern inherent in the historical paradigm of the "original bastard." The national attention placed on the children of rape exposes the discrimination inherent within the social order, threatening the state's legitimacy. Through the public hearings, the state reclothes itself in "heterosexuality's garb,"[43] applauding maternal expressions of unconditional and selfless love and recognizing the children in a symbolic reconciliation of the national family. Including the children in the performance, and having the commissioners embrace and kiss them along with their mothers after the testimony, indicates state recognition and acceptance. This public act even seems to absolve the stigma of illegitimacy and to resolve the problem of the "original bastard," facilitating closure on the issue.

The extremely conflicted relationship Magdalena Monteza and Georgina Gamboa Garcia have with their pregnancy due to rape and unintended maternity troubles the reconciliation narrative. Magdalena Monteza Benavides highlights in her testimony that she was pregnant against her will and she found it unacceptable to be a mother due to rape. Yet she qualified her comments by saying the baby was not at fault and she could not make her daughter suffer due to this. In the statement, "I learned to love her," she reaffirmed both identities of long-suffering victim and self-sacrificing mother. Georgina Gamboa Garcia, in her testimony, wondered what kind of monster could be growing inside of her as a product of the beatings, rapes, and abuses she suffered at the hands of seven officers. She wanted to commit suicide or at least to abort, but it was too late. So she wanted to give the child up for adoption. She explains how she was separated from her daughter but was able to get her back, yet her daughter has no paternal last name. She ended her testimony without speaking the words of full acceptance and love for her daughter who sat next to her. This failure to express her maternal commitment endangered the reconciliation narrative.

Georgina Gamboa Garcia exemplifies the effort on the part of a *testimoniante* to break the representational framework that thwarts the desired effect of her message. Her testimony, according to Rocío Silva Santiesteban, utilized the power of interpretation to demand a reciprocal exchange with her audience. "I give you my story/you give me your indignation."[44] This approach does everything possible to deny pity as an appropriate response, forcing the audience to negotiate an alternative emotional terrain with the goal of restitution and distributive justice. However, at the end of this testimony, a commissioner forced the *testimoniante* back into the maternal role with the following closing comment: "The love between you and your daughter goes beyond all the terror that happened." This insertion sutured the narrative loop to achieve full reconciliation between the mother and the state as symbolic father.

The hearings put faces and stories to the statistics. As a civic ritual, the public hearings were a success in that they carved a new national space for victims to tell of their experiences during the internal armed conflict. However, the range of representational frames mobilized by the PTRC limited the ways the *testimoniantes* could communicate. The representational framing ended up reifying the victim, as did the dominant cultural, temporal, and linguistic references. These factors influence the extent to which the audience could break out of emotional responses based on social hierarchies to experience humanizing emotions, such as the indignation Georgina Gamboa Garcia demanded. This intimate bridging of social distance would require the audience to identify with the *testimoniante*, thereby overcoming discrimination, transforming "relationships among former antagonists,"[45] and truly moving toward reconciliation.

The Politics of Reception

The hearings elicited pity at the national level and, according to the *testimoniantes*, even among some commissioners.

> In general the participants felt they were the objects of attention of the commissioners and it affected them to see that their stories had the power to move them and inspire words of support. *"The Commissioners of the Truth looked anguished when we told them everything that happened. They looked at me in a sad way because of all the things that have happened here. They looked at me with sadness and pain"* (Ayacucho, woman, seventy-three years old, family of disappeared).[46]

Although there are multiple levels of reception, the PTRC placed emphasis on the national public opinion of the hearings, with the goal of swaying the opinions of the privileged and Spanish-literate sectors of Peruvian society.[47] This unidirectionality reflects an economy of emotion in which the historically marginalized produce testimonies that conform to dominant linguistic and temporal frames for mainstream consumption.[48]

In an effort to maintain social order during the hearings and also reach as much of the population as possible, the commissioners divided the public hearing audience into three main sectors. First, the audience present during the actual public hearing could be completely controlled. For the first hearings, the audience was handpicked until such time the public-hearing working group determined that they could ensure safety and order. The regional audience made up the second level, those who lived in the region where the hearing was to be held. The public-hearing working group and local NGOs opened additional spaces to view the hearings through live broadcast. This was the most complicated audience to reach, and the cultural and artistic work of *Grupo Cultural Yuyachkani* and others accompanied the population and created a space of reflection, memorialization, and healing. The third level of audience included the national public, which could be reached through television and radio transmission.[49]

An analysis of the regional reception of the public hearings and related activities brings critical perspective to an examination of reception at the national level. Efforts on the part of the PTRC to prepare the regional audience for the public hearings had begun months ahead with a three-week artistic and cultural tour of the regional cities where the public hearings were to take place. Javier Torres from the NGO Rural Education Services organized the cultural tour of the selected locations for the public hearings several months in advance of the hearings themselves. Artists, musicians, and actors performed popular theater, organized street events, and gave concerts. The tour disseminated information regarding the hearings to come and built interest, awareness, and curiosity.

Grupo Cultural Yuyachkani participated in this tour. Embodied in the name *Yuyachkani* (in Quechua) is the interconnected I/you, thereby breaking out of binary logic of self/other.[50] Since its establishment in 1971, *Yuyachkani* has contributed to a liberatory social-political project in Peru. Its cultural politics come out of the tradition of popular theater collectives in Latin America.[51] Reflecting on the composition of theater groups in the 1970s, Miguel Rubio writes, "Our groups were families whose theater pieces announced the possibility of gaining our happiness and our livelihood. Our works, which reflected the political and social reality of our countries, were full of hope, and little by little they were converted into inventories of horror; victims of violence, migrants, displaced, and disappeared people populated our stages."[52] A central topic of their work has been political violence and its aftermath. Harnessing the power of memory, *Yuyachkani* contributes to a tradition of breaking complicit silences around national trauma, oblivion, horror, and pain.

Grupo Cultural Yuyachkani organized a vigil the night before every hearing. Compared with to the foreignness of the formal public hearing, the vigil is part of the traditional community-based expression. The vigil brought together the regional groups working on issues of disappearances, kidnappings, and extrajudicial assassinations, memorializing their family members with pictures and crosses. In addition, members of *Yuyachkani* welcomed people as they arrived for the hearings.[53]

During the public hearings *Yuyachkani* performed popular theater pieces in markets, main squares, and the atriums of churches. The three main pieces included *Adiós, Ayacucho, Antígona,* and *Rosa Cuchillo,* all of which revolve around absent bodies: the struggle to find the body of a loved one (or the pieces of one's own body, in the case of *Adiós, Ayacucho*) and to properly mourn and bury the remains. These actions make palpable the accumulation of trauma through symbolism, repetition, and a call to collectively witness, remember, and take responsibility for one's position in society.

Yuyachkani's cultural and artistic work contributed to reconciliation on the micro level by accompanying the public hearings and intimately engaging with the community. The local population commonly assumed that they were an extension of the PTRC, offering their testimonies. These impromptu truth-telling circles both raised consciousness about the conflict and inspired mutual support and healing.[54] While the public hearings introduced a new channel through which victims could express themselves at the regional level, many people questioned why they could not speak and why only a handful of people were chosen to give testimony. The seeming lack of transparency regarding who could speak generated complaints. People wanted their dead to be registered by the state, their names written and published with indelible ink on paper. Given the impossibility of responding to all the popular

"Rosa Cuchillo," *el Grupo Cultural Yuyachkani* theater piece performed by Ana Correa at Trinity College in Connecticut, 2005. (Photograph by Pablo Delano.)

demand, the cultural and artistic community work opened a space for spontaneous moments of healing, memorializing, and public truth telling.[55]

The performance piece *Rosa Cuchillo*, with its use of flower water in a closing act of ritual healing, was well received by local communities. *Rosa Cuchillo* enacts the apparition of a woman who died years ago yet still searches for her disappeared son. This character is a composite of many mothers who lost their children; there are many Rosa Cuchillos in Peru to whom this book is dedicated. The story of my encounter with one such woman in the garden of broken trees opens this book. In the performance, as Rosa Cuchillo's spirit comes to peace, she dances and throws flower water out to the audience in an act of blessing and healing citational of Andean medicinal practices. At the end of the performance, the whole audience approaches her, asking for more water to moisten their heads in a self-curative gesture.

Besides performing the piece, the actress who played Rosa Cuchillo, Ana Correa, took her character through markets and city streets greeting people. These moments of blurred boundaries between fiction and reality opened extraordinary communicational spaces. Correa recalls the remarkable level of mutual recognition that she established with people who received her with great love and respect, gifting her corn, bread, and other goods. The intensely intimate experiences of public truth telling, deep recognition, and collective healing that took place at the margins of the public hearings contrast sharply with the disidentification that characterized the national public reception.

Public opinion polls, such as the one taken in 2001 by the PTRC, concluded that people from Lima perceive the abuses related to the conflict as distant, abstract statistics. Therefore, the PTRC's main communicational objective should be to move public opinion from a perfunctory approval of the PTRC investigation to a deeper level of comprehension. To this end, during the public hearings advocates made explicit calls to shift public opinion. Directly after the last testimony of the thematic public hearing on women, for example, Ana Maria Rebaza, a psychologist on the panel "Impact and Experience of Political Violence on Women," opened her presentation with an exhortation to the audience: "Our gaze should not dwell in either commiseration or idealization." This comment reflects the problematic positioning of the audience in relation to the two main representations of women during the testimonies. On the one hand, the representation of women as long-suffering victims produces a powerful sense of pity within the audience. On the other hand, the representation of strong women community leaders produces a romanticized idealization of a superhuman capacity to overcome trauma and persist in struggle. Neither representation is fully accurate, as the testimonies illustrate through the multiple and overlapping roles, events, experiences, feelings, and reactions that each woman recounts.

Sofia Macher explains the problem of lack of identification on the part of the Peruvian populace with regard to the thematic hearing on women.

> We measured the impact of the public hearings and it was very impressive. Such a significant communication instrument had never been used—it was the first time. The women, majority poor, indigenous, excluded, and invisible, could speak in their language and be listened to with total serenity. As a professional instrument, it was impressive, it had a huge impact and was greatly respected throughout the country. Not one newspaper shed doubt on a testimony . . . the problem was that even though it had a great impact, the public opinion did not reflect the establishment of a relationship of equal citizenship with the testimoniantes. The personal connection and the civic responsibility in the face of such atrocity were lacking. So, in the end it did not produce any change. Public opinion reflected that the hearings had an impact on immediate feelings but did not achieve any changes in attitudes or behavior. . . . In the end, public opinion was of sadness, but it stayed there, reproducing pity separated from personal identification and responsibility . . . and that is not enough.[56]

Upon the bedrock of historic exclusion, the public hearings had little chance of marking a significant shift in public opinion, given that they mobilized a representational repertoire that reaffirmed the status quo.

The PTRC's assumption that the national public did not know of the effects of the conflict was erroneous, according to Javier Torres.[57] He argues that everyone knew what was happening. One had only to glance at the newsstand. The real issue was the willful turning away—in other words, percepticide, "the self-blinding of the general population."[58] The public already knew about the pain and suffering and had chosen to avert their gaze in an act of denial and social erasure. The PTRC representational frames and procedural oversights triggered a repetition of this response given their consistency with hierarchies embedded in the emotional terrain.

In 2003 the PTRC contracted Imasen to conduct a qualitative evaluation of the PTRC's work in Lima in the regional cities of Huánuco and Tingo Maria, in the department of Huánuco. The comparison of responses from the capital city and the regional cities underscores the social distance of Lima in relation to the consequenses of the conflict and the distrust of the PTRC intentions on the part of people in the regional cities. The deepest critique leveled at the PTRC by the regional evaluation claimed that the PTRC put its interests and internal logic first without any regard to the well being of the victims and the additional suffering the public hearings could cause. Similar to the questions raised by people in Ayacucho, the evaluation in Huánuco and Tingo María demonstrated suspicion regarding the case selections for the public hearings and the preparation of the *testimoniantes*. Those who gave testimony felt deceived because they were not informed of the overall process, the followup, and outcome of the public hearings. Another sector believed that the hearings could have positive effects, such as exposing the truth and increasing consciousness about the impact of the conflict. The report concluded that positive perceptions were the result of an additional process of reflection on the hearings, which suggested that a campaign to disseminate and interpret the hearings would assist the population in understanding the hearings.

The same study in Lima concluded that the population in favor of the hearings did not necessarily comprehend the testimonies or their implications. Neither did the population assume any shared responsibility for what happened. Given these results of the study, the PTRC commissioner directing the public hearings incorporated a public discussion group at the end of the hearings to develop a collective reflection on the hearing. According to Commissioner Macher, there were not enough resources to add a discussion group to all the hearings, but when possible, they were very successful in furthering the educational objective of the PTRC, such as the Citizen Dialogue the last day of the Thematic Public Hearing on Women.

The key piece of the puzzle left out of these evaluations has to do with the representational frames deployed within the public hearings and further emphasized through the editing process. The individual story of suffering, designed to create the greatest potency for the audience also tends to foreground the pain while the subject enduring the abuses recedes from the frame. Furthermore, as Lisa Laplante and Kelly Phenicie assert regarding the media response to the PTRC, "When the media focuses on an individual's story, it avoids the more systemic, causal explanation of societal problems or situations. This can even shift the public agenda away from confronting pressing social, political and economic challenges."[59] Such an approach elicits the response of pity while recentering the intended audience and further marginalizing the suffering subject.[60]

Press coverage contributed to the problem of public opinion in that access to the full public hearings was mediated at various levels. While the first public hearings in Ayacucho and Huanta were transmitted nationally in their full length, the subsequent transmissions consisted of one-hour edited segments. Ana Correa recalls walking the streets of these cities during the hearings: everyone had televisions or radios tuned to the testimonies. This prompted a collective need to tell their stories and revisit their own experiences. Since only sixteen testimoniantes spoke on the national stage, the rest of those with the need to speak initiated a spontaneous public truth-telling process. This outpouring of public expression exceeded the expectations of the commissioners and the public-hearing working group. Ana Correa notes that after that initial full-length transmission of the public hearing, "from then on they only broadcasted edited clips of the hearings."[61] Given the need to contain the audience and avoid negative outcomes, the full transmission of the hearings became a liability.

There were several different organizations editing the hearings for public dissemination. The PTRC contracted Channel 7 to film the hearings in their entirety. Their journalists determined the first cut with oversight from the PTRC communications team. They produced a one-hour clip and broadcast it the night after the hearings and on the weekends. Channel N also edited and compiled audio/video records of the public hearings. The Peruvian state radio and television channels, along with cable channel N, transmitted the public hearings. The channels with open signals demanded to be paid to broadcast the public hearings, an attitude shared even by the state television channel. Manrique suspects that the owners may have taken this position out of a sense that the hearings would not attract much of a viewing audience. The decisions made regarding the dissemination of the testimonies limited the possible reach of symbolic and vicarious restoration of victims' dignity by viewing the recognition of their country folk by the state. "Some participants evidenced dissatisfaction regarding the lack of press coverage received by the public hearings, explaining that in their communities there is no access to cable television and newspapers."[62] In the rural parts of Peru, radio was the only way to access information regarding the hearings.

Conclusion

In a general sense, the PTRC public hearings educated the populace about the how the internal armed conflict affected women and offered recognition to the *testimoniantes*. Yet, as I argue throughout, problematic reassertions of Peruvian social hierarchies, combined with the victim focus, compromise the potential contributions to national reconciliation. Commissioner Macher comments that given the transitional justice framework, the public hearings focused only on victims. Yet in retrospect Commissioner Macher notes that she wishes she could have widened the scope to include the military, for example.[63] Therefore, one lesson learned from the Peruvian public hearings is the need to broaden the representative repertoire beyond the victim.

When read closely, the testimonies consistently give voice to a variety of experiences that go far beyond victimhood. A partial composite that blends elements of the eight testimonies underscores the overwhelming variety of stories told at the public hearing.

> . . . *receiving third degree burns all over my body due to a terrorist attack and not having insurance to cover the cost of medical care, demanding social equality, having my house burned, living scared, being detained by the armed forces and accused of being a terrorist, being raped by twenty-five soldiers, searching in vain for an authority to report these violations, having my partner shot while lying beside him in bed, having to care for the thirty-six orphaned children left in the community, denouncing the captain responsible for these crimes, witnessing the beating of my blind mother, refusing to sign a paper accusing my husband of terrorism, being raped by six soldiers while trying to protect my one-and-a-half-year-old baby, feeling sick and crazy, being blamed by a doctor for not taking proper care of my children while detained and on the run, having my two daughters, fifteen and eighteen years of age, taken by soldiers (who knows what they did to them), watching my children search for employment and finding no opportunities, witnessing the public assassination of my husband, being enslaved by the Shining Path, having my baby taken from me while in detention, keeping silent, being forcibly displaced, becoming terminally ill, having all my livestock taken, exercising community leadership, never finding loving kindness again in the world after all my family was killed and demanding of the commissioners that these testimonies lead to a proper investigation of the causes for so much abuse of humble peasants.*

This staccato recitation blurs the individual voices of *testimoniantes* to elucidate the sense of imbricated collectivity that defies categorization and underscores the systemic and structural aspects of violence.

The selection of testimonies and the testimonies themselves demonstrate the restricted qualities of both victimhood and motherhood. Magdalena Monteza Benavides's and Georgina Gamboa Garcia's ambivalent motherhood in the face of pregnancy due to rape and the shadow figure of the imprisoned subversive women illustrate both the narrative overflow and erasure of the hearings. Dorisa Ccellccascca Llesca and Maria Cecilia Malpartida embody the limits of reconciliation. Their excesses, similar to the previous composite of testimonies, point toward violence beyond gross violations of human rights and demand attention to the histories of discrimination.

The fact that the PTRC named the dynamic of historic oppressions in the final report marks a significant step. To incorporate these insights into the preparation, implementation, and dissemination of the public hearings demands a willingness to transform the existing social order and deeply question the state's investment in linear progress toward modernity. Had the PTRC broken with the representational repertoire, going beyond the victims voicing their pain to better attend to linguistic, temporal, and cultural differences, the audience would have had to adjust its assumptions about the "other," thereby reconfiguring their emotional response beyond pity.[64]

By contemplating Yuyachkani's work in collaboration with the Peruvian transitional justice project, a tension arises out of the transitional justice concept of a linear and bounded temporality for social transformation. Yuyachkani's cultural politics of performance engages with spiral and cyclical forms of temporality. Simultaneously engaging with the state-initiated public hearings and infusing them with new meanings and referents, they go beyond the frame and call upon their spectators to take the next step of embracing cultural difference. They claim self-referential approaches to voice, express creativity, and construct life-affirming spaces where possible. At an epistemological level, *Yuyachkani* offers an alternative of multiple temporalities and spatialities grounded in Andean cosmovision.

In his reflections on the work of the PTRC, Commissioner Degregori makes the following statement.

> To construct citizenship in any country, and even more in a pluricultural country, implies not only legal equality but also a scrupulous respect for differences. The recognition of the "Other." The "Other" that in our case is interwoven with youth, women, the poor, and indigenous, even though racial and ethnic-cultural "othering" is more prominent. For the construction of a national community this recognition implies passing from tolerance to respect and esteem, which are opposite from the mix of fear and scorn that has predominated in our history.

The problems of social exclusion were not solved by the PTRC. However, the PTRC did bring difficult and controversial histories to light, placing them on the national stage for state and civil society followup. The role of sexual violence within the internal armed conflict embodies one of those difficult and controversial histories. The next chapter analyzes the PTRC's treatment of this issue, both in the preparation of an emblematic case and through its final report.

4

Sexual Violence beyond
Consent and Coercion

Prosecuting cases of sexual violence during internal armed conflict has become part of the international transitional justice agenda. Although the PTRC was not mandated to investigate sexual violence, it included the violation under the umbrella of torture[1] and other grave violations in compliance with international human rights law. According to the Rome Statute of the International Criminal Court, which Peru ratified November 10, 2001, "rape, sexual slavery, enforced prostitution, forced pregnancy, enforced sterilization, or any other form of sexual violence of comparable gravity are crimes against humanity."[2] Examining the PTRC investigation of sexual violence provides insights into the limits and possibilities of utilizing the international human rights law to address violence against marginalized populations, the victims' subjectivity, and the institutional utility of sexual violence for the military. This feminist analysis of state responses to sexual violence during the internal armed conflict draws from the PTRC Manta and Vilca (military bases) legal case, the PTRC final report chapter "Sexual Violence against Women," and fieldwork conducted between 2005 and 2012. Elucidating the state's treatment of sexual violence exposes how the state both opens the possibility for radically rethinking its parameters and reconsolidates as coherent and singular by reinforcing gender and racial hierarchies.

Of the forty-seven legal cases that the PTRC prepared for prosecution and passed to the state prosecutor, two cases address rape. The PTRC labeled the Manta and Vilca case as emblematic of sexual violence as it took place in the rural context by military personnel. The case is a compilation of twenty-six victims assaulted by soldiers both during military incursions and in and

The department of Huancavelica in Peru. (Map created by John A.
Stevenson using ArcGIS)

around military bases.[3] Military personnel perpetrated sexual violence in a
persistent and reiterated manner, yet the violation is largely understood as
a secondary effect of armed conflict: it's collateral damage. The armed forces
and police, responsible for 83 percent of sexual violence, exercised domination by violating women's corporal integrity while the subversive groups,

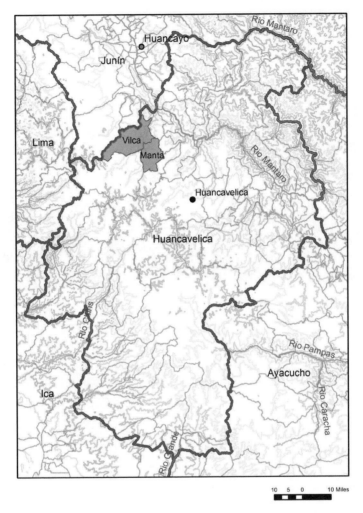

The districts of Manta and Vilca in the department of Huancavelica.
(Map created by John A. Stevenson using ArcGIS.)

Shining Path—Communist Party of Peru (PCP-SL) and Túpac Amaru Revolutionary Movement (MRTA), were responsible for 11 percent.[4]

In the early years of the conflict, the Shining Path began to have a presence
in the northern cone of Huancavelica where Manta is located. The conflict
most strongly affected the poorest areas of the southern Andes, including

The community of Manta with the military base on the hill. (Photograph by author.)

the regions of Ayacucho, Huancavelica, and Apurimac. The district of Manta is part of Huancavelica, the poorest region of Peru, with 88 percent of the population living in poverty and 74 percent in extreme poverty.[5] It sits at 3,532 meters above sea level, and the community is largely composed of subsistence farmers and herders who supplement their livelihood with seasonal labor migration to cities.

In 1984 the Political Military Command[6] established a counterguerrilla military base in the district of Manta as a result of subversive action in the area. When the armed forces entered the community of Manta, they came in shooting, burning homes, and sacking provisions. Community members took refuge in the surrounding mountains. Then, when they tried to reestablish themselves in what remained of their homes, the military obliged the community to build the military base out of what was left of their homes and buildings. The military presence dominated the community for eleven years, during which time the whole region was under a state of emergency (between 1983 and 1999).[7] The Manta Vilca case is emblematic of how the military perpetrated the majority of sexual violence against women from Andean Quechua-speaking or Amazonian ethnolinguistic communities in and around military installations. The systematic and generalized nature of

The military base in the community of Manta. (Photograph by author.)

the military perpetration of sexual violence suggests the need to examine the internal utility of this practice for the military.

The Manta and Vilca case investigates sexual violence under the rubric of torture and also as perpetrated through the individual initiative of soldiers on their days off and when they escaped from the base at night. This violation under individual initiative could not fit into the rubric of torture, yet its occurrence was directly related to the military presence. The inclusion of sexual violence perpetrated by soldiers acting on individual initiative opens up an important legal and sociopolitical discussion regarding historical power asymmetries as they take form under military occupation. In addition to the goal of prosecution utilizing the rubric of torture, feminist legal advocates working in the PTRC placed this issue of individual initiative onto the national stage to challenge legal frameworks and sociopolitical consciousness. This case and the debates surrounding it—regarding the social context in which soldiers could act with such impunity—imply an underlying militarized heteropatriarchal order. Within this order, conflicts exist among differing expressions of masculinity: those of the benevolent state promising justice, the hyperaggressive soldier/rapist-soldier, and the community leaders.

The state's use of the international human rights law to address violations facilitates the potential expansion of citizenship and national inclusion of historically marginalized populations. This development marks an important opening on the part of the protective and paternalist state. On a practical level, as illustrated in chapter 2, the scale of the PTRC work, the short timeframe, and the lack of resources made it impossible to attend to the individual and collective subjectivities of the victims. At the conceptual level, heteropatri-archal norms—such as the private and public spheres embedded in inter-national human rights law—undermine the goals of transitional justice by circumscribing the conceptual optic through which to document and address abuses, specifically sexual violence.

The binary of consent/coercion and conceptual myopia around sexual violence are the two most significant limiting factors regarding the imple-mentation of the international human rights regime to investigate and pros-ecute sexual violence. With regard to the binary of consent/coercion, the PTRC draws its understanding of sexual violence from the Rome Statute, article 7, as "a sexual act realized against one or more people or when these individuals are forced to realize a sexual act among themselves: by force or threat of force or coercion due to fear of violence intimidation, detention, psychological oppression or abuse of power against these persons or others or taking advantage of an environment of coercion or the incapacity of these persons to give their free consent."

A decolonial feminist approach aims to deconstruct binary logics. Applied here, such an approach highlights how the conditions for consent and coer-cion are assumed to be mutually exclusive. Consent requires the possibility and relevance of individual free will, which comes under question in the context of rural Andean-highland, Quechua-speaking communities with long-term military occupation. While the binary of consent/coercion is fundamental to proving that sexual violence has taken place, this violation is embedded in a dense matrix of historic power relations that fall beyond the scope of adjudication. The legal case provides an entry point to "iden-tify a much broader array of enabling phenomena resulting in women's experiences of systematic violence."[8] Exploring power relations through a community-based analysis presses beyond the limits of linear temporal-ity to contextualize sexual violence relationally across different historical moments. This community-based analysis aligns with a decolonial analyti-cal approach to highlight patterns of domination rooted in coloniality and heteropatriarchy.

Conceptual myopia, that of reducing women to the violation of sexual violence, develops in part because sexual violence is the only direct human rights violation committed against women more than against men.[9] The rigors of the human rights regime demand a focus on the violation rather than on the person(s) and their subjective interpretation of such violation. The conceptual myopia attached to investigating sexual violence denies recognition of the way victims of this violation understand and express themselves. The process of designating the Manta and Vilca case as emblematic further underscores the fragility of the state's commitment to recognize victims as subjects. Nevertheless, a combination of local, national, and international pressures created the conditions for the insertion of the Manta Vilca case into the PTRC investigation.

Incorporating the Emblematic Case of Manta and Vilca

The Manta and Vilca case came to the PTRC through an essay titled "Women and the Armed Forces in a Context of Political Violence: The Case of Manta and Vilca, Huancavelica" written by anthropologist Mercedes Crisóstomo in 2002.[10] Crisostomo's report came into contact with the PTRC and, given the international and national pressure to address sexual violence, provided an opportunity for the state to demonstrate its adherence to the latest developments in the human rights regime. The fact that the PTRC included cases of sexual violence builds upon an important shift in the work of commissions across the globe after 2000, following on the Guatemalan Commission for Historical Clarification and the War Tribunals of Rwanda and Ex-Yugoslavia.

The Juridical Unit prepared the Manta and Vilca legal case, and the Regional Histories Unit performed an in-depth investigation.[11] Before the PTRC took up the legal case, Crisóstomo and a group of PTRC employees returned to Manta and Vilca to ask the victims for permission to investigate their cases and prepare them for prosecution. Most consented, and the PTRC went forward with those cases.[12] The inclusion of this collective case offers the opportunity to write women in as subjects of the national historical narrative. At the public event *Nunca Mas* in 2006, Sofia Macher, PTRC commissioner, reflected on the PTRC's decision-making process regarding the inclusion of the Manta and Vilca case. She asserts, "For us in the TRC there was a big discussion about whether it was legitimate or not to put all the attention on the one case of Manta and Vilca. Was it legitimate to present the case to the state prosecutor when the women were not adequately informed about the juridical process? At the end it was decided that if we had the information about the injustice and violation, it was our duty to report it."

Macher's version of the events somewhat contradicts Crisóstomo's version, since Crisóstomo went back to the community with the PTRC staff and asked permission to represent the cases. This discrepancy might be explained by the lack of follow-up communication with the victims after Crisóstomo's trip with the PTRC employees to request their initial consent. Legally, the victim's permission is not necessary to forward sexual violence cases because the violence is considered a public action. As Peruvian feminist lawyer Diana Portal comments, while women do not have to present their cases personally, the process can take the victim's agency away.[13]

What is made clear through these passages is that the PTRC's treatment of the Manta and Vilca case contains a certain level of ambiguity with regard to positioning women as *subjects* with the capacity of making decisions regarding the use of their testimonies for legal ends in the service of national justice processes. The moments of self-doubt and questioning reflected in Macher's comments are important opportunities to explore how exclusionary practices are reinforced for the "greater good" of transitional justice. These exclusionary practices have a long legacy and are not new to the people who live in the Andean highlands. Crisóstomo's insistence in returning to the community to discuss the possibility of taking up the legal case with the victims was an important step of recognition that positioned the victims as subjects. The ambiguity that followed during the PTRC process illustrates the contradictory position of the PTRC. On the one hand, the PTRC had taken the step to include sexual violence. On the other hand, given the mountain of tasks and tight timeline, the PTRC could not always guarantee a commitment to the recognition of victims as subjects.

An analysis of the PTRC legal case, "Sexual Violence in Huancavelica: The Military Bases in Manta and Vilca," shows how women's subjectivity is eclipsed and how a vast amount of sexual violence remains invisible because the characteristics of the violation fall outside the purview of the law. The opening pages of the PTRC Manta and Vilca legal case centrally position two quotes that reflect the dominant characteristics the PTRC wishes to highlight regarding this case: the rape of virgins and children of rape. The case finds strength by building on the ultimate symbol of innocence, virginity, and the proof that it has been taken: children born of rape. This optic reinforces stereotypical depictions of victims, thereby reifying historic power asymmetries. The paternal and protective state reconsolidates itself through heteropatriarchal logics, such as the innocent raped virgin and children born of rape as evidence of the crime. Indeed, the state uses the human rights regime to fold "its own interests into a disciplining narrative that it could later claim as evidence of its benevolent paternalism."[14] Positioning these themes as central to building a legal case further marginalizes the subjectivity of the women victims.

While the focus of this analysis on the harm and victim's subjectivity is critical to both achieving justice and making visible marginalized peoples, it has the potential of eclipsing another question. Given the systemic and generalized nature of the violation, what function does sexual violence serve for the internal workings of the military? The worthy goal of exposing the limits of heteropatriarchal norms within international human rights law, such as the public/private divide, can be paired with an inquiry into the heteropatriarchal norms and practices within the military.[15] The instrumentalization of sexual violence on the part of the military functions as a socialization process to form and maintain soldiers capable of extreme brutality. In this chapter I offer suggestive insights on this topic, which demands much more research. Opening this second line of inquiry, however tentative, underscores the different faces of the state, the paternal protective masculinity expressed through the PTRC and its underbelly, military socialization into hyperaggressive masculinity through the practice of sexual violence.[16] Meanwhile, communities such as Manta leverage the institution of marriage against the state. Exploring the solution of marriage with the soldier-rapist illuminates the grey areas between community complicity with national heteropatriarchal logics and the communal-based logic of marriage as a means of economic justice.[17] Community-based perspectives on sexual violence offer the historical context to this practice.

Historically Contextualizing Sexual Violence in Manta

Manta has experienced a chain of vertical relations, which included abusive *patrones*, or powerful regional landowners. The account of one *patrón*, Pacheco, stands out in the collective memory of Manta for his unbridled exploitation of *campesinos*, forced recruitment of young men for military service, theft of animals, and sexual abuse of women.[18] He acted with complete impunity as a result of his association with the regional elite.[19] *El patrón* had a central role not only in economic production but also in the political and ideological arena to keep the labor in place through a feudal order based on racialized hierarchies and heteropatriarchy.

El patrón has multiple meanings. In addition to a powerful landowner, *el patrón* is also a pattern, like that used to cut material into the pieces necessary to sew a piece of clothing. Most significant, the theory/metaphor *el patrón* as developed by communities in the southern Andes critically identifies patterns of illegitimate authority, economic exploitation, and cultural domination. It "constitutes a form of synthesizing the hierarchical character of the social relations still present in Peruvian society."[20] The theory/metaphor exposes patterns of social relations across time, connecting historical moments that modernity posits as distinct through a naturalized order of progression.

This temporal bridging of the theory/metaphor *el patrón* challenges linear temporality. Such an approach aligns with decolonial feminisms as exemplified by Jacqui Alexander's concept of palimpsestic time—reading for social, economic, political patterns of exploitation and illegitimacy as attached to the affective and emotional worlds of those subjects who bear the brunt of these patterns.[21] The idea of palimpsest evokes the image of a paper that has been written and erased many times. Traces of the older writings remain through their indentations in the paper, so the newer writings are overlaid on the older ones. Thinking about temporality in this way suggests that older practices influence how we understand newer practices. The practices, if seen together, create continuity, a pattern across time. Patterns also hold discontinuities, in that actors, actions, and contexts may vary. By bridging historical moments seen as separate, Alexander argues that "the ideological traffic between and among formations that are otherwise positioned as dissimilar" come into view.[22]

Communities in the southern Andes affected by the internal armed conflict understand sexual violence in relation to its perpetration in other historical moments, echoing the decolonial sensibility Alexander underscores in her concept of palimpsestic time. Ruiz Bravo, Neira and Rosales assert that within the rural communities of the Southern Andes, *el patrón* theory/metaphor "politicizes illegitimate situations that take an emotional toll, that coerce desire and impede the consolidation of citizenship and democracy."[23] The collective case of Manta and Vilca exemplifies such illegitimate situations in that the pattern of sexual violence echoes colonial legacies manifest in a continuity of violence experienced through Pacheco's rule and the internal armed conflict. These legacies "evoke the imagery of an inheritance" and trace the "continuities and discontinuities between contemporary and inherited practices."[24] Critical attention to colonial legacies implies a rethinking of history that challenges basic assumptions such as linear progression and the separation of historical moments.

El patrón as a metaphor elucidates the way class, race, ethnicity, and gender function within the local social imaginary to map a paternalist system, "marked by power, domination and coloniality."[25] As discussed in the introduction of this book, coloniality paired with modernity indicates the colonization of the Américas, the enduring ways of knowing imposed by colonization and its current manifestations. Decolonial feminist Lugones brings attention to the gendered aspects of coloniality/modernity. Alexander's decolonial feminist concept of palimpsestic time offers an analytic frame to trace the modern/colonial gender system while prioritizing Andean-based ways of knowing—which foreground the patterns of domination embedded in the practice of sexual violence across time and space. This approach anchors an intersectional analytic sensibility in the historical roots of legitimated inequalities in Peru.

Quechua-speaking campesinas find themselves in a precarious position of vulnerability to abuse and humiliation with no recourse. This pattern of social relations naturalizes sexual abuse. "*El patrón* was the owner of both the land and the people that inhabited it. In the case of women, they were obligated to submit themselves to sexual practices against their will as a form of 'pleasing' the owner."[26] For generation upon generation, ruling elites have imposed multiple social exclusions upon rural Quechua-speaking women, and the practice of sexual violence epitomizes this dehumanizing logic.

In other words, sexual violence during the internal armed conflict can be understood as a continuation of violence with a new perpetrator, or *patrón*. This approach looks at the historical specificity of each set of social relations while attending to continuities and discontinuities. The next sections scrutinize the specificity of social relations that create the context for systematic and generalized practice of sexual violence on the part of the military. The population maintains that with the establishment of the base came the beginning of a "permanent practice of detentions, abuse and executions against men and women assumed to be collaborating with the Shining Path. In the case of women, torture commonly included sexual violence, which was regularly perpetrated by groups of military."[27] The victims of sexual violence occupy the bottom ranks of the social hierarchy. The profile of the victims of sexual violence reflect 75 percent Quechua-speaking women, 83 percent from rural areas, the majority with primary education or less and between ages ten and twenty-nine.[28] The pattern of sexual violence perpetrated during the internal armed conflict reproduces gendered and racialized hierarchies.[29]

Individual Initiative

Of the twenty-six cases of sexual violence documented in Manta and Vilca through the PTRC legal case between 1984 and 1988, the majority of sexual violence was perpetrated in the form of torture, occurring at the base or during searches in the community. During the latter years of military presence, between 1988–1992, sexual violence took place more frequently under the individual initiative of military personnel. Soldiers exploited their power with complete impunity and with complicity on the part of military officials. As Crisóstomo explains, "When women in the community were attending to their daily activities, soldiers' common operating procedure was capricious exploitation. Because of their position as military, they had license to abuse and arbitrarily use their power."[30] One example from the legal case offers a common illustration.

* * *

A soldier came to her house looking for her. On various opportunities he had come to court her. This time the soldier got her out of her house under false pretenses and raped her.

> . . . he said "the lieutenant has called you, I don't know why, come quickly," he was visibly angry, and the subject obeyed, she came out of her house and was taken far from her home. The soldier tried to hug her and she refused him. In that moment, the subject said that the soldier knocked her down and said, "I am in love with you, why don't you want to be with me?" and she answered, "why should I be with you, I don't know you." The soldier forced her to have sexual relations with him, holding her arms and the subject could not resist due to the difference in their strength. The soldier put his knee on her chest and lifted up her skirts, took off her underwear and forced her to have sexual relations with penetration.

She did not report the event due to fear that the soldier would get mad and shoot her or take her to the base under the suspicion of terrorism and also because the soldier promised to marry her.

> . . . once the sexual act was finished, the soldier sat next to her and seeing her cry, he consoled her and promised her that he would help her so that the other military did not bother her. . . . "I will not trick you, I want you to be my wife, I won't abandon you."

She accepted to be his girlfriend and maintained a relationship with him for five months. She got pregnant and the soldier signed an act promising to marry her and legally recognize the child. Nevertheless, he abandoned her and her new-born, when he got off duty in June 1985.[31]

* * *

The military base functioned in Manta for eleven years. A generation of girls grew into womanhood in this context of coercion. This case demonstrates the vulnerability of women in Manta and the asymmetric social relations wherein the soldier could act with complete impunity. Sexual violence of individual initiative included the attempt on the part of the soldier to convince his victim to be sexually used, which turned to threats and overwhelming force when she refused.[32] These kinds of cases become very complicated to prove since the victim "consented" to maintaining a relationship after the violation. Therefore, it is especially laudable that the PTRC included this violation in the collective case because it places these complex issues under the national legal gaze.

Bringing the theory/metaphor of *el patrón* to bear illuminates both tension and complicity among legalistic, military, and rural community perspectives, thereby illuminating what the gaze of the law cannot. There is an implied ambivalence in the relationship between women and the military given this legacy of "hierarchical relations in which one person conducts himself as *patrón* [master] while positioning the other as *siervo* [servant]."[33] Women entering into a relationship with a soldier weighted out the promised gains, such as protection, against the negative aspects of objectification through a series of calculations. Liz Kelly calls these types of decisions "'patriarchal bargains' women make in circumstances not of their choosing."[34] A woman who enters into a relationship with a soldier brings a level of prestige to herself and her family that raises their status in the community. The family gains a higher level of protection against military aggression due to the daughter's relationship.[35] These "patriarchal bargains" are embedded in an authoritarian and paternalist social structure in which clientalism becomes a strategy of survival in search of the "good" *patrón*.[36] Yet in the majority of cases the women who choose marriage, hoping to have found a "good" *patrón*, were abandoned and left in extreme poverty with the bitter remains of a frustrated life project and social and familial humiliation.

Under these conditions of long-term military occupation, how does one determine consent? On what basis is consent given? Tesania Velázquez, psychologist, reflects on the complicated relations that developed in Manta between the military base and the community. "The years of occupation insert other forms of interrelating; Guilia Tamayo's image of a concentration camp is useful for understanding that the concepts of consent or will disappear when relations are marked by such power asymmetries."[37] Under military occupation, free will is undercut by fear of the military, vulnerability under the conditions of long-term coercion, and the need to find allies within the armed forces for protection.[38] This context can be seen as part of a pattern of extreme exploitation under the logic of militarized heteropatriarchal order.

The Children of Rape

Much like the public hearings, the children of rape hold significant symbolic weight in the Manta and Vilca case. The first paragraph of the summary of the PTRC Manta and Vilca case foregrounds this issue before any other aspect in an effort to reposition the state as benevolent and empathetic. "The PTRC has determined that sexual violence was a repeated practice on the part of the Military against women in the districts of Manta and Vilca (department of Huancavelica), where military bases where installed from 1984 until 1995. As a consequence of the rapes, there exist a large number of boys and girls that have not been recognized by their fathers and are thereby denied their fundamental rights."[39] As discussed in the previous chapter, soldiers produced children and abandoned them, thereby denying them recognition. The proliferation of children of rape threatens the national heteropatriarchal order in that children do not have a paternal last name and are thereby denied legitimacy. Recognition of these children reestablishes the state's paternal protective image.

The heteropatriarchal logic embedded in the legal framework reduces children of rape to evidence of the violation. To illustrate community-level complicity, Crisóstomo points out that the members of the community know that women were raped when there is a child to evidence the violation. In this situation, the attitude they assume is concern for the child.[40] Who will provide for the child? While the recognition of these children's plight is significant, it contains a disciplining narrative that writes women's realities out. The state's recognition of this social scar effectively obscures the women who suffered the violation and the varied ways they interpret their life experiences. The next case allows for further exploration into the overlapping logics that victims had to navigate.

* * *

A community leader, Aurelio[41] reported that his daughter and sister were sexually violated by military. " . . . his daughter and sister, who were both 15 years old, were violated sexually by soldiers." He was able to identify the perpetrators by name and presented his complaint to the chief of the military base.

The military chief denied the occurrence, claiming that it must have been terrorists, but when the daughter pointed out the perpetrator, the chief obligated the soldier to marry her. The same happened with the sister. They both became pregnant from the sexual abuse . . . but the sister's pregnancy did not coincide with the date of the sexual violence because after the sexual violence, they became boyfriend and girlfriend, which didn't happen with the daughter.

As a product of the rape, his daughter had a child.[42]

* * *

Demonstrating the community level logic, Aurelio became furious with the lieutenant in charge when he came to find out that one of the perpetrating soldiers had been allowed to move to another base, thereby escaping responsibility for their child.[43] Here, Aurelio reflects a concern for the abandoned children produced through rape that translates into single mothers with insufficient resources to care for them, ultimately affecting the overall functioning of the community. As Henríquez and Mantilla explain, a single woman in the southern Andes holds little value in rural communities.[44] In comparison, the couple is highly valued because it insures productivity, familial subsistence, and communal order. Furthermore, marriage continues to be arranged and the husband's work contributes to the wife's family, as does the work of the children. Arranged marriages serve to "broaden relations of reciprocity among families in agricultural tasks, join small parcels of land, or raise a family's social status."[45] Marriage functions as an organizational unit within the communal logic of gender complementarity.

Since marriage affords economic security and belonging within the communal order, Aurelio insisted on marriage as the solution, especially if his daughter and sister were found pregnant. The difference between Aurelio's sister and daughter is telling. His sister accepted a relationship with the rapist-soldier because her family had determined that was the best solution. The fact that she got pregnant after the rape incident made the pregnancy a product of consensual relations. So when she was abandoned, she lost all legitimacy as a victim *and* had a child under coercive circumstances with no financial support. This point is made clear by the fact that only the daughter's child is mentioned in the PTRC legal case since it was conceived during the act of rape.

Aurelio has documented at least thirty-two children who suffer the social stigma of being products of rape. To be abandoned by one's father marks that one's status for life, as without a paternal last name, without a legitimate family and consequently materially poor. Many mothers registered their children of rape under their last names, which positioned them as siblings to their mother. Others used the soldier's nickname such as "*puma*" or just "*militar*" in the place of a paternal last name. The children of rape embody the unresolved legacy of the conflict that reverberates against the unstable foundations of the state as discussed in chapter 3. Both through public hearings and the legal case, the PTRC aims to rectify these harms and thereby relegitimate the state.

The implications of the children of rape are engraved in the collective memory of the community, as exemplified in the narration of Manta's history by a high school student.[46]

> The campesinos got accustomed to the military presence and built the base and worked with the military for days and days and would sometimes get out of it. The military lived in the base that the community built and started to abuse some of the young women and got them pregnant and did not recognize their children and left the district of Manta. There exist children that are now young men and women, that do not know their fathers and justice should be focused on them. First the Senderistas [Shining Path] abused people and then the military came and also abused and that was the worst because they left Manta without recognizing their children. Within the people of Manta there is no trust and we search for justice for those boys and girls without fathers. That is the history of Manta and now they are psychologically traumatized.

Ruiz Bravo and Neira argue that the representations presented by schoolchildren can be seen as an allegory that allows insights into the collective imaginary of the community.[47] The psychological trauma sits at the intersection of heteropatriarchal norms that marginalize the abandoned children and the ways not having a father materially and socially affects children in rural communities, as well as the community as a whole. More research must be done regarding the lives of children of rape, their agency, victimization and subjectivity.[48]

Within the logics of the community, national legislation, and the military, marriage between perpetrator and victim resolves sexual violence and the children of rape.[49] The acceptance on the part of the perpetrator of parental economic responsibility also ameliorates the issue in many circumstances. Since economic and social survival exists within a communal context, individuality does not figure significantly. Therefore, individual cases of sexual violence that have the goal of seeking justice do not receive much support. Practically speaking, the justice that the Peruvian legal system has yet to produce does not put food in the belly. At every level, this causes outrage among feminists. Specifically with regard to the rural community level, Barrig explains that customary law tends to protect patriarchal relations "that restrict women's freedoms."[50]

While Aurelio's demand for marriage could be read as a demand for economic justice, it also demonstrates the complicity of the rural community with state heteropatriarchal order in an effort to gain recognition and receive reparations. The state embodies a dominant masculine power while rural community members such as Aurelio enact a subordinated masculinity. The theory/metaphor of *el patrón* highlights how the social relations of *patrón*/master and *siervo*/servant are marked by a patriarchal orthodoxy, which establishes a hierarchical relation between dominant and subordinate masculinity.[51] The struggle between dominant and subordinate masculinity condenses around mobilizing the institution of marriage. Therefore, patriarchy, as it manifests at both the rural and national levels, denies subject status to the person who sustained the violation, the woman victim.

Women's Perspectives under Erasure

One of the most complex examples that tests the bounds of consent/coercion and conceptual myopia is that of women who traded sex, or access to their bodies, for the freedom of their family member. In conversations with women in Manta during my visits to the community,[52] they were divided on this issue. Some said that women were forced into doing this as the only way to save their family member. Others argued that the women chose to do this and that choice was a sign of courage, family loyalty, and bravery. By allowing sexual access to one's body, one could potentially save a husband, brother, or son. Some women saw themselves as protagonists in the decision to utilize this sexual currency as a means to an end.[53] Historically, women's bodies have been objects of exchange. In feudal times, "women were given to the [land]owner by their parents as a way to avoid retribution or fines for lost livestock."[54] This relation repeats itself in the context of the internal armed conflict with different actors. By listening to the women's debates on the issue, the multiple subject positions of women come to the surface. They do not understand their experiences as singularly under the framework of victimhood.

This issue of exchanging sex for the freedom of their loved ones was not isolated to Manta: it was a generalized practice in which military actors took advantage of their power to set the rules and the modes of currency.[55] This practice highlights the paradox of the consent/coercion binary. It is clear that the military presence in rural communities significantly altered the power relations to the point of establishing a generalized environment of terror, coercion, and intimidation. Under these conditions is consent possible? The legal framework of establishing individual consent or coercion makes it difficult to read for this environment and the historic patterns that underlie it. Women's perspectives under erasure highlight the "incoherence between the rationalism of the juridical procedure and the violence of the state."[56] By exploring the question of how women engage the state, or how they respond when engaged by the state, the two faces of the state appear more clearly: that of paternalistic protector and hyperaggressive rapist-soldier.

Interpreting the exchange of sex for a family member's freedom as a violation aligns with liberal feminist and human rights perceptions. Yet how can one make sense of the view that a woman is making a courageous and brave decision to give military officers and/or soldiers access to her body as means to a desired end—the freedom of her loved one? In taking the analysis of patterns of hierarchical relations seriously, it forces a conceptual opening to make space for simultaneous and incongruous readings. Through the critical practice of conceptual capaciousness, one can value the legal tools to end impunity, acknowledge historic power relations, and honor the subjectivities of women maneuvering within such contexts. These women are protagonists, witnesses, survivors, victims, and at times perpetrators, but by no means are they reduced to any of these as a singular identity. By focusing on these patterns rather than the individual cases, the multiple and seemingly contradictory types of responses made by women have become intelligible.

Sexual violence is an act that is commonly not spoken of, yet whether through silence or public testimony, its affective, personal, and emotional impact is undeniable. As a practice with historical antecedents, the response of silence functions as a collective sensibility that allows for social cohesion at the community level.[57] Given the perpetrator's threats of retaliation if the victim speaks of the violation, silence can be a strategy of self-protection.

The state apparatus and society are prepared for women to be silent.[58] Moreover, women must remain silent to maintain the patriarchal system.[59] When women speak out and report these abuses, it exposes the incapacity of the state apparatus and the society to guarantee women's human rights. The Peruvian judicial system is complicit in maintaining military misogyny due to its inability to guarantee the security of judges and other judicial functionaries that would be willing to stray from this norm. In the case of sexual violence during the internal armed conflict, there has yet to be a sentence given by a Peruvian court. Therefore, the state's investigation into sexual violence presents a site of contestation and instability, "the mobilization of an unstable heteropatriarchy, re-elaborating and reinventing itself at a moment of crisis."[60] Inclusion of sexual violence in the PTRC investigation creates a significant opening, yet the judicial system has allowed impunity to reign.

When women do speak, their linguistic and communicational choices are multiple and varied and not always intelligible within a legal framework. Dreams offer an alternative realm of expression for women, particularly around sexual violence. Crisóstomo found many women in Manta discussed dreams involving unknown men attempting to force a sexual encounter. The unknown man presents as *el Apu* (the mountain god within the Andean cosmovision) and/or soldier and/or *patrón*. The telling of these dreams marks the profound influence of the internal armed conflict in the communal collective imaginary and expresses the fragile integration of different logics, that of *el Apu*/the mountain god, *el patrón* and soldier/military through a nonlinear concept of time. "These are transformations that seem to reflect historical changes in the identities of the rapists."[61] The women's dreams reflect the shifting representations of those who exercise power over them, echoing the theory/metaphor *el patrón*. Speaking through dreams also underscores women's agency and effort to narrate their experiences in their own terms.

The slippage of meaning between *violencia sexual* in Spanish and the lack of a translatable term in Quechua, leads to other ways of formulating an understanding of what happened. This challenge of incommensurability tends to undermine the possibility of collecting the coherent narrative necessary to mount a case with the hope of achieving justice. Legal frameworks attempt to designate meanings neatly, snipping off extra information from testimonies that stray. An example from the PTRC final report chapter "Sexual Violence Against Women" further demonstrates the difficulty of rendering women's subjectivities legible through the law. The subsection "In the language of the victims" retains the legalistic notion of naming actions explicitly rather than positioning the women victims as subjects with reasons for their language choices. "It is common that victims use confusing terms or their own interpretations when describing the acts of sexual violence that were forced upon them."[62] From the legal perspective, the indirect references to being abused or made fun of (*abusaron de mi, burlaron de mi*) or lack of explicit reference to penetration make building a legal case difficult because the language is imprecise. From the victims' perspective, they may be using indirect terms for any variety of reasons, including different cultural and linguistic references, a sense that such terms as "my condition as a woman" or "my dignity" more aptly communicate their understanding of what was violated, or an explicit desire not to name the violation directly. The exigency to selectively align narrative elements to construct a strong case overrides attention to the series of calculations victims make given a context of coercion.[63]

Sexual Violence as Multipurpose Military Practice

The PTRC chose the Manta and Vilca case as emblematic because of the systematic and generalized nature of sexual violence in rural areas in and around military bases throughout the areas afflicted with violence. This analysis prioritizes the victims to bring them justice for the harm done and to shed light on them as subjects. Feminist analysis of sexual violence during internal armed conflict generally focuses on women victims and the social context that allows for its proliferation. As feminist legal scholar Rhonda Copelon writes, "Sexualized violence in war and conflict is thus inseparable from violence, abuse, gender inequality, racisms, and poverty—all of which contribute to the oppression of women in daily life and form a matrix that can exacerbate violence in war."[64]

Not just an act of gender-based violence, sexual violence is an organizing and regulating principle of state power and control. The armed forces enacted and (re)produced a militarized misogyny in which sexual violence was a tool to gain state domination in the region through terror and repression. Sexual violence was used as a method of torture for women who supposedly had connections to subversive groups. According to the armed forces, that is what they deserved as terrorists. As one woman relates in her testimony, the soldier who detained her said, "Since you don't want to talk, we will do what is customary, what we usually do."[65] If the women survived, they were usually threatened with death to ensure their silence.

Yet contrary to some feminist generalizations, sexual violence is not a constant in armed conflict, and masculinity is not inherently violent. Elizabeth Wood asserts that great variation exists over different conflicts. Variation consists of who is targeted, where it occurs, who perpetrates, if the perpetrator is an individual or a gang, the duration of the violence, and whether it is related to other perpetration of violence.[66] Therefore, studies of sexual violence must pay attention to specificity of context to shed light on the logics that support its perpetration.

The PTRC reports that sexual violence went beyond isolated acts to constitute a systematic practice generally tolerated by superior officers.[67] All the military bases in the department of Huancavelica practiced this abuse of authority.[68] Officers in charge of the bases committed these violations, ordered their subordinates to take part, tolerated such criminal behavior among the ranks, and did not sanction these violations when they were brought to public attention.[69] Indeed, within the military hierarchy, soldiers were expected to participate in collective violations. If they didn't want to participate, Theidon explains that they were gang raped.[70] Therefore, soldiers that perpetrated sexual violence due to individual initiative knew that they acted with impunity. The armed forces and police not only tolerated those responsible for such violations, but also protected them and gave them promotions.[71]

Research suggests that in some cases sexual violence perpetrated by the armed forces is a practice through which to construct masculine identities consistent with military ideology and strengthen soldiers' social cohesion.[72] Political scientist Dara Cohen argues that wartime rape is linked to a type of military recruitment mechanism. If soldiers are recruited by force, sexual violence is a method of socialization to create cohesion. The institutionalized and instrumental practice of sexual violence reinforces the internal hierarchy of armed forces through the collective degradation of women. Since recruits were largely rural youth with no other choice, and since the Peruvian military did practice forced recruitment,[73] Cohen's findings hold potential implications in the case of Peru.

The Manta and Vilca case is therefore emblematic of the multipurpose function of sexual violence. This practice is not just a method of torture to gain information, a weapon of war, a human rights violation, and a crime against humanity. It also serves an important purpose *within* the military. The consistent practice of sexual violence, especially in its collective form of gang rape, establishes and reinforces internal hierarchies as well as a highly aggressive form of masculine expression. As feminist international relations scholar Laura Sjoberg explains, militarized masculinity refers to "war's reliance on militarism and militarism's reliance on commanding and transforming masculinity/ies in times of war."[74] To understand the internal workings of this military practice, Wood suggests analyzing the repertoire of violence, the opportunities and access the soldiers have to perpetrate, and the guiding norms, sanctions, and/or incentive structures.[75] In the case of Manta, soldiers had access and no sanctions or norms that inhibited their perpetration of the crime. Therefore, sexual violence resulting from individual initiative became commonplace.

The practice of giving/gifting women to the troops, *pichana*,[76] during searches or incursions and the order by which the gang rape would occur demands a nuanced analysis of the gendered and racialized dynamics of the military. As Wood indicates, paying attention to the leadership, the hierarchy, the units of combatants, and individual combatants allows for such an analysis. Furthermore, Sjoberg underscores how hegemonic and subordinate masculinities are reinforced through military indoctrination. The practice of gang rape buttresses social hierarchies. The perpetrator's social position determines his access to the women being violated. In addition, women are valued more or less for their social position.[77] Depending on where women were situated along the gender and racial hierarchy, some "were less dehumanized than others, some women deserved more respect and also some soldiers deserved 'better versions of women' than others."[78] An intersectional sensibility brings attention to these military rituals of domination and submission as (re)producing race and sexual hierarchies.

The more "desirable" lighter-skinned, higher-class women were reserved for the officers, reinforcing hegemonic masculinity. The soldiers were given the "less desirable" campesinas, reinforcing subordinate masculinity. Most soldiers, being young men from rural areas, were obligated to participate in the abuse of rural young women. The racialized insults they spoke while raping were similar to those insults that they received at other moments in their own lives. Soldiers distanced themselves from the discrimination they received by displacing it onto women, thereby reinforcing racialized and gendered hierarchies as the basis of social cohesion and expression of militarized masculinity. Theidon explains how this shared experience of brutalizing women unites soldiers through a collective sense of guilt that also shifts the social norm around shame.[79] Collectively losing a sense of shame results in their heightened capacity for brutality. More research must be done to document the military's practice of constructing a hyperaggressive expression of masculinity that soldiers, as agents of the state, must adopt.

Categorizing sexual violence as systematic and generalized facilitates the legal objective of holding superior officers accountable for ordering the strategy and/or tolerating the actions rather than focusing on the individual soldiers who perpetrated the violations.[80] Clearly, sexual violence appears as the military's modus operandi during the internal armed conflict. This line of inquiry into the multipurpose use of sexual violence by the military highlights the heteropatriarchal structure underpinning the militaristic expressions of masculinity in the case of Peru and its direct link to the systematic and general perpetration of sexual violence. This practice served primary goals of degrading, humiliating, and controlling the population to gain cooperation, and of social cohesion and a heightened capacity for brutality within the military. At both levels, the practice reinforces social hierarchies and imposes racialized and gendered identities.

Conclusion

The PTRC's response to sexual violence represents an important step in addressing the historic marginalization of women in Peruvian society and advances international endeavors to bring these issues to light. The legal cases challenge impunity and create small fissures through which to expose the difficulties of accounting for rigid, vertical social relations, the perspectives of women who suffer such violations, and the multipurpose utility of sexual violence for the military. The PTRC's inclusion of sexual violence due to individual initiative exposes ongoing conditions of coercion. This fissure marks a critical opening to access how victims negotiate their relationship with agents and institutions of the state. However, conceptual myopia and the consent/coercion framework for evaluating cases of sexual violence make only a thin slice of reality legible. Rendering visible the historical context shows the paradoxical nature of state efforts to redress sexual violence and the disciplining practices that limit the legal goal of justice.

Demystifying the blueprint of historic power relations upon which the state is constructed makes visible the blurred line between consent and coercion and how community members navigate such situations. The concept of coloniality/modernity encompasses the entanglement between colonial systems of knowing and national narratives,[81] which are expressed through the law in the Manta and Vilca case. This colonial legacy is not frozen or static; it shifts across time and space. Similarly, heteropatriarchy also shifts across time and space, influencing the multiple expressions of masculinity. As Cahn and Ní Aoláin argue, "the end of violence is not a superficial engagement, but may require deep and difficult entanglement with the masculine construction of self in many societies."[82] Indeed, a serious engagement with coloniality, heteropatriarchy, and masculinity expose the deeply embedded roots of violence.

Mobilizing the theory/metaphor of *el patrón* uncovers the complexity of historic power asymmetries and the effects of long-term occupation. Rural community members in the southern Andes speak about themselves and their struggles through this theory/metaphor, which in turn reflects the ongoing experience, effect, and sentiment of resistance. Transmitted across generations orally and through representations, it contains a subjective dimension—a rejection of the dominant order and hatred of the dominant figure, *el patrón*.[83] As Mignolo argues, "decolonial possible futures can no longer be conceived from a universal perspective, anchored in a hegemonic imaginary managed by linear time and final destination."[84] Alternative ways of knowing, such as the theory/metaphor of *el patrón*, illuminate decolonial futures. Women victims' understandings of their experiences have a chance to emerge from the erasure of conceptual myopia, the consent-and-coercion binary, and linear temporal logic.

This analysis elucidates what the law is ill prepared to redress and, simultaneously, what the legal case introduced into the national political debate. Serious attention to community perspectives holds the potential to radically reframe the parameters of the state. The nature of the legal cases makes it very difficult to address the context of long-term coercion while the base was active in Manta, much less the vertical relations that undergird society and naturalize gender-based violence. This curtailed the PTRC's ability to expose the colonial roots of the state violence during long-term military occupation. The PTRC approach has limited tools for addressing the intersections of historical vertical relations based on gender, class, culture, ethnicity, geography, and language. Therefore, the PTRC efforts were compromised by discursive reassertions of Peruvian social hierarchies, combined with the limits of the legal frameworks to grasp the intricacies of the rural community context.

The state is directly implicated through both the generalized practice of sexual violence perpetrated by the armed forces and the state reconsolidation based on heteropatriarchal logics that reduce the victims to a singular reading of their personhood and subjectivity. This chapter illustrates feminist legal scholar Copelon's following assertion: "The recovery of the state" by utilizing international criminal law "obscures the violence of the state-based order. The state may, for example, have been instrumental in perpetuating the systemic gender inequality that influenced the conditions for large-scale rape in the first place."[85] Discussions of democracy, and I would add human rights, transitional justice, and nation building, must address the nexus of violence that constitutes the state and its disciplining practices.[86]

In thinking carefully about the transitional justice process, the PTRC was founded on the promise of the state as guarantor of truth and reconciliation, with a deep investment in putting the atrocities committed by the armed forces firmly in the past. Yet rural communities such as Manta are weary of both the arbitrary violence of the military arm of the state and the promises of the PTRC that passed through in trucks, waving banners of justice and reparations and taking testimonies with clipboard and recorder in hand. Recognizing how victims engage in a complex set of negotiations when deciding how to respond to militarized masculinity or the guarantee of national inclusion forces a reconfiguration of the relationship between the state and society. The PTRC struggled to address this level of state, civil society, military, and victim relations because such an analysis holds the potential of unraveling its project of state reconsolidation.

5

Finding Each Other's Hearts

Weaving Interculturality into
Gender and Human Rights

When the PTRC finished its mandate to research the causes and consequences of the internal armed conflict, it submitted the final report with recommendations for reform and reparations to President Alejandro Toledo and passed forty-seven human rights cases to the state prosecutor. In 2004 the collective Manta and Vilca case came to rest among the stacks of human rights cases in the Office of the State Prosecutor in Huancavelica. Currently, feminist and human rights organizations represent those women who decided to pursue their cases through the Peruvian judicial system. Cases of sexual violence during the internal armed conflict pose a challenge to the NGOs associated with both the feminist and human rights movements due to the narrow legal, political, sociocultural, and linguistic avenues available for addressing this violation. This is the story of how one feminist NGO became intimately acquainted with these challenges and, in an effort to transform the culture of law, wove interculturality into its feminist human rights work.

The Study and Defense of Women's Rights[1] (DEMUS) was the first feminist NGO in Peru to develop programming that directly responds to the effects of the internal armed conflict on women. Four Peruvian feminist lawyers established DEMUS in 1987 as a space where the feminist movement could focus on legal strategy, including the defense of women's rights, legal advocacy, and the transformation of the law. (The main feminist organizations in Lima were established in the late 1970s and early 1980s, as noted in chapter 1.) With time, DEMUS's work expanded to encompass social, political, juridical, and cultural components.[2] DEMUS's programming in response to the consequences of the internal armed conflict on women started with a juridical focus on the Manta and Vilca case of sexual violence, which quickly presented new challenges, given that it was DEMUS's first project based in a rural Andean community.

When the issue of sexual violence during internal armed conflict first gained notoriety, DEMUS became involved. Distrust between feminist and human rights advocates quickly surfaced.[3] The feminists accused the human rights groups of not addressing women's issues. The human rights advocates accused the feminists of bias, pointing out that they did not attend to victims directly or represent any cases. Moreover, the feminists were not present in the rural areas where the worst violations occurred. In the post-PTRC period various NGOs have taken up the issue of sexual violence because global attention made funding available. Both feminist and human rights advocates search out spaces and resources to advance their work.[4] Various human rights NGOs represent sexual violence cases in which the attorneys focus on the legal matters and psychologists work in parallel to offer support to the victims.

In 2004 DEMUS initiated its project in Manta based on the PTRC legal case. DEMUS's interdisciplinary fieldwork team created a model in which attorneys, psychologists, and sociologists worked together in Manta and produced theoretical reflections on their fieldwork. DEMUS's theorizing practice, or praxis, negotiated across levels of scale, power asymmetries, and sociocultural and linguistic reference points to build a feminist inter-cultural approach that prioritized community mental health in the quest for justice. An intercultural approach signals an ethical and political project to (re)construct channels of communication across differences in and through asymmetrical contexts. The goal is to "transform the symbolic structures upon which social relations of difference are built."[5] On a practical level, an intercultural approach refers to the translation and interaction across culture and language embedded within historical inequalities.

As chapter 4 of this book argues, narrowing the effect of internal armed conflict on women to sexual violence and reducing the women victims to the violation, especially when paired with the urgency to prosecute these cases, shuts down the space for recognizing women victim's subjectivity. Similar dynamics influence the work of NGOs. Timeframes stipulated by funders obligate NGOs to produce results that assume cooperation from women victims as compulsory counterparts. Feminist NGOs have difficulty sustaining relationships with Andean communities, largely because their locations are absolutely separated within the national geographic imaginary. Given these social dynamics, DEMUS contributes to the elimination of violence against women and all forms of discrimination based on gender, class, and ethnicity/race.[6] Through political advocacy and pressure DEMUS's mission is to strengthen the defense and recognition of women's human rights, in particular sexual and reproductive rights.

Based on research with the DEMUS fieldwork team in Manta from March to September 2006 and from January to March 2007, this chapter traces DEMUS's confrontation with the legacy of colonialism and subsequent efforts to rework its project given linguistic and sociocultural gaps. My inability to speak Quechua and my affiliation with DEMUS compromised my capacity to map the relationship from the perspective of the Manta community.[7] The community perceived me as another *señorita de* DEMUS because of my Peruvian heritage and the way I incorporated myself into their programming. While I asserted my independent researcher role, the fact that I came and went with the fieldwork team seemed to override my proclamations of autonomy. In practice, it looked like I worked for DEMUS.

Through long, candle-lit conversations in the evenings in Manta, research team debriefings after trips, and monthly supervision meetings with senior psychologists, I came to participate in the fieldwork team's collaborative theorizing practice. As we developed workshops together, attended community events, and discussed interactions, we analyzed power dynamics. I brought an intersectional sensibility to the discussion of intercultural relations and the gendered nature of coloniality. Coloniality names the racialization of colonial relations for the purpose of labor exploitation and wealth accumulation. This systematic process of dehumanization interweaves with gender-based exploitation. Recognition of the victim's full personhood requires attention not only to gender but also to coloniality and intercultural relations.

Our discussions demanded recognition of the varied genealogies that inform differently situated conceptual frames and methodological approaches, as explored in the introduction. Indeed, these conversations inspired me to elaborate on the interface between an intersectional sensibility and decolonial feminism as the productive analytical tension that underlies this study. The fieldwork team consistently wrote up their empirically based theoretical reflections, which I cite throughout this chapter. In other words, this chapter traces the DEMUS Manta Project's crisis and metamorphosis through the reflections recorded in the Manta fieldwork team's writings. Since the initial research I did with DEMUS, I have conducted follow-up research, shared my writing, organized panels at academic conferences that included DEMUS staff, facilitated workshops for DEMUS staff, and will continue to collaborate with them into the future.[8]

The DEMUS Manta Project

DEMUS became aware of the collective case of twenty-six rapes in Manta and Vilca because it had an employee, Cecilia Reynoso, who also worked part time for the PTRC Gender Unit. As a lawyer, she saw the possibilities of legal followup on this case. Reynoso developed a project proposal with a colleague trained in psychology, Pilar Aguilar, and they presented it to DEMUS. The vision behind the project was to create continuity with the work of the PTRC by positioning the emblematic case on the national stage as a crime against humanity, thereby sustaining public debate on the issue. When the funding for the project came through from UNIFEM, Reynoso and Aguilar had distanced themselves from DEMUS. While the staff person subsequently assigned to direct the Manta Project was unfamiliar with it,[9] the lawyer assigned to the Manta Project had worked for the PTRC and was familiar with the case.

DECENTRALIZING THE DEMUS MANTA PROJECT

In the post-PTRC period, NGOs of all types descended upon Manta after it gained attention through the emblematic collective rape case. DEMUS broke new ground on the national level by initiating the first feminist project to address the consequences of the internal armed conflict on women. This innovative, precedent-setting project made conducting research with DEMUS extremely appealing. Two senior sociologists who speak Quechua and were from the neighboring department of Cuzco facilitated the introduction of the fieldwork team to the community.[10] The other four fieldwork team members were young women from Lima, just starting their first job or still finishing up their degree in law, sociology, psychology, and/or gender studies. During the first visits to Manta, the DEMUS fieldwork team encountered deep distrust.

When I approached DEMUS about accompanying the Manta project, the executive director and program director were very receptive, but suggested that I talk to the fieldwork team. On a sunny afternoon on the back patio of the DEMUS office, I perspired as I explained to the fieldwork team my current research project in addition to my Peruvian background, feminist NGO work experience, and previous research in Peru. They seemed uncertain and very protective of their project, which might be seen as an extension of the distrust and apprehension that dominated the project and its reception in Manta. Nevertheless, they decided to accept my research proposal, and I began to learn about their unique approach to addressing sexual violence during the internal armed conflict.

In June 2005 the communal assembly of Manta permitted DEMUS a space for staff to use one week every month. On April 20, 2006, I embarked on my first trip to Manta with the fieldwork team. We met at 11:30 P.M. and boarded the bus to Huancayo, arriving at 5:30 A.M. After waiting in the morning's biting cold until 7:00 A.M., our driver picked us up. We loaded the car, bought big containers of water, and headed out to Manta, a five-hour drive on steep, winding dirt roads. As the many trips to Manta blend together, I remember the driver stopped at least once each trip to change a flat, bald tire for a patched inflated one or work his mechanical genius under the hood to keep us running. Sometimes we all had to get out while he maneuvered over a washout, admiring his composed demeanor as he came a hair's breadth from plummeting down the cliff. The anxiety of the drive was only quelled when exhaustion overtook us. By the time we reached Manta, it was early afternoon, and we moved slowly in the high elevation. I recount these details not only to highlight geographic distance but also to give a sense of the social distance associated with the geographic imaginary of *el Perú profundo*.[11]

DEMUS's decentralization strategy suggests that through *convivencia*—sharing life with the possibility of getting to know each other on an intimate, day-to-day level, building trust and mutual caring—it is possible to create a model for social relations that respond to the need for a transformation in the culture of law. This implied establishing a branch office in Manta, thereby challenging the concentration of power and decision making in the capital and the implicit geographic imaginary based on colonial mappings of difference. DEMUS established agreements to work with local leaders, health workers, women, and adolescents in school. The Manta Project also included working with regional judges and district attorneys. Initially, the relationship with local leaders was based on information exchange. They requested hard-to-access information regarding regional and national programs and policies that would affect them and/or hold potential opportunities. The fieldwork team needed to gather information about the community, find out what they needed, and build trust to gain access. DEMUS offered workshops on issues of interest. With local health workers, the fieldwork team constructed a project to document local concepts of health, sickness, and well being, as well as forms of treatment. Besides sharing academic concepts, this project opened a space to valorize local concepts and healing practices.

A key part of the programming consisted of establishing a workshop for women through which they eventually could broach the issue of sexual violence. Since the school requested that DEMUS work with parents, the fieldwork team invited mothers to take part in what started as a space of play, jokes, games, and songs. Then, through familiarity and trust, they began to discuss issues relevant to the participants, share requested information, and move toward discussions of violence, gender, and sexuality. To maintain the exchange model, the fieldwork team always brought yarn for knitting, and the participants would knit and teach the fieldwork team how to knit. This brought a productive value to the workshops. For example, if a woman's husband questioned her participation, she could show him the sweater she was working on as a product of the workshop. Finally, the community requested that DEMUS work with adolescents in the school. While this request went beyond the scope of the initial project, DEMUS decided to extend programming to fulfill the community's request. The work with youth consisted of group discussions, games, and art/writing projects with a focus on addressing transgenerational trauma related to the internal armed conflict.

While DEMUS worked at multiple levels in the community, the main goal was to construct and prosecute cases of sexual violence that highlight the patterned, systematic, and generalized nature of these violations.[12] DEMUS's efforts to engage in a relationship of *convivencia* with the community of Manta are reflected in DEMUS's 2007 internal document on juridical strategy. "We look to create the necessary conditions for the women affected by the conflict to take the initiative to report cases of sexual violence and initiate the legal process. For this reason, the first steps have been to build trust with the community through community work." DEMUS accompanied the women and the community of Manta in their struggle for justice and reparations, shared information about human rights, the PTRC, justice, and reparations, and they facilitated communication across national and community justice processes.

DEMUS's interdisciplinary Manta Project drew from law, psychology, and sociology. The psychological strategy worked from an intersubjective community mental-health framework to recognize both self and other as subjects, offering individual and collective therapeutic spaces to women victims and the population in general. The sociological aspect of the project assisted in rebuilding the social fabric of the community. DEMUS complemented these efforts on the regional and national level through public campaigns to generate new ways of understanding sexual violence before, during, and after the internal armed conflict.

While DEMUS's decentralizing efforts were laudable, *convivencia* is not simply about physical relocation; it also presented the fieldwork team and the people of Manta with a sociocultural and linguistic gap. During my first trip, it became amply clear that the fieldwork team suffered from a language barrier, despite ongoing Quechua classes. They spoke Spanish and the most rudimentary Quechua, while the majority of women in Manta prefer to speak or only speak Quechua. At least three times in my presence a community member implored a DEMUS fieldwork team member to learn Quechua and/ or bring back the senior Quechua speaking staff. As the months passed and the senior Quechua-speaking staff did not return, the potential of the project narrowed significantly.

The language barrier extends into cultural reference points for interpersonal communication. Tesania Velázquez, the program director, writes about this. On one of her first trips to Manta, she heard about a woman with mental health problems, and as a psychologist, she sought Martha (a pseudonym) out. "We simulated communication: I listened and she spoke. I asked and she responded, but we did not understand each other. . . . [F]or me, meeting Martha presupposed a conversation, an interview, an application of a psychological test. For her, it seemed to be an introduction to her home, her animals, her plants, her histories, her jokes, and herself. This difference generated chaos between us."[13] As much as decentralization worked against the geographical concentration of power, the linguistic and sociocultural distances remained.

The linguistic limitation narrowed the DEMUS project to include the community members from Manta who spoke Spanish. The DEMUS team could work well in the school, with the municipal authorities, and with women community leaders. Yet the language barrier made the population of sexual violence victims a challenge to reach. The majority of women between age ten and age forty during the eleven-year military occupation (1984–95) were now at least thirty, with very limited educational opportunities, and therefore less likely to be comfortable communicating in Spanish. Furthermore, Spanish is the language of military occupation, making it ill suited for communicating delicate and painful memories. However, the sociocultural distance between the fieldwork team and the community of Manta has been mitigated through an ongoing process of constructing critical methodological approaches that include an exploration of community notions of justice, reparations, and health.

NAVIGATING REFERENCES TO JUSTICE

After returning from a trip to Manta (that did not include me), the fieldwork team explained how, in a popular theater contest, one skit had portrayed a judge holding a hearing for a sexual violence case. After much discussion between the judge and the accused, the judge did not sentence him and the accused walked free. While the fieldwork team was excited about the issue coming up in a public forum and the possibilities of building from this reference point to explore the issue of sexual violence further, they were also perturbed by the message of impunity. It was easy to extrapolate assumptions about community resignation, leading to further permissibility of sexual violence.

Discussing this popular theater piece with the justice of the peace during my next stay in Manta revealed divergent interpretations of what the skit represented. He explained that the skit did touch upon sexual violence but the underlying message was not impunity, it was corruption. He added details of a certain moment in the skit when the accused discretely passed money to the judge, at which point the accused was pronounced not guilty. Therefore, the dual interpretations of the skit highlight the potential distance between the foci of DEMUS and the community of Manta: DEMUS was most concerned with impunity and sexual violence, while the community members (the justice of the peace claimed) were more concerned with corruption and the arbitrary nature of state justice. This disjuncture hints at the incommensurable meanings of justice across international human rights law, national justice, and rural community justice systems. DEMUS faced political, sociocultural, and linguistic challenges when preparing to prosecute cases of sexual violence, which dovetail with the limitations of gender essentialism.

The fieldwork team searched for answers to a vexing set of questions regarding the meaning(s) of justice. What informs the subject's ambivalence about engaging in the formal justice system? What issues are most important to her, given that she may have never seen or experienced the justice that the PTRC or NGOs promise? The answers continually seem to recede, thereby testing the NGO's commitment to a process that defies containment. As anthropologist Deborah Poole explains, "Although the state and NGOs assure them that 'the law' is universal and impartial, peasants—like many other Peruvians—negotiate their daily lives as a series of calculations involving individuals and spaces that everyone knows exist 'outside the law.'"[14] Exploring the meaning of justice at the community level, as DEMUS does, sheds stark light on the promises of inclusive citizenship, thereby questioning the legitimacy of legal processes and the promise of a transition to democracy. As Peruvian sociologist Narda Henríquez states, "The tension between juridical frameworks and the lived experiences of injustice is expressed in the de-legitimization of [state] institutions."[15] This bleak picture underscores the need to work with multiple epistemological references, thereby facilitating a potential transformation in the culture of law.

As the popular theater piece underscores, one of the most significant issues in DEMUS's quest to understand community notions was to grasp the disconnection between rural community and state justice systems. DEMUS suffered from conceptual confusion in its initial programming with regard to the state. DEMUS emphasized the state as guarantor of rights without full acknowledgement of the ever-present shadow of state terrorism and arbitrary violence. Theidon finds this dynamic present in her research in Ayacucho. "The capricious, horrendous state, sometimes benevolent, sometimes malignant, provokes in campesinos the need to combine various routes in the search for justice. They discern how the state and its representatives are useful and how they are not useful. The popular legal consciousness includes a conceptualization of the state as both protector and aggressor, which informs the communal mechanisms to resolve conflicts."[16] The DEMUS Manta Project had to critically reassess the role of the state and their own position in relation to both the state and the victim/subjects.

The limited relevance of state justice to the resolution of conflicts in Manta presents a major challenge to national juridical processes. Municipal authorities such as the president of the community and the justice of the peace address the social and legal issues that arise. At the community level, justices of the peace administrate daily tasks such as marriage and disputes regarding livestock, property, and domestic violence. In each regional capital, the first level of judges can be found; the superior courts are situated in the most significant regional capitals; the supreme court is located in Lima. Article 149 of the constitution recognizes Andean and Amazonian communities' special jurisdiction in accordance with their customs and consuetudinary laws as long as they honor human rights. Unfortunately, the lack of clear channels of communication between the special jurisdiction at the community level and the other judicial instances compound inequalities based on sociocultural and linguistic differences.

Justices of the peace have strong legitimacy because they are proximal (usually a community member), they offer low-cost services, and they have a conciliatory role. They apply law with no formal legal training, mixing customary and traditional norms with information garnered from workshops sponsored by NGOs or regional authorities. The justices of the peace suffer from a lack of training and resources because the state system disregards their role.

The communal system's components include the communal assembly and the president of the community. Through this system, decisions are made that hold legitimacy among community members. The communal assembly is the maximum authoritative space, over which the president of the community presides, as does a facilitator elected at the meeting. All community members participate, yet only the male heads of family, widows, and single mothers vote. The president of the community maintains order at meetings, coordinates tasks, and organizes collective labor.

Returning to the national level, DEMUS works with legal rubrics marked by gender discrimination, framing rape as singular and isolated. The national legal codes addressing sexual violence during internal armed conflict are limited to the crime of rape and aggravated kidnapping. National legislation narrows the legal options for mounting cases, especially due to the criteria for proof. The international human rights rubric of torture within the context of internal armed conflict, which was included in the penal code in 1998, also falls short. According to the UN Convention against Torture, "torture is the willful infliction of severe physical or mental pain or suffering not only to elicit information, but also to punish, intimidate, or discriminate, to obliterate the victim's personality or diminish her personal capacities." This code cannot apply to cases before 1998, and the vast majority of sexual violence happened between 1980 and 1997. Moreover, the 1998 law applies only to rape, which limits the recognition of the wide scope of sexual violence that takes place during internal armed conflict. Furthermore, the PTRC Manta Vilca legal case identifies rape as also occurring due to the individual initiative of the soldiers who practiced sexual predation as individuals and/or groups. These rapes do not constitute torture, according to the PTRC legal analysis (see chapter 4).

Given the shortcomings of the national legal codes, DEMUS asserts that international human rights law offers a favorable framework to address sexual violence during internal armed conflict in that it recognizes the massive and systematic perpetration of crimes against humanity and obliges states to sanction and prevent such crimes. To address the variation of violations, feminists draw from the 1998 Rome Statute of the International Criminal Court, article 7, which defines sexual violence as including rape, sexual slavery, forced prostitution, forced pregnancy, forced sterilization, and other sexual abuses of comparable gravity as crimes against humanity.[17] This enumeration stands during peacetime and wartime and recognizes state and private actors alike. Article 7 also prohibits discrimination based on gender. Three important benefits to framing sexual violence during internal armed conflict as a crime against humanity include: there is no statute of limitations; there is the possibility of trying the superior officers (not only the direct perpetrators); and the sentences are more severe when perpetrators are tried under these conditions.

Peru ratified the Rome Statute nine days after establishing the presidential decree mandating the TRC in 2001. Although more than a decade has passed, this international law has yet to be adopted into Peruvian penal code. The Red Cross, Amnesty International, the Commission of Andean Jurists, the Commission of Human Rights (COMISEDH), DEMUS, and other NGOs advocated strongly for a legislative bill to introduce a new book into the penal code. The Third Book would include genocide, crimes against humanity, and crimes against international humanitarian law.[18] Although Peru is required to adjust its national legislation to the Rome Statute, the initial 2003 proposal died in the Congressional Justice and Human Rights Committee.[19] There have been some advances with a recent majority report that recognizes crimes arising from human rights violations, yet that same majority report includes higher penalties for abortion, even in cases of incest and rape. While advocacy continues, those political forces that value impunity hold this important legal tool out of reach on the national level.

While feminist activism has been integral to the recognition of women's rights as human rights and has aided in the development and expansion of international frameworks for justice, it has yet to adequately address racial, ethnic, and/or cultural differences *among* women. Gender essentialism compounds the incommensurability between international, national, and community justice systems. The baseline unit of the human rights model, the individual, does not speak to rural, Quechua-speaking *campesinas'* lives. Collective notions of the family and community trump individual notions of rights, as discussed in chapter 4, regarding the children of rape. As Peruvian social researcher Mary Carbovella explains:

> We know that the values of Andean and Amazonian societies are collective because their lives are based on reciprocity. A person is nobody if they do not form part of a community. Ethics are not limited to human beings and the individual; they are linked to a cosmic order and obey the principles of complementarity and reciprocity. The ethical subject is the collective and communitarian 'we,' not the sovereign and autonomous 'I' of the West. To not understand how difference functions in intercultural relations produces a confounding interpretive problem, which is one of the most critical social problems Latin America faces today.[20]

DEMUS has not been alone in these struggles with the multidimensional challenges of addressing sexual violence during the internal armed conflict. While NGOs respond to the injustice and impunity inherent in these cases of sexual violence, a deep ambivalence tinges their efforts because interlaced manifestations of historic social exclusion have effectively foreclosed legal advances in this area. The Manta case advances very slowly due to myriad problems, including difficulties with identifying the perpetrators, the national legislation's limits in classifying the crimes committed, and faulty psychological examinations wherein the doctor casts doubt on the victim's honesty and questions her sexual behavior. There is a lack of training for regional state prosecutors, especially in international human rights and humanitarian law; they also lack the resources and staff to address all the cases. Cases are left to the side because it is difficult to gather proof of sexual violation that occurred up to twenty-five years ago (no more physical evidence, no medical exam record, and so on). Finally, the Defense Ministry refuses to release necessary information requested of them to mount the cases, and there exist no channels obligating them to do so.

Much of the ambivalence manifested by state and civil society institutions and actors stems from the confounding legal, political, sociocultural, psychological, and linguistic issues entwined in these cases. Working with rural Andean communities around sexual violence during internal armed conflict demands not only a long-term commitment to build trust but also a combination of skills that commonly evade the human rights and feminist NGO staff. These skills include Quechua language facility and cultural and gender sensitivity as related to sexuality and violence against women. These demands overwhelm the capacity of staff, especially when higher education, whether it is in law, sociology, or psychology, lacks attention to these overlapping issues of gender and coloniality as they present themselves in this case.[21]

To address the challenges inherent in the legal case, the DEMUS Manta Project dedicated a year to discussing the concepts of justice, reparations, and health with the community of Manta within the frame of *convivencia*. This would be the basis for developing a culturally appropriate approach to legal cases. With regard to formal justice processes, the community has great distrust due to their lack of impartiality, credibility, and transparency, as reflected in the popular theater skit. They assert that justice does not exist for poor people and that corruption benefits the most powerful. As the popular theater piece suggests, people with resources can bend the law in their favor. The fieldwork team reflects, "We encounter distrust, resentment, and resignation due to the absence of a functioning state justice system and its lack of response to human rights violations."[22] These obstacles are even more staggering for women. "For women, in particular women affected by sexual violence, state juridical processes are seen as distant and complicated; the formal justice system is perceived as a direct confrontation with people that hold more power. Therefore, initiating such a process requires support."[23] In response to this harsh reality, DEMUS reworks its concept of justice by placing it in the context of Manta, which is characterized by poverty and marginalization. Therefore, justice must center on the lived reality of the women.

The DEMUS Manta Project highlights how the challenge of legal incommensurability across national and communal levels demands attention to the multiple reference points for the concept of justice. The fieldwork team synthesized the key aspects of justice for the community after their year of intensive research. "Justice and reparations are linked to the reconstruction of the community and also the development they hope to reach. Justice is related to truth, discrimination and respect for norms. For men and women, reparation signifies an opportunity to gain support from the State to improve the community's social wellbeing."[24] Therefore, it is necessary to balance the goal of sanctioning the perpetrators of human rights violations with the recognition of what happened as the victims told it. Respectful support of the internal processes of both the victim and the community balances with the goal of prosecuting human rights violations. By centering the woman's subjectivity and by taking her calculations between the state's guarantee of justice and the ongoing threat of retaliation and/or humiliation seriously, the DEMUS Manta Project moved toward the transformation of the culture of law. Another key aspect of their methodology was collective self-reflection through an intercultural optic.

NEGOTIATING DIFFERENCE: INTERCULTURAL RELATIONS

The incommensurability between how they first arrived and the reality of their arrival for the community plunged them into a deep collective reflection. Institutional consideration of social positioning demonstrates DEMUS's commitment to constructing intentional and respectful relations across difference. Monthly supervision meetings conducted by two senior psychologists opened a space for debriefing about the trips to Manta. Collective narratives emerged out of these discussions to make sense of chaotic moments, such as Velazquez's initial interaction with Martha. Working through the fieldwork team's initial ambivalence of stepping into unknown terrain—literal, linguistic, and psychic—they redefined the Manta Project. As the fieldwork team explains:

> We arrived in Manta with the idea of creating psychotherapeutic and legal services for victims of violence in response to the PTRC's call to civil society organizations. We arrived with the modern/colonial knowledge systems that we received through our professional training. Although we arrived with the flags of the human rights struggle flying high, our presence could easily be

understood as yet another incursion/intervention (like that of the military or the Shining Path). This has brought us to the practice of constant critical reflection of our assumptions, of our formation, and of the convictions we have been socialized to act upon.[25]

The institutional space for critical reflection allowed for a process of shifting epistemic reference points. Through this process, the fieldwork team seriously engaged the implications of coloniality and the possibilities of interculturality.

In addition to reflecting on the cultural differences as they took shape when the fieldwork team went to Manta, the flip side is when the women of Manta (*Mantinas*) came to DEMUS's office in Lima. Despite the linguistic limitations, five Mantinas decided to accept DEMUS's invitation. They arrived at the DEMUS office in the morning and were seated in the couches in the lobby. Everyone went around preparing for a mobilization to be held in front of the Palace of Justice to further expose the issue of sexual violence during the internal armed conflict and to denounce impunity. Throughout the morning, DEMUS staff from other programs came over to say hello, asking, "First time in Lima?" The women would smile, giggle, and look at each other. The fact that this occurred repeatedly made me question the underlying assumptions behind the question, especially since I knew that most of the women had traveled repeatedly to Lima yet did not venture to explain this to their hosts. A truthful, yet negative response, would challenge the geographic and temporal imaginary that placed these women from Manta in the category of people bound to their land and stuck to their traditions.

The second issue involved another set of repeated assertions that DEMUS would take the women to the beach, assuming it would be their first time seeing the ocean. The women were excited and insisted on going to the beach, not to see it for the first time but to collect seawater for medicinal purposes. This made itself clear to all of us when we got to the beach and the women took out the plastic bottles they were saving and began to fill them as they played with the waves, attempting not to get their shoes wet. Again, dominant geographic imaginary did not correspond with the reality of the situation. Rather than standing before the ocean in awe, the women from Manta took the opportunity to add to their medicinal supply.

In discussions following the mobilization and visit by the Mantinas, both the assertions "First time in Lima?" and "We are going to take you to the beach!" were brought up and considered. There was much discussion regarding the problem of putting on the intercultural optic only when in Manta, as if that is the only place where it would be necessary to pay close attention to sociocultural differences and multiple epistemological reference points. Everyone came to the conclusion that while intercultural relations were first introduced by the Manta Project, these lessons should apply to all interactions, irrespective of the location. The staff discussion echoes the comments of Nora Cárdenas, a consultant to the Manta Project. "It is necessary to place the emphasis on relationships of *convivencia* with members of all the different cultures that make up this country—looking to meet people where they are, take on conflict and resolve it. Our work from an intercultural and gender perspective, should be an essential transversal axis for the construction of democracy."[26] Through the debriefing, DEMUS staff reassessed their assumptions regarding the Mantinas, analyzed their social positioning, and reevaluated future interactive practices with the Mantinas with the goal of establishing respectful intercultural relations through *convivencia*. Furthermore, they broadened the relevance of the insights to include an approach to interactions with anyone they might perceive as culturally different.

While the reasons for DEMUS's bringing the women of Manta to Lima and the reasons why the women from Manta came to Lima with DEMUS were never made completely explicit, the time shared was another level of *convivencia* that deepened the bonds between DEMUS and the Mantinas. In line with their programmatic goals, the visit exposed the Mantinas to the particulars of DEMUS in Lima, specifically their public campaign on sexual violence during the internal armed conflict. The public protest and the popular theater performance by *Grupo Cultural Yuyachkani*,[27] in Quechua, in front of the Palace of Justice, introduced the issue of sexual violence during internal armed conflict into the conversation with Mantinas. This shared experience created a context for the issue that did not directly implicate the women participating and established a point of reference for future programming in Manta. Furthermore, DEMUS counted on the Mantinas to tell stories about their trip and create further awareness in the community about DEMUS's concern for sexual violence during the internal armed conflict.

To untangle DEMUS's social positioning in relation to historical and structural relations of violence, the fieldwork team drew from Peruvian decolonial theorist Aníbal Quijano's theorization of the coloniality of power. Quijano writes of new "intersubjective relations of domination" based on a European concentration of "the control of subjectivity, culture and especially knowledge and the production of knowledge under its hegemony."[28] New "intersubjective relations of domination" trap the colonized population in the past along a linear temporal trajectory that glorifies Europe as modern. Indigenous languages were deemed inferior to Spanish. This systematic control of social relations and communication functions through to the present day and continues to serve Euro-centered capitalism and the European *criollo* descendants in Peru. The dehumanization and exploitation of colonial subjects blocks the radical redistribution of power and full citizenship through the valorization of all peoples.

The DEMUS Manta Project confronts and attempts to counteract the ways multiple social hierarchies of colonialism manifest themselves in the contemporary nation-building context.[29] Modern patriarchy in Latin America, and in Peru in particular, can be understood only by holding the two analytical elements together, that of gender and coloniality. The representative of Peruvian modern patriarchy, the literate Limeño of colonial descent, can exist only in contrast and opposition to the abject subject of the nation-state, the indianized woman.[30] Race and gender are at the heart of colonization. Drawing upon Third World and women-of-color feminisms, Lugones argues that biological dimorphism, heterosexualism, and patriarchy are at the core of this colonial gendered system.[31] This system aimed to dismantle precolonial, communal, and sociopolitical organizations and knowledge production based on multiple and dynamic genders and sexualities. While the European "light" side of the gender system constructs and exalts the "sexual purity and passivity" of colonizer women, the indigenous and African "dark" side of the gender system is construed as intrinsically violent and serves to subjugate colonialized women through "their reduction to animality, forced sex with white colonizers and labor exploitation."[32]

A rigid sexual morality enforced by the Catholic Church legitimated these inequalities in Peru.[33] During the colonial period, European/white women did not commonly travel to Peru. When they did, they were prized for their purity. Sexual relations with such European/white women would occur only in the context of marriage with a European/white man recognized by the Church and only for reproductive purposes. The flip side of this rigid sexual morality was the utter permissibility for European/white men to access, use, and abuse women of lower classes and darker complexions. This is the historical context to Silva Santiesteban's assertion of the hallmark of Peruvianness, the original bastard/*bastardia originaría* complex, as noted in chapter 3. This Peruvian sexual morality and its enduring influence embody the colonial gender system, or what Lugones calls the coloniality of gender.

Sexual violence during internal armed conflict and the impunity surrounding it should be understood in relation to the coloniality of gender. Analyses that take only gender or coloniality into consideration are frightfully limited. On the one hand, gender analyses that do not consider racialization "tend to recreate geopolitical power relations inaugurated with the colonization of the Americas."[34] On the other hand, analyses based on the coloniality that overlook gender tend to naturalize gender binaries and other colonial gender imaginaries. The DEMUS Manta Project explores the possibilities of interculturality to address how coloniality manifested itself in their early programmatic attempts and foiled their initial efforts.

DEMUS wrestled with the concept of interculturality as both a method of analysis and political project. Interculturality is generally understood as a political project committed to respecting the plurality of rationalities and the heterogeneity of forms of life. A plurality of rationalities refers to the multiple ways groups of people may represent, code, and make comprehensible the elements that symbolize their lived realities. Respect for this plurality of rationalities carves a space beyond the universalizing and totalizing Occidental rationality. Furthermore, this respect positions Occidental rationality as one among many and looks for ways of establishing communication across different rationalities. The respect for the heterogeneity of forms of life orients the intercultural political project toward horizontal dialogue, reciprocal enrichment, and self-discovery. In turn, this orientation counteracts authoritarian attitudes engrained in Occidental rationality that reduce and transform interpersonal and intergroup interactions into vertical power negotiations. At its heart, interculturality implies an expanded understanding of citizenship and belonging, beyond Occidental reference points.

Interculturality emerged within the context of state education policy and in response to the undeniable plurality of languages and cultures in Peru and the crisis of the paradigm of state homogenization. In the late 1980s and 1990s in Peru, the intercultural approach to education functioned to address a turn towards equal opportunities, budgeting more resources to rural and urban-marginal primary education. The Peruvian state adopted intercultural bilingual education[35] to address the problems that arise in the education of indigenous groups.

Yet over the past decades Peruvian state discourse has come to institutionalize interculturality in its bilingual educational policy as a technical instrument. Nation-states are constructed on the negation of cultural and ethnic differences and the assumption of universal principles for social and political order. The state's patchy implementation of the intercultural bilingual education policy in the 1990s exemplifies its disinterest in the liberatory capacity of this approach. The state typically implements a watered down, add-on version that fits its liberal constraints. Furthermore, intercultural policy and programming do not incorporate gender analysis.

As with any concept, interculturality can be discursively manipulated and quickly lose its critical capacity and liberatory potential. For example, the intercultural political project gets read as a normative principle. "An ethic-political proposal that looks to perfect the concept of citizenship with the goal of adding to the rights of liberty and equality before the law, the recognition of the cultural rights of indigenous peoples, ethnic groups or cultures, that live within the borders of the nation-state."[36] The key word is "add." Similar to the shortcomings of adding gender to the PTRC investigation, adding cultural rights does not realign the overall singular rationality upon which the state is built. At the same time, state intercultural policies and programs come with a message for indigenous communities: participate with the designated program or lose the resources all together.

While NGOs generally take on the state-centric approach, earning them the name of "neo" rather than "non" governmental organizations, DEMUS began in the realm of the "neo" and then reworked its project with a liberatory intention.[37] This is not immediately apparent, given that DEMUS responded to the call of the state to follow up on the findings of the TRC. Therefore, the state and other actors and institutions take up interculturality in a number of ways that serve varied, and sometimes oppositional, political projects. NGOs such as DEMUS, and movements for and/or by indigenous peoples that work with this concept, must be vigilant to maintain their political edge.

DEMUS drew upon interculturality as a political project in its liberatory sense, as well as a method of analysis to acknowledge the enduring presence of coloniality, the homogenizing tendency of gender essentialism, and the incommensurability of international, national, and communal justice systems. As a method of analysis, interculturality emphasizes interactions or dialogue across difference rather than focusing on preexisting or static entities. Within intercultural dialogue, participants are understood as inter-related rather than separate. This approach assumes a process of reciprocal transformation that happens on the micro-interpersonal and macro-social/symbolic levels simultaneously and is definitely not limited to the arena of education. As Norma Fuller, Peruvian anthropologist and cultural theorist explains, "Intercultural dialogue affirms cultural diversity, generates channels to establish horizontal dialogue. This dialogue permits the recognition of mutual influence through 'convivencia' and the acceptance of cultural interchange as an open process that constantly generates new forms of expression and organization."[38] DEMUS wove the liberatory potential of interculturality and gender analysis into the interpretation of international human rights, national, and community-based legal frameworks.

In response to the deep challenges faced in constructing a viable project in Manta and their attention to coloniality and the potential of an intercultural approach, the fieldwork team made the following assertion and asked a set of key questions: "We cannot fragment the subject [either] as an individual [detached from the collective] [or] into the components of her identity; each woman comes to voice through her gender, culture, class, race, and ethnicity, and it is by acknowledging this that we propose the interaction between DEMUS and Manta. How do we construct this interaction from a point of acknowledging difference? How do we recreate language to make space for the voices of subaltern/colonized women? How do we break with the rational-ethnocentric-phallocentric logic that defines us?"[39] These are the questions that underlie the Manta project's internal process and reorient their methodological approach.

DEMUS's gender and intercultural approach to human rights aligns conceptually with intersectional sensibility. Furthermore, they incorporate an account of the historical, social, and spatial dynamics of coloniality as manifest in the postconflict context. Through a process of collective analysis and reflection, the fieldwork team elaborated a three-dimensional conceptual framework for their programmatic work in Manta, addressing the inequalities of culture, race, and place, and critically rethinking their decentralization. "The DEMUS project in Manta is a political proposal that addresses three dimensions of inequality present in our society: the inequality of gender, the inequality of culture and race and the inequality of 'place'" (Lima-provinces, urban-rural). In general terms, the project is engaged in the ongoing construction of social relations founded on gender equality, intercultural relations, and decentralization of civil society. This implies that the DEMUS project in Manta understands itself as a learning process in creating local alternatives while also producing outcomes relevant to broader contexts and realities."[40] The PTRC recommendation 171 grounds this programmatic orientation, stating that reconciliation demands the construction of the nation-state that positively recognizes diversity (multiethnic, pluricultural, and multilingual). In addition, the fieldwork team worked with gender as a sociocultural and historical construction, situating it in relation to culture, race, and place.

DEMUS's three-dimensional approach demanded revisiting disciplinary assumptions about timeframes, differing modes of interaction with the community, and disparate understandings of the path toward justice and reparations. One of the main goals was to build bridges between state and community notions of justice. To this end, the fieldwork team works toward the reconceptualization of justice and reparations *with* the Manta community. DEMUS's approach was to break purposefully from their familiar frameworks. This shift opens a space for new ways of relating and new ways of constructing knowledge based on respect and integrity. As the fieldwork team wrote, "It is necessary to distance ourselves from the global modern/colonial order and its form of patriarchy that reproduces inequality and hegemonic knowledge systems. It is important to come to know the voices of the people that have been affected by the conflict. By recognizing their forms of knowing and thinking and organizing, it becomes possible to develop an inclusive justice and reparations process."[41]

The psychologists of the team fundamentally reworked their individualistic approach to respond to the communal context of Manta, focusing less on spoken words and more on an ongoing series of interactions in any place or moment. For example, the prerequisite of a neutral clinical context for therapy did not fit with the spatial geography of Manta. Most conversations took place during visits either in a woman's house, at the DEMUS office, or on a bench in the plaza. While none of these spaces necessarily guarantees confidentiality, exchanges took place, stories were told, and trust was built. These interactions created an intersubjective connection, which necessarily transformed both. DEMUS framed this connection within the concept of *convivencia*, wherein each subject engaged in the moment reconfigures self-perception through interactions with the other. In light of Quijano's analysis of "intersubjective relations of domination," DEMUS moves toward an intersubjective decolonial connection.

At the end of my research with the fieldwork team in Manta, I presented my work to the DEMUS staff. We had a long discussion of the use of the term "us" (*nosotras*) in working with target populations such as the women of Manta. The use of "we" (also *nosotras*) creates a myth of horizontality that erases differences. As one person pointed out, "the fear is that by recognizing difference one automatically reasserts the power differential, so using an undifferentiated 'we' is the way out of that moment of fear. Yet, we can only construct a horizontal relationship by first recognizing our differences and that one does not negate the other. . . . It is possible to find the similarities and common aspects but first recognizing the differences, not starting from an abstract assertion of an ungrounded 'we.'"

Indeed, the fiction of horizontality creeps into daily life as an easy escape for people in a privileged position to avoid recognition of social power differentials in the context of coloniality, or colonial difference. The DEMUS fieldwork team worked through the tasks of decolonizing, which include seeing colonial difference and "emphatically resisting her epistemological habit of erasing it. Seeing it, she sees the world anew, and then she requires herself to drop her enchantment with 'woman,' the universal, and begins to learn about other resisters at the colonial difference."[42] This process of recognizing and holding difference as the basis for constructing relationships is particularly significant for feminists in that it rejects the violent maneuver of claiming "global sisterhood."

Instead of assuming sameness, a critical part of the Manta fieldwork team's shift was to listen to what the community has to say and to understand the context of their comments. When the DEMUS team first went to Manta they were told, "We don't know who you are; we don't know what you are thinking; you could be telling us many things but we don't know what is in your heart." The heart is the center of the Quechua emotional world and deeply related to well being, sickness, and the possibility of reconciliation. The internal armed conflict brought with it fear, terror, distrust, and hate, which in turn hardened and irritated the hearts of those who lived through it. In the fieldwork teams' reflections, they wrote, "If we take into consideration that the heart is the center of emotions and thoughts that determines everything, it would be important to show our hearts. Our question to ourselves was, 'How do we establish this trust building process?'"[43]

In developing an answer to this question, the fieldwork team has come up with the following: construct a space of dialogue and communication based on the recognition and respect of differences and a focus on the relationship and the interaction instead of on the other. This space of dialogue has the goal of finding each other's hearts through integral healing relationships based on recognition. Through collective self-reflection they embarked on a process of completely reorienting the Manta project. "The initial plan of going to Manta to attend to the victims was based on a model of healing and/or ordering the victims and their difference. Yet the goal, as Gavina Córdova— Quechua teacher—helped us understand—is to heal the relationship, heal the relationship with the other . . . and with oneself."[44]

Conclusion

The DEMUS Manta Project focused on the issue of sexual violence during internal armed conflict and the women who have suffered this violation. After going through a long process of reframing their approach to include the recognition of coloniality and the potential of interculturality, DEMUS reworked their juridical strategy: "We begin by recognizing the women, their decision-making capacity and their ability to engage with reparations and justice, always respecting their timeframes and internal processes." Sexual violence is understood through the embodied experience of the women who suffered it, rather than as a decontextualized abstraction buried by silence or hijacked by sexist and racist narratives. Fundamental to this approach is learning the community notions of justice and establishing common references upon which to build legal cases, in the event that a victim, after working through the series of calculations between the possible threat and guarantee of engaging in state justice mechanisms, chooses to approach DEMUS to begin legal proceedings. Despite the language barrier, many women have approached the fieldwork team for legal and psychological consultation, usually bringing along a grown child to translate between Spanish and Quechua. Three women have decided to move forward with their legal cases with the support of DEMUS. These cases of sexual violence were the first to be denounced as crimes against humanity in 2009 with the district attorney of the Fourth Supraprovincial Criminal Court.[45]

Currently, women's and human rights organizations are pursing justice for cases of sexual violence during the internal armed conflict. In addition, some organizations give psychological support to women victims, and others have developed contracts with the police to train them in human rights.[46] The issue of sexual violence during the internal armed conflict poses a challenge to the NGOs associated with both feminist and human rights movements. In response they have worked together on specific projects such as a collective public hearing regarding the issue at the Organization of American States (OAS) 128th Regular Session of the Inter-American Commission on Human Rights (IACHR) in mid-2007. At this public hearing they voiced their joint concerns regarding the legal procedural impasse that has stalled all their cases of sexual violence during internal armed conflict. Despite continuous advocacy at local, subregional, national, regional, and international levels over the years, not one case has gone to trial. Human rights and feminist organizations share the challenges of a resistant judicial system and lack of political will to advance the cases, which offers a possible opening for further situational collaboration.

The fact that sexual violence during internal armed conflict has gained international attention is an important victory. However, the question of *how* to proceed legally troubles current transitional justice agendas and feminist and human rights advocates. DEMUS steps past initial ambivalence to make itself accountable to the workings of coloniality, setting a precedent for NGOs working with sexual violence during internal armed conflict in Peru. Going beyond the limits of gender essentialism, it works to bridge the conceptual gaps between community and state justice systems. Nonetheless, DEMUS's language constraint crippled its intercultural relationship with Manta. This linguistic limitation mirrors my own and circumscribes my capacity to map the full workings of the intercultural relationship from the perspective of the Mantinas/os. Given these obstacles, I assert that the DEMUS Manta Project contributes to establishing a new relationship between the state and civil society and between the state and the victims, by constructing an optic that holds human rights, gender and intercultural relations in productive tension.

The Manta project highlights the promise of a method and theorizing practice that responds to the need for a new culture of law and democratic inclusion:

> The deepening and widening of democracy in a country such as ours, characterized by great gaps, requires a change in how political power is exercised, thereby generating new ways of relating among the state and civil society, promoting popular participation, especially of women and other traditionally excluded groups. This necessitates embracing cultural diversity and generating forms and channels for horizontal dialogue that permits the recognition of mutual influence in the space of *convivencia*. In addition, this change requires that cultural interchange be understood as an open process that constantly generates new forms of expression that enriches all involved parties.[47]

Their work illustrates the challenge of advancing responsibly in such contexts and reflects the hallmark of decolonial feminism according to Marcelle Maese-Cohen: "The acknowledgement of 'materialities, power across scales'" and "a completely intimate relation of subject formation under conditions of colonialism."[48] As sexual violence presents itself during internal armed conflict in ways specific to the historic context of the nation-state and coloniality, as well as the particularities of the armed actors, this question of how to proceed legally will continue to demand accountable activist, advocate, and scholarly collaborations with affected communities.

Paradox and Temporality

Rosa Cuchillo, the woman I met in the garden of broken trees, lives in suspended time, in an interstitial space between Heaven and Hell. What the state registers as a legal case of disappearance manifests in her life as an endless search for her daughter. Over the years she has found support from human rights advocates as well as local community and church groups. Rosa Cuchillo's unending quest reveals the endurance of love, the importance of legal avenues to register such violations, and the critical role played by human rights advocates. This book positions itself within the paradox of rights: the tension between the need for human rights law to document and prosecute violations and the inability of the human rights framework to address the full scope of harm.

Since the roots of transitional justice grow out of international human rights law, transitional justice mechanisms, such as the PTRC, manifest this same paradox. An interdisciplinary conversation informed the PTRC's approach, which straddled historical and juridical perspectives.

1. The violence that took place in Peru could only be understood and analyzed by taking into account the nation's history. The CVR was ideally placed to understand the context in which a crime was committed and should focus on that instead of the facts of the crime itself. Thus, the CVR should follow the example of commissions that prioritized the clarification of the "historical truth," such as the Commission for Historical Clarification in Guatemala.

2. The events the CVR had to investigate constituted human rights crimes and violations, so it was appropriate and crucial to gather probative

material in connection with "cases," reconstructing them sufficiently to identify victims and alleged perpetrators. The historical context—while important—should only be reconstructed if relevant to demonstrate the criminal responsibility of the suspects. According to this approach, the CVR should follow the example of the Chilean Truth and Reconciliation Commission, which concentrated on "judicial truth."[1]

Therefore, a historical "mode of enunciation"[2] facilitated an explanation of the context in which the conflict unfolded. This approach speaks to the urgency of constructing a framework that orients the political force of human rights institutions toward a "serious consideration of the wider political, social or cultural contexts which produced violence in the first place."[3] Accordingly, the PTRC worked with "the conviction that the violence was first and foremost a fact that ruled out ethical neutrality: it was the result of a serious moral failure by Peruvian society, which obliged the Commission to search for an ethically motivated and emotionally committed truth."[4]

Rosa Cuchillo's life experience presses further upon this "mode of enunciation" by bringing into question the sense of linear time applied to transitional justice. While she is among the living, her spirit inhabits the restless in-between where her disappeared daughter hovers. Yuyachkani's popular theater production of *Rosa Cuchillo* further blurs these temporal and spatial bounds. From death the character continues her quest for her disappeared child, walking among the living as an apparition. She accompanies the PTRC public hearings, facilitating alternative paths to healing, peace, and well being.

Ana Correa, the Yuyachkani actress and playwright who interprets Rosa Cuchillo, asks the question,

> How do we close this cycle of pain to start to find happiness again? If the painful wound stays open one cannot be reborn. The cycle must be closed. For that reason the PTRC and the public hearings are important. One must relive the pain to be able to heal and close the wound and start anew. We are cyclical; everything in us is cyclical, just as nature is cyclical.[5]

Transitional justice efforts hold the possibility of synchronizing with alternative temporal cartographies and of breaking from coloniality and heteropatriarchy to assist in closing a cycle of pain. Greater attention and support for community-based justice, memory making, and reconciliation processes hold the key to such an alternative approach.

In these blurred spaces beyond the logic of the state and international human rights law, time is anything but linear. A palimpsestic temporality acknowledges the ongoing patterns of domination elucidated by Andean conceptual frameworks such as *el patrón*. What would such an alternative transitional justice process look like? Under what conditions would a nation-state enact a process that lays bare its regulatory and disciplining practices? While this seems impossible, each chapter demonstrates how visionary social actors expand the parameters of the transitional justice process.

Structural, Procedural, Methodological, and Conceptual Implications

This examination of feminist and human rights movements, the PTRC, and a feminist NGO's follow-up project to one of the emblematic cases of sexual violence provides insights for future transitional justice endeavors both within and outside of Peru. These insights can be grouped into three main areas. Structural implications address policy, legal, and normative frameworks. Procedural implications consider processes embedded within transitional justice efforts. The methodological and conceptual implications direct attention to the underlying logic. The three areas mutually inform each other.

Transitional justice processes provide a unique opportunity to examine the dynamics that surround how the state-in-crisis responds to its instability through a contradictory mix of retrenchment and emancipatory reconfiguration. The advances the PTRC made in addressing sexual violence and including a gender perspective contribute to shifting the international transitional justice agenda. Although the PTRC did not move past the "add-on" model, it did include more add-ons than previous commissions. Therefore, the PTRC furthers the international recognition for the need to incorporate gender and sexual violence in future commission mandates. The next step on the international transitional justice agenda, integrating an analysis of multiple oppressions into the research agenda of all transitional justice mechanisms, will come about only with sustained advocacy.

Lessons learned from this experience suggest the need to establish a gender analysis at the inception of the transitional justice process, with a shared definition of gender and clearly outlined practices and policies. All commissioners, staff, and volunteers need to learn and implement a gender analysis. To counteract how gender gets reduced to women, a social interpretive definition of gender includes men/masculinity and does not focus only on bodies.[6]

At the Peruvian national level, a new legal doctrine regarding crimes against sexual liberty expresses agreement on this issue by all members of the Peruvian Supreme Court. Acuerdo Plenario N° 1-2011/CJ-116 established a new reference point regarding gender-based violence and gender analysis more broadly. This legal doctrine embodies a major victory for feminist legal advocates and exemplifies the kind of framework that would facilitate the implementation of the above lessons learned. Although there are many aspects of this legal doctrine worth mentioning, the definition of a gender perspective offers a fundamental starting point.

> Recognize gender power relations, which in general favor adult men as a social group and discriminate against women and children. Such relations have been socially and historically constructed and constitute how people are defined. Such relations cut across all aspects of society and intersect with other social relations based on class, ethnicity, age, sexual orientation, etc. Gender-based violence, rooted in cultural norms within an androcentric logic common in different societies and cultures, includes, according to the UN: family violence (physical, sexual, or psychological), including not only abuse but also violence related to the practice of dowry, female genital mutilation, exploitation; violence (physical, sexual, or psychological) perpetrated within a community including sexual abuse, harassment or intimidation in workplace, trafficking of women and forced prostitution; and violence (physical, sexual, or psychological) tolerated by the State—which is the most grave and difficult to address.[7]

This definition of a gender perspective incorporates an intersectional analytical sensibility that provides a legal reference point for future transitional justice endeavors. The last point regarding gender-based violence tolerated by the State offers a way to legally scrutinize the military instrumentalization of sexual violence.

Circling back to lessons learned from the feminist NGO followup to the PTRC emblematic case of sexual violence in Manta and Vilca, a key step was to take the discussion of sexual violence beyond the rubric of torture. This step initiated a dialogue about the permissibility of such violent acts within the military, the overarching coercive environment created by long-term military occupation, and the false dichotomy of consent and coercion. This false dichotomy is by no means limited to Peru. A study of transitional justice in Timor Leste and Sri Lanka, for example, also highlights the difficulty of claiming consensual relations given contexts of ongoing coercion.[8]

In Peru, feminist advocates made headway by incorporating into national legal doctrine, ACUERDO PLENARIO N° 1-2011/CJ-116, the International Criminal Court's Rules of Procedure and Evidence regarding consent in cases of sexual violence.

> (a) Consent cannot be inferred by reason of any words or conduct of a victim where force, threat of force, coercion or taking advantage of a coercive environment undermined the victim's ability to give voluntary and genuine

consent; Consent cannot be inferred by reason of any words or conduct of a victim where the victim is incapable of giving genuine consent; Consent cannot be inferred by reason of the silence of, or lack of resistance by, a victim to the alleged sexual violence.[9]

This definition provides a legal reference point to place under strict scrutiny the cases of rape perpetrated by soldiers acting on their individual initiative.

In terms of future commissions' procedures and processes, naming commissioners who are culturally and linguistically competent would constitute an important first step. Commissioners should ideally represent all sectors of society, as well as reflect gender parity. A participatory process of developing the research design, the design of hearings or other public events, data collection, and definition of products would encourage more social investment. Analyzing relevant vectors of oppression such as gender and race/ethnicity relationally as transversal axes throughout the research design, data analysis, public events, and final products would be paramount.

Such a participatory process would allow the commission to account for linguistic and geographic obstacles. One key lesson learned with regard to public hearings is that language interpretation should be in both directions, avoiding situations such as the PTRC, which provided Quechua to Spanish, but not Spanish to Quechua. This step would further the potential of creating horizontal relations between victims and commissioners.

Including artistic and cultural work more prominently in the transitional justice process would offer another entry point for community involvement. The close of *Rosa Cuchillo* enacts a *limpia*, a ritual to cleanse the wounds and initiate healing. Rosa Cuchillo brings forth a sense of rebirth by splashing flower water and sprinkling flower petals on herself and the audience. Through revisiting the deepest abyss of the wound, mourning the loss and letting go, collective rebirth through the flowering ritual starts the new cycle. Popular theater presentations such as *Rosa Cuchillo* inspired public truth telling on the survivors' own terms, tempo, and language, which in turn produced powerful moments of spontaneous, collective healing.

In terms of the public hearings, moving past the stereotypical gendered representations of motherhood and victimhood would further humanize the *testimoniantes*. This step, in conjunction with more sensibility toward linguistic, temporal, and cultural differences, would honor *testimoniantes'* ways of knowing as well as force certain members of the audience to adjust their assumptions and reconfigure their emotional response beyond pity.[10] Finally, the public ritual of reconciliation should be a communicative space that does not necessitate closure. Leaving things undone and uncomfortable is preferable to forcing closure at the cost of the *testimoniante*.

Conceptual considerations suggest that mapping the ways transitional justice mechanisms "entrench old fault lines of marginalization"[11] and uncovering the strategies social actors implement to make change requires a methodological approach that reads for linguistic, representational, historical, spatial, and temporal power relations. The approach developed at the interface of intersectional sensibility and decolonial feminisms challenges the "hegemonic reach of legal liberalism as represented by mainstream transitional justice."[12]

Bridging the divide between object and subject sets the tone for democratizing knowledge production and opening space for alternative ways of framing what happened during the internal armed conflict. Strategies for examining transitional justice from this approach include taking the long view to contextualize historically,[13] analyzing power relations, honoring subaltern subjectivities,[14] moving from an essentialist either/or logic toward an integrated both/and logic,[15] thinking across levels of scale, and reflecting on social positioning, at the same time assuring researcher accountability and responsibility.[16]

This approach brings attention to gender and race as well as coloniality/modernity, heteropatriarchy, temporality, binary logic inherent in the private/public sphere, political/criminal violence and extraordinary/ordinary violence, the colonial mappings of difference within the Peruvian geopolitical imaginary, and language interpretation/translation. Regarding temporality, the key implication includes moving toward acknowledgement of a continuum of violence rather than a linear temporal split from violence to peace. This optic elucidates indigenous cosmovisions while recognizing the inherent incommensurability and inability to contain and fully know.

Finally, MUDE's work at the intersection of women's rights and human rights demonstrates the potential of coalition building between these two movements' agendas to respect historically marginalized women's rights. Great potential for political change resides in alliance building among these movements, popular women's organizations, and nascent national indigenous women's organizations. Developing a feminist intercultural human rights approach[17] is key to creating a new culture of law capable of addressing sexual violence during armed conflict.

The Struggle against Impunity Continues

Embarking on this project of ending the impunity surrounding sexual violence during internal armed conflict demands extended time commitments, as DEMUS came to understand in its followup work. Through much struggle and turmoil, the DEMUS Manta Project decentered colonial reference points in their interdisciplinary approach to practicing law. Their intercultural, gender, and human rights framework responds to the cultural and gender politics of Peru. DEMUS's approach produced limited success, as the practice of intercultural relations cannot escape the fragility of efforts to reach across centuries of intentional cruelty and disregard.

In the beginning of 2008, Manta's general assembly ended the contract with DEMUS and effectively kicked them out of the community. The year 2007 had proved to be a difficult one, in that few people participated in DEMUS's activities, and some men in the community complained that DEMUS's presence made the women and children more rebellious. In this strained climate, DEMUS found it more and more difficult to broach the issue of sexual violence. Furthermore, the mayor did not handle the distribution of collective reparations with transparency. When DEMUS brought attention to this, the fieldwork team fell out of the mayor's favor. A new mayor came to power with a strong anti-NGO agenda, which sealed DEMUS's fate. The new mayor also came from a powerful old family with a history of authoritarian relations.

DEMUS was framed as the hated *patrón* that needed to be expelled from the community.[18] The community leveled serious critiques at DEMUS regarding lack of transparency about project budget and expenditures, utilizing images of community members, representing them in ways they did not approve of, and using the term indigenous to describe them. By mid-2008, DEMUS had transitioned to organizing monthly workshops and events in the regional capital of Huancavelica for the people of Manta who wanted to continue working together, specifically workshops for women and health workers.

With regard to the goal of prosecuting sexual violence during the internal armed conflict, the same three victims DEMUS represents (see chapter 5) await trial in the Manta and Vilca military collective case along with numerous other victims. Seventeen other sexual violence cases represented by other NGOs, including the Pro-Human Rights Association (APRODEH), the Episcopal Commission of Social Action (CEAS), the Commission on Human Rights (COMISEDH), the Legal Defense Institute (IDL), and Paz y Esperanza inch their way through the judicial system.[19] The following table reflecting the status of sexual violence cases can be found in the 2011 CEDAW report on "Violence against Women during Internal Armed Conflict." The Manta and Vilca Military Base case has been updated to December 2014.

Table 1. Cases of sexual violence during the internal armed conflict under investigation.

Name of case	Department	Nongovernmental organization	Status of case
Manta and Vilca Military bases	Huancavelica	IDL DEMUS	State Prosecutor's decision pending
M.M.M.B.	Lima	IDL	Judicial investigation
Chumbivilcas	Cuzco	APRODEH	Judicial investigation
G.G.	Ayacucho	COMISEDH	Formalized official complaint
R.M.M.	Junín	APRODEH	Preliminary investigation
Capaya, Santa Rosa and Abancay military bases	Apurimac	APRODEH	Preliminary investigation
L.Q.I.	Apurimac	APRODEH	Preliminary investigation
Putis peasant slaughter	Ayacucho	Paz y Esperanza	Preliminary investigation
Llusita	Ayacucho	COMISEDH	Formalized official complaint
Totos military base	Ayacucho	CEAS	Preliminary investigation
Pampagallo: D.C.O.	Ayacucho	APRODEH	Preliminary investigation
Pampagallo: Q.H.	Ayacucho	APRODEH	Preliminary investigation
Pampagallo: A.H.R.	Ayacucho	APRODEH	Preliminary investigation
Los Cabitos military base	Ayacucho	APRODEH	In trial, yet the sexual violence included within the crime of torture has been left aside.

Translated to English and partially updated from the "Informe CEDAW violencia contra las mujeres en Conflicto Armado Interno" by Gloria Cano and Rossy Salazar. December 2011.
The Manta and Vilca Military Bases case has been updated to December 2014.

The first three cases on the list have advanced past preliminary investigation and await trial. Within the Manta and Vilca Military Base case, DEMUS represents three victims and utilizes international human rights law to argue that the sexual violence sustained by the victims constitutes crimes of humanity. The Legal Defense Institute (IDL) represents the rest of the victims and argues that the sexual violence sustained by the victims constitutes torture. These two arguments imply differing yet complementary approaches.[20]

The eighteen defendants are mostly soldiers and several low-ranking officers. DEMUS projects the future possibility of extending the claims up the chain of command to senior military officials. Because no legal precedent has been set, and because the defendants represent the lower rungs of military

Table 2. Additional cases of sexual violence during the internal armed conflict under investigation without the representation of a nongovernmental organization.

Name of case	Department	Status of case
Huancapi military base	Ayacucho	Preliminary investigation
Huanta - Virú	Ayacucho	Preliminary investigation
Huancaraylla	Ayacucho	Preliminary investigation
C.V.C.	Ayacucho	Preliminary investigation
M.E.L.T.	Lima	Closed due to expiration of statute of limitations

Translated to English and updated from the "Informe CEDAW violencia contra las mujeres en Conflicto Armado Interno" by Gloria Cano and Rossy Salazar. December 2011.

hierarchy, the military has not mobilized its formidable legal team. So far, the defendants have claimed that there is no crime, as the women were their girlfriends at the time and have since become angry with them. This argument reactivates the vexing binary of consent and coercion. The defendants claim also that the incidents, which occurred approximately two decades ago, have passed the statute of limitations. DEMUS argues that because the crimes are understood as crimes against humanity, there is no statute of limitations.[21]

For the past year, the Manta and Vilca Military Base case has been awaiting the state prosecutor's decision to issue an indictment or not. This matter of due process overlaps with concerns about due diligence in sexual violence cases. In regard to gender-based violence, the Shadow report at the Seventh and Eighth Periodic Report of the Peruvian State, for the 58th Session of CEDAW Committee in 2014 asserts that "the State does not comply with due diligence . . . so that impunity, lack of access to justice, and . . . structural discrimination remain in place."[22] The CEDAW committee's concluding observations recommend that "the State party should identify all women who were victims of violence during the internal armed conflict, investigate, prosecute and punish perpetrators and provide individual reparations to those women who experiences any form of violence."[23] Feminist and human rights advocates leverage these regional level findings against the state.

The cases lurch along in the arduous process toward trial. The judiciary has struggled to move human rights cases through the system with continuous delays and stall-outs. Recent rulings mark significant setbacks in the application of international human rights law.[24] The last in the above table, that of M.E.L.T., is particularly troublesome. This case was won in the

Inter-American Court of Human Rights. At the national level, the case was closed. Of the 191 charged with grave human rights violations in the Peruvian justice system between 2005 and 2012, 113 have been acquitted, 66 were condemned, and 12 are missing.[25]

While a specialized subsystem of human rights courts has been consolidated, they find themselves overwhelmed with other types of cases, such as drug trafficking and intellectual property rights. The concentration of cases in Lima makes access to justice all that more difficult for the victims in the Andean and Amazonian departments, given long distances, lack of adequate interpretation services as well as gender and intercultural sensitivity, the emotional toll of retelling the story multiple times, and their high level of undocumented status.[26] Another very troublesome issue is that the victims are vulnerable to acts of revenge within an ineffective victim protection system. In response to this last problem, DEMUS utilized a participatory process to develop an elaborate security plan with the victims it represents, as well as the attorneys litigating the cases.

The DEMUS attorney representing the three victims expresses optimism that the state prosecutor will press charges against the eighteen defendants for crimes against humanity.[27] When the case goes to trial, the security plan will be critical. In addition, DEMUS has identified the prevalence of gender- and culture-based stereotypes throughout the judicial process of sexual violence cases. Leveraging articles 2, 3, and 5 of the Convention on the Elimination of All Forms of Discrimination against Women, DEMUS recommends that the State Prosecutor and Judiciary weigh these cases fairly, without gender or cultural prejudice.[28] Moreover, DEMUS calls for a trial that recognizes the context of terror and generalized gender-based violence and discrimination, as well as the broad power of the military forces within the occupied communities; that honors the voices of the victims, their families and the community members; and that provides expert psychologists to support the victims though the trial.[29]

The legal process works in conjunction with a national plan for reparations. Reparations refer to state's actions in favor of victims and their families that facilitate their access to justice, their exercise of rights, resolution of the consequences of the human rights violations, and the material, moral, and symbolic reparation of harms suffered. The Integral Plan for Reparations (PIR), established by law in 2006 and implemented in 2007, has succeeded in distributing collective reparations, as in the case of Manta. Feminist advocates have been fighting hard to get victims of sexual violence recognized as beneficiaries of reparations. In 2008 several congresspeople, including

María Sumire and Marisol Espinoza, presented the bill 2906-2008/CR that proposed modifying the Integral Reparations Plan (PIR) to include victims of sexual violence as beneficiaries. Conservative congresspeople in the Human Rights and Justice Committee blocked the proposal. In 2010 the minister of justice prepared an opinion on the issue, coming down against the proposal, indicating that there was no internal armed conflict and that sexual violence cannot be repaired since it does not exist as a crime in the penal code.[30] The struggle continues to recognize survivors of sexual violence as beneficiaries of reparations.

At the same time, other types of sexual violence besides rape were included as categories in the National Registry of Victims. In 2013, the Registry cumulatively documented 2,383 rape cases and 603 rape cases in the process of registration. Additionally, 1,274 cases of other forms of sexual violence have been registered, and 289 cases of sexual violence are in the process of legal classification.[31] The results are widely understood to be a subregister of cases. While documenting these cases demanded a herculean effort, the Integral Reparations Plan law as it stands only offers economic and not integral reparations to victims of rape. Furthermore, the law does not consider victims of sexual violence (other than rape) as beneficiaries of reparations. This is a deeply incoherent situation that needs to be corrected.

Political will determines which aspects of the PTRC recommendations see the light of day and which get buried for good. While there have been some advances in the area of reparations, Peru lacks the political will to implement all the PTRC suggested recommendations and reforms. The PTRC itself cannot be blamed for political inaction. As a PTRC commissioner asserts,

> Truth commissions were not designed to substitute for justice, but to initiate a process of social mobilization to strengthen a strong and lasting process towards justice. Nevertheless, the empirical reality of transitions indicates that many times, besides the initial enthusiasm for the restoration of justice, commissions' recommendations are left aside. This situation harms the possibility of rebuilding upon a solid base of democracy and rule of law.[32]

At the PTRC's five-year anniversary, ex-president of the PTRC Salomón Lerner affirmed that Peruvian politics maintains existing inequalities and serves the interests of the privileged sectors of society.[33] In effect, Peru has experienced a retrenchment of the state. Given that human rights and feminist attorneys share the challenges of a resistant judicial system and a lack of national political will, further situational collaboration will be necessary to make legal headway on sexual violence cases, as well as the full integration of the Rome Statute into the penal system. A sentence in the Manta and Vilca Military Bases case against the eighteen defendants for sexual violence as a crime against humanity would be precedent-setting in Peru as well as globally.

This book traces the ragged edge where good intentions collapse under the weight of historic exclusionary practices and celebrates the exemplary attempts to forge just relations within the Peruvian transitional justice process. As long as patterns of domination persist, there will always be those who struggle for justice, dignity, and recognition.

Notes

Introduction

1. Citational of the popular theater piece of the same name performed by Ana Correa of Grupo Cultural Yuyachkani (2002). See http://www.yuyachkani.org/web_obras/rosa_cuchillo.html (accessed December 30, 2014).

2. Burt, "Transitional Justice in Post-Conflict Peru."

3. See Reilly, "Cosmopolitan Feminism and Human Rights," for more on such an approach, which she calls "cosmopolitan feminism."

4. Boesten, *Sexual Violence*; Boesten, "Marrying Your Rapist"; Mantilla Falcón, "Gender and Human Rights"; and Theidon, "Gender in Transition".

5. Lugones, "Toward a Decolonial Feminism," 747.

6. Balasco, "Transitions of Transitional Justice," 205.

7. Paramilitaries called *Sinchis* and community-based self-defense groups called *Rondas campesinas* also played important roles.

8. Ní Aoláin, Fionnuala. "Advancing Feminist Positioning."

9. Arthur, "How 'Transitions' Reshaped Human Rights," 326.

10. President Alejandro Toledo's Supreme Decree No. 065-2001-PCM. There is significant literature on the internal armed conflict in Peru, which focuses primarily on the Shining Path. See Root, *Transitional Justice in Peru*; Degregori, *Qué difícil es ser Dios*; McClintock, "Peru's Sendero Luminoso Rebellion"; Gorriti, *The Shining Path*; Stern, *Shining and Other Paths*; and Starn, Degregori, and Kirk, *Peru Reader*.

11. "La verdad que ha revelado la CVR ha cuestionado esta hegemonía públicamente por primera vez en la historia del Perú. Hecha pública, esta verdad nos obliga por lo menos comenzar a interrogar la historia de la modernidad en el país, y a ver cómo ha legitimado la desigualdad." de la Cadena, "Discriminación Étnica," 9.

12. Ibid., 1–9. Also, see Franco, "Crisis of Liberalism."

13. Ní Aoláin, Haynes, and Cahn, eds. *On the Frontlines*, 177.

14. The 1995 law no. 26749 granted amnesty to all military and police for crimes committed during the conflict.

15. See Otto, "Lost in Translation." The following list of declarations, platforms of action, conventions, international jurisprudence, and statutes illustrates the *normative shifts* in the way gender and violence against women in particular are understood within international human rights: Declaration and Program of Action of the 1993 U.N. Human Rights Conference in Vienna; Declaration and Platform of Action of the 1995 U.N. Women's Conference in Beijing; Convention for the Elimination of All Forms of Discrimination against Women (CEDAW); The Convention of Belém do Pará; the international jurisprudence of the Rwanda and Ex-Yugoslavia War Tribunals and the Rome Statute. See Keck and Sikkink, *Activists beyond Borders*, 35.

16. Mantilla, "Peruvian Case."

17. PTRC Final Report, vol. 6, 1.5.

18. Otto, "Exile of Inclusion."; Buss, "Performing Legal Order"; Ní Aoláin, Haynes, and Cahn, *On the Frontlines*. For the regime of International Humanitarian Law's response to women and armed conflict, see Gardam and Jarvis, *Women, Armed Conflict and International Law*. Women suffered a wide range of violations, including torture, disappearance, and assassination. Moreover, women suffer greatly from loss of family, loved ones, property, and livestock; displacement; and having to assume head of household, among other indirect effects. For a full review of the impact of armed conflict on women, see Lindsey-Curtet, *Women Facing War*.

19. Ní Aoláin, Haynes, and Cahn, *On the Frontlines*, 163.

20. Buckley-Zistel and Stanley, "Introduction."

21. See Ní Aoláin, Haynes, and Cahn, *On the Frontlines*, and Copelon, "Toward Accountability," for extended discussions of these nascent efforts to prosecute crimes against women.

22. Dhawan, "Transitions to Justice," 278. See Copelon, "Toward Accountability" for a discussion of women's NGOs and movement's role in transforming law to recognize women's rights.

23. Also note that sexual violence can constitute grave breaches of the Geneva Conventions and are recognized as war crimes under article eight. See Rome Statute, http://legal.un.org/icc/statute/romefra.htm (accessed December 30, 2014).

24. Brown, "Suffering Rights as Paradoxes."

25. TRC archival material SCO 0102, Pleno de Comisionados "Pautas generales de discusión sobre el enfoque jurídico—Derechos humanos de la Comisión de la Verdad y Reconciliación," August 1, 2002.

26. Goodale and Merry, *Practice of Human Rights*.

27. Buss, "Performing Legal Order," 411.

28. 1993; see article 1 at http://www.un.org/documents/ga/res/48/a48r104.htm (accessed November 10, 2014).

29. CEDAW established the obligation of states to guarantee the development and advancement of women, including the full exercise of rights. In 1992, article 19 was added to CEDAW, which specified violence against women as a form of gender discrimination.

30. Lagarde y de los Ríos, "Preface," 3.

31. While attributed to Crenshaw, "Mapping the Margins," intersectionality comes out of U.S. women-of-color feminist praxis.

32. Cho, Crenshaw, and McCall, "Toward a Field of Intersectionality Studies," 795.

33. See Nash, "Re-thinking Intersectionality," for historical context of intersectionality.

34. Arya, "Imagining Alternative Univeralisms."

35. McEvoy, "Beyond Legalism," 413.

36. See de la Cadena, "Alternative Indigeneities," for a historicization of indigeneity in Peru.

37. Hays-Mitchell, "Who Are the Victims?"

38. Oliart, "Indigenous Women's Organizations."

39. See works by de la Cadena. For literature on the debates surrounding the "Peruvian paradox," or lack of an articulated indigenous movement, see Albó, "Ethnic Identity and Politics"; Degregori, "Identidad étnica"; Montoya, "¿Por qué?"; and works by Garcia; Garcia and Lucero; Greene; and Yashar.

40. Hays-Mitchell, "Who Are the Victims?" 200.

41. From a comparative perspective, Menjívar's study of violence against women in eastern Guatemala assists in framing this expansive approach to studying gender-based violence. Menjívar notes that the transition to peace in Guatemala did not markedly change the lives of Eastern Guatamalan women and their experiences of violence, lending further support to the continuum of violence.

42. See works by Boesten; see also Pankhurst, *Gendered Peace*; Sigsworth and Valji. "Continuities of Violence."; Theidon, "Reconstructing Masculinities"; and Turshen and Twagiramariya, *What Women Do in Wartime*.

43. See works by Boesten.

44. Manrique, "Memoria y violencia," 430.

45. Buckley-Zistel and Stanley, "Introduction," 8.

46. Arthur, "How 'Transitions' Reshaped Human Rights."

47. Sriram, "Introduction," 5.

48. Sriram, Martin-Ortega, and Herman, *War, Conflict and Rights*.

49. McEvoy, "Beyond Legalism," 417.

50. Arthur, "How 'Transitions' Reshaped Human Rights," 333.

51. Sriram, Martin-Ortega, and Herman, *War, Conflict and Rights*. Also see UN Secretary-General's 2004 Report on the Rule of Law and Transitional Justice in Post-Conflict Societies, available at http://www.unrol.org/doc.aspx?n=2004+report.pdf (accessed November 10, 2014).

52. Arthur, "How 'Transitions' Reshaped Human Rights," 342.

53. Ní Aoláin, Haynes, and Cahn, *On the Frontlines*; Gready, *Era of Transitional Justice*; Hayner, *Unspeakable Truths*; Muvingi, "Sitting on Powder Kegs"; Teitel, *Transitional Justice*; Wilson, *Politics of Truth*.

54. van der Merwe, Baxter, and Chapman, *Assessing the Impact*.

55. Balasco, "Transitions of Transitional Justice," 205.

56. Barria, and Roper, *Development of Institutions*, 4. Also see van der Merwe, Baxter, and Chapman, *Assessing the Impact*.

57. Balasco, "Transitions of Transitional Justice," 206–7.

58. ICTJ website, http://ictj.org/about/transitional-justice (accessed November 10, 2014).

59. Mignolo, "Epistemic Disobedience," 160.

60. Santa Cruz Feminist of Color Collaborative, "Building on the Edges."

61. There is also a rich Europe-based body of literature on intersectionality, including Yuval-Davis, "Intersectionality and Feminist Politics"; Grabham et al., *Intersectionality and Beyond*; Lutz, Viva, and Supik, *Framing Intersectionality*.

62. Yarwood, *Women and Transitional Justice*, 7.

63. Ní Aoláin, Haynes, and Cahn, *On the Frontlines*, 20.

64. Ní Aoláin and Hamilton, "Rule of Law Symposium."

65. For a discussion of the "additive analytical paradigm," see Crooms, "Indivisible Rights," 624.

66. Harris, "Race and Essentialism," 585.

67. Cahn and Ní Aoláin, "Hirsch Lecture"; Giles and Hyndman. *Sites of Violence*; Moser and Clark. *Victims, Perpetrators or Actors?*; Rimmer, *Gender and Transitional Justice*.

68. Leebaw, "Irreconcilable Goals of Transitional Justice."

69. Ibid., 97.

70. Spade, "Intersectional Resistance and Law Reform," 1031.

71. Dhawan, "Transitions to Justice," 266. Regarding transitional justice, Dhawan asserts that "colonial relations still inform how problems are perceived and what solutions are offered" (264). While she refers to Asia and Africa, this assertion echoes Latin American decolonial theory and provokes an important question regarding the effects of the colonial legacy on Peruvian transitional justice. "Most theories of justice have been criticized for being Eurocentric and Androcentric, a criticism that can also be extended to transitional justice since it is firmly grounded in a Western (hetero)normative framework" (265).

72. Tlostanova and Mignolo, *Learning to Unlearn*, 38.

73. Mignolo, *Darker Side of Western Modernity*, xviii.

74. Mignolo and Schiwy further support the connections between systems of domination across time. "Modern nation-states reproduced, within the territorial frontiers, the structure of power put in place by the colonial model. That is why the coloniality of power is not a question related only to colonial 'periods,' here and there, but also to the entire modern/colonial world-system from its inception to its current form

of global and transnational coloniality." Mignolo and Schiwy, "Double Translation," 20.

75. Ewig, *Second-Wave Neoliberalism*.

76. Schutte, "Engaging." My attention to the transnational translation of feminist theory derives from years of collaboration with the Transloca research cluster. The conceptual framework is presented in Alvarez et al., *Translocalities/Translocalidades*.

77. Francke, "Género, clase y etnía," 85.

78. The four spheres of the colonial matrix of power include: *economic control*: appropriation of land, exploitation of resources, and human labor; *control of authority*: political, military, legal, financial systems; *control of gender and sexuality*: nuclear family, binary, normative sexuality, patriarchal superiority; and *control of knowledge and subjectivity* through education and colonizing existing knowledge. Tlostanova and Mignolo, *Learning to Unlearn*, 44.

79. Lugones, "Heterosexualism," 189.

80. Sigsworth and Valji, "Continuities of Violence," 117.

Chapter 1. Parallel Tracks and Fraught Encounters

1. Henríquez Ayín, "Codigos de género," 3.

2. Coral-Cordero, "Women in War," 356.

3. Hays-Mitchell, "Women's Struggles," 593.

4. Tamayo, "ANFASEP."

5. Henríquez Ayín, "Cuestiones de género y poder," 12.

6. For a full mapping of social movements in Peru, see Bebbington, Scurrah, and Bielich, *Movimientos Sociales*.

7. Reynaga Farfán, "Cambios."

8. Personal interview with José Coronel, long-time human rights advocate and coordinator of the PTRC.

9. Tamayo, "ANFASEP."

10. Coral-Cordero, "Women in War," 357.

11. Hays-Mitchell, "Women's Struggles."

12. Coral-Cordero, "Women in War," 359; and CEPRODEP, "Las mujeres en la guerra."

13. Coral-Cordero, "Women in War," 372.

14. There are plentiful examples of smaller organizations that worked with women affected by the conflict that do not identify readily with either the feminist or human rights movement. Research must be done to make visible these efforts.

15. Degregori, "Desiguadades persistentes."

16. Drinot, *The Allure of Labor*.

17. de la Cadena, "Alternative Indigeneities," 343.

18. Radcliffe, "Indigenous Women."

19. Henríquez Ayín, "Movimientos sociales," 27.

20. Hays-Mitchell, "Women's Struggles," 590.

21. Sikkink, "Emergence," 64.

22. Acosta Vargas, "Derechos humanos," 139.

23. Basombrío, "Sendero Luminoso and Human Rights," 425.

24. Fujimori had recently made statements supporting the death penalty, especially in cases of terrorism, which he announced after his self-coup in 1992.

25. In 1992, eighteen women's groups in Peru, mostly grassroots groups, prepared a document that listed the six main areas of concern to be personal security and integrity, liberty, health, food security, housing, and education. While their demands gave balanced attention to political and civil rights and economic rights, they did not mention the armed conflict: see "Documento elaborado por mujeres." In Vásquez Sotelo, *Vientos del sur*, an anthology of essays written by feminists from Peru and other parts of Latin America and the Caribbean, the issue of armed conflict is also absent.

26. *CLADEM's Declaration.*

27. Henríquez, "Codigos de género," and Burt, "'Quien habla es terrorista.'"

28. Personal interview with Silvia Loli.

29. Personal interview with Roxana Vásquez Sotelo.

30. Friedman, "Women's Human Rights," 28–29.

31. According to the declaration: "Violence against women is defined by the draft declaration as "any act of gender-based violence that results in, or is likely to result in, physical, sexual or psychological harm or suffering to women, including threats of such acts, coercion or arbitrary deprivation of liberty, whether occurring in public or private life." Also see Sullivan, "Women's Human Rights." Advances in Vienna were made by proposing that the special rapporteur on violence against women also investigate its causes, "in light of the interrelationship between violence and women's subordinate status in public and private life" (Sullivan, 157). This focus brings out the interconnections with gender-based inequalities at all levels. Like article 19 of CEDAW, this step furthers the framework of analysis that connects violent abuses of women with gender discrimination (167).

32. Sullivan, "Women's Human Rights," 155.

33. See Copelon, "Toward Accountability."

34. Personal interview with Silvia Loli.

35. Henríquez Ayín and Alfaro, *Mujeres, violencia*, 16.

36. Personal interview with Silvia Loli.

37. Vásquez Sotelo, "Los un@s y las otr@s."

38. Burt, *Political Violence.*

39. The more conservative sectors, which include Opus Dei, have historically been in opposition to human rights work. COMISEDH, *Memoria*, 155.

40. Vásquez Sotelo, "Los un@s y las otr@s."

41. Henríquez, *Mujeres, violencia*, 16.

42. Personal interview with Roxana Vásquez.

43. Personal interview Pablo Rojas, human rights advocate.

44. Personal interview with Liliana Panizo, human rights advocate.

45. Ibid.

46. Personal interview with Francisco Soberón, human rights advocate.

47. Vargas, *Movimiento feminista*.

48. Vargas, Ibid., 21.

49. Personal interview with Narda Henríquez. Also see the work of Centro de Promoción y Desarrollo Poblacional (CEPRODEP) in Ayacucho.

50. Personal interview with Ofelia Antezana.

51. For a detailed description of this problem regarding women's popular organizations, see Moser, "Happy Heterogeneity?"

52. Barrig, "Difficult Equilibrium."

53. Barrig, "Persistencia de la memoria," 582.

54. Henríquez, "Movimientos sociales," 28.

55. "Feminismo y mujeres," 4.

56. Personal interview with Roxana Vásquez.

57. "Feminismo y mujeres," 13.

58. Interview with Gissy Cedamanos, feminist activist, March 15, 2007.

59. Escalante, "Warmi Kay," 18.

60. Ruiz Bravo, Patricia. "Andinas y criollas," 283.

61. Henríquez, *Mujeres, violencia*, 14.

62. Ibid., 18.

63. Drzewieniecki, "Coordinadora Nacional."

64. Youngers, *Violencia política*.

65. Rodriguez Beruff, "Right-Wing Offensive."

66. Youngers, *Violencia política*, 31.

67. Ibid., 58.

68. Hinojosa, "Poor Relations," 61.

69. Youngers, *Violencia política*, 53.

70. Cano and Ninasquipe, "Role of Civil Society."

71. Basombrío, "Sendero Luminoso and Human Rights," 436.

72. Burt, *Political Violence*, 176.

73. PTRC final report, 295.

74. In a personal communication, Drzewienciecki points out that APRODEH was a clear exception, having come out of a strongly secular leftist party.

75. Youngers, *Violencia política*, 48.

76. Basombrío, "Sendero Luminoso and Human Rights," 438–39; COMISEDH, "Movimiento."

77. COMISEDH, *Memoria*, 152.

78. CNDDHH, *Análisis*.

79. Schmidt, "All the President's Women," 170.

80. Barrig, "Latin American Feminism," 29.

81. Vargas, *Movimiento Feminista*, 56.

82. Personal interview with Liliana Panizo.

83. For a full discussion of women's political participation during this period, see work by Rousseau; Schmidt, "All the President's Women" and Blondet, "'Devil's Deal.'"

84. For literature on forced sterilizations, see work by Boesten; Ballón, "Memorias del caso peruano de esterilización forzada"; Barrig, "Persistencia de la memoria"; Ewig, "Hijacking Global Feminism"; Burt, "Sterilization and Its Discontents," 5; Caceres, Cueto, and Palomino. "Sexual and Reproductive Rights"; Coe, "Anti-Natalist"; Getgen, "Untold Truths"; Pieper Mooney, "Re-Visiting Histories."

85. Personal interview with Javier Ciurlizza.

86. Ibid.

87. Drzewieniecki, "Coordinadora Nacional," 533.

88. Personal interview with Sofia Macher.

89. Ibid.

90. Burt, "Quien habla es terrorista," 55.

91. Personal interview with Liliana Panizo.

92. Personal interview with Carmen Lora; personal interview with Virginia Vargas.

93. Influenced by the global Women in Black movement.

94. Personal interview with Maruja Barrig.

95. Ibid.

96. Barrig, "Latin American Feminism," 31.

97. Vargas, "Mujeres por la Democracia."

98. "30 puntos para la transición democrática: Opiniones de mujeres por la democracia." Mujeres por la Democracia MUDE. Lima, diciembre de 1998. Translated from Spanish to English by author.

99. Cooper and Legler, "OAS in Peru."

100. Personal interview with Carmen Lora.

101. Youngers, *Violencia política*, 427. See Carrión, *Fujimori Legacy*, for an analysis of the Fujimori regime, its rise and fall.

102. Krauss, "Peru Congress."

103. Root, *Transitional Justice in Peru*.

104. "Compromiso ciudadano," 2001, Mujeres por la Democracia MUDE.

105. Letter from MUDE to Alejandro Toledo, February 16, 2001.

106. Poole and Renique, "Popular Movements," 64.

107. Root, *Transitional Justice*, 44.

108. Ibid., 45.

109. Personal interview with Sophia Macher.

110. Root, *Transitional Justice*.

111. Arthur, "How 'Transitions' Reshaped Human Rights," 340.

Chapter 2. Gender Implementation in the Peruvian Truth and Reconciliation Commission

1. See Mantilla, *Gender, Justice, and Truth Commissions*, 425–28. Also, between 1998 and 2000 the Red Cross conducted a study of the situation of women in conflict zones, thoroughly documenting the constellation of issues that confront women during conflict.

2. Personal interview with Julissa Mantilla, 2005.

3. See Buss, "Performing Legal Order"; and Bell and O'Rourke, "Does Feminism Need a Theory of Transitional Justice?" "Whether there is one conflict or many and how levels of public and private conflict intertwine in women's lives, about the silences around the sexualized dimensions of war and about the gendered fall-out of the consequences of war. In contrast, attenuating justice during transition with reference to a goal of liberalization in practice tends to narrow rather than expand the 'crimes' under consideration—with reference to thresholds such as the most serious offenders and the most serious offences, which often make the job of battling for inclusion more difficult" (38).

4. Conversation with Julissa Mantilla at the USIP symposium in Washington, D.C., February 2013.

5. Henríquez, *Cuestiones de género y poder*, 7–8.

6. Schiwy, *Indianizing Film*, 111.

7. TRC archival material SCO 0103, Pleno de Comisionados, December 19, 2002. First national and international contacts in developing the TRC were made with the U.S. National Security Archive, the International Center for Transitional Justice, la Asociación Civil de Transparencia, and the Coordinadora Nacional de Derechos Humanos. (TRC archival material SCO 0101, Pleno de Comisionados, August 1, 2001.) Also consulted with the Inter-American Court on Human Rights regarding relevant cases. Funding was channeled through NGOs, such as the Open Society fund and the Ford Foundation funding through the Institute for Peruvian Studies for an international seminar.

Funding was part national and international. In 2002–2003, funders included USAID (Office of Transitional Initiatives), Canada, European Union, Switzerland, Norway, Ford Foundation, UNDH, and OSI. Other funders included the German Embassy, UN Development Program, and Deutsche Gesellschaft für Technische Zusammenarbeit (GTZ).

8. TRC archival material SCO 0103, Pleno de Comisionados, December 19, 2002.

9. The five key objectives included: analysis of the political, social, and cultural processes and conditions of the political violence; analysis of the behavior of society and institutions in relation to the political violence; contribution to juridical entities by clarifying crimes and human rights violations by terrorists and state agents; identification and analysis of the impact of crimes and human rights violations on people and collectivities; and elaboration of reparation proposals for victims and recommendations for institutional and educational reforms.

10. Sriram, "Introduction."

11. Mantilla, "Perspectiva," 418. See Mantilla's chapter for specific references to "the right to the truth" in International Human Rights Law, the Tribunal Constitucional del Perú, and the Inter-American Commission on Human Rights.

12. TRC archival material SCO 0103 Pleno de Comisionados: "Propuesta para orientar la discusión sobre temas de justicia transicional" Eduardo González (5).

13. TRC archival material SCO 0101, Pleno de Comisionados, October 19, 2001, statement by Carlos Iván Degregori.

14. Fujimori already granted amnesty in the early 1990s.

15. TRC archival material, Pleno de Comisionados, Carlos Iván Degregori, "Sobre el diseño de la investigación," documento de discusión pendientes de aprobación por los comisionados.

16. TRC archival material SCO 0102, Pleno de Comisionados, "Pautas generales de discusión sobre el enfoque juridico—Derechos humanos de la Comisión de la Verdad y Reconciliación," January 8, 2002.

17. Baden and Goetz, "Who Needs [Sex]?," 7.

18. The first meetings between state entities and civil society groups to form the PTRC included the CNDDHH (more than half were religious institutions), Defensoría del Pueblo, Comisión Episcopal de Acción Social, El Concilio National Evangélico and Paz y Esperanza (TRC archival material SCO 0101, Pleno de Comisionados, August 1, 2001). Other civil-society entities involved were PUCP, Instituto Bartolome de las Casas, IDL, IEP, Equipo Peruano de Antropología Forense (EPAF), CAAP, APRO-DEH.

19. On an international level, Buss highlights these issues within the position of the Vatican at the UN Conference on Women. Buss, "Robes, Relics and Rights."

20. See http://www.promsex.org/notas-de-prensa/item/2559-retroceso-comision -de-justicia-del-congreso-aprueba-dictamen-que-aumenta-penas-en-casos-de -aborto.html (accessed December 30, 2014).

21. See Gegten, "Untold Truths," for a full critique of this decision. Internal to the PTRC, Narda Henríquez points out that since forced sterilizations already had achieved recognition on the national public stage, they put more emphasis on sexual violence, which at that point had not been publicized. She reflects that limited time and energy didn't allow for a full treatment of forced sterilizations within the PTRC process.

22. The other woman commissioner, Beatriz Alva Hart, was a politically conservative lawyer who served as Vice-Minister of Labor under Fujimori in 1999.

23. See Ross, *Bearing Witness*, for details on the South African special hearings on women.

24. Julissa Mantilla's presentation at DEMUS.

25. TRC archival material, Informe de actividades en materia de género, December 12, 2001.

26. One example is the project "Women Finding the Truth," which the Peruvian Women's Center's "Flora Tristan" proposed to Jorge Salazar of the PTRC on October 2, 2001. This proposal had international focus to bring together women activists from Guatemala, Kosovo, and South Africa. The proposal's target audience included the human rights community, commissioners and staff of the PTRC, and functionaries of the state.

27. TRC archival material, Memorandum 023-2002-CVR-SE from Javier Ciurlizza, Executive Secretary, to all head staff, January 18, 2002.

28. TRC archival material, "Incorporación de la perspectiva de género al trabajo de la comisión de la verdad y reconciliación." Propuesta preliminar del trabajo, Julissa Mantilla, January 2002.

29. For more discussion, see Nesiah, "Truth Commissions and Gender."

30. Mantilla, "Perspectiva," 435. They developed a civil-society support group that included APRODEH, DEMUS, Flora Tristan, and MUDE.

31. Interview with Julissa Mantilla, 2005. The Gender Unit solicited financial support for additional activities such as producing materials for outreach, receiving funds from USAID, AECI from Spain, and the Canadian Embassy. In September 2002, the Gender Unit gained its own small budget; the unit developed through the end of 2002 and grew in staff. Toward the end of 2002, the TRC restructured and downsized to prepare for ending the mandate and re-contracted some staff as consultants to see the project through.

32. The psychologists include Viviana Valz Gen and Elisa León. Commissioner Ronaldo Ames also supported Mantilla's efforts. Julissa Mantilla interview, Washington, D.C., May 31, 2013.

33. Ibid.

34. Mantilla's presentation at DEMUS.

35. Mantilla, May 31, 2013, Washington D.C.

36. Thanks to Cynthia Enloe for attuning my analysis to this point in her keynote address at the International Studies Association Northeast Conference, Providence R.I., November 2013.

37. The Rome Statute, article 7, provides the following definition: "For the purposes of this Statute, it is understood that the term 'gender' refers to the two sexes, male and female, within the context of society. The term 'gender' does not indicate any meaning different from the above." See Oosterveld, "Definition of 'Gender.'" This definition of gender holds a level of "constructive ambiguity" that leaves unresolved the ongoing debates regarding the meaning of gender and increases the stakes involved in interpreting and implementing its usage (57). A struggle over meaning continues between the position taken by states to leave the term undefined and the approach taken by the UN and its agencies, which understand gender to be socially constructed, highly influenced by culture and the roles and relationships between men and women. The definition of gender in the Rome Statute "seems to fall heavily on the side of the 'sex'-as-a-starting-point approach" (73). This echoes the debates that took place within the PTRC.

38. TRC archival material, Propuesta de folleto Género y CVR, Equipo de Género en la CVR, July 2002.

39. Mantilla, "Perspectiva," 422.

40. Henríquez, Narda, and Mantilla Falcón, Contra viento y marea, 121.

41. Ruiz Bravo and Velázquez, "Violencia política."

42. TRC archival material, Comunicación y género, Línea de Género de la CVR, July 2002.

43. TRC archival material, Perspectiva de género y CVR.

44. TRC archival material, "Guía breve para el uso no sexista del lenguaje."

45. TRC archival material, Memorandum 449-2002-CVR/I, from Julissa Mantilla, Gender Unit, to Elisabeth Acha, In-depth study team; regarding the Boletín CVR, September 16, 2002.

46. TRC archival material, Memorandum from Commissioner Ing. Alberto Morote to Julissa Mantilla, Gender Unit, February 8, 2002. Emphasis in the original.

47. Zinsstag, "Sexual Violence."

48. See Charlesworth, "Symposium." As Charlesworth highlights, "international criminal law incorporates a problematic public/private distinction: it operates in the public realm of the collectivity, leaving the private sphere of the individual untouched" (387).

49. Charlesworth, "Symposium," 384.

50. Mani, "Editorial Dilemmas," 260.

51. Sigsworth and Valji, "Continuities of Violence," 121.

52. Charlesworth, "Symposium," further explains this problem: "In the statutes of the Yugoslav Tribunal and the ICC at least, all three categories of international crimes are concerned only with acts forming part of a widespread, systematic or large-scale attack. Thus, the 'new' international criminal law engages sexual violence only when it is an aspect of the destruction of a community" (387).

53. Sigsworth and Valji, "Continuities of Violence," 127.

54. See Brems, "Globalisation and Social Rights," 112–13, for her transformational approach breaching the public/private divide.

55. Brems, "Protecting," 117.

56. David Sulmont (sociologist) and Carlos Iván Degregori (anthropologist) worked on the methodological design. The debates between them illustrate the differing disciplinary foci around qualitative versus quantitative methods and analysis based on statistics or more ethnographic interpretive approaches.

57. The register of individual violations was modeled after the Guatemalan CEH. Degregori, "Sobre el diseño de la investigación," documento de discusión pendiente de aprobación por los comisionados.

58. Nevertheless, victims hold onto hope of reparations and justice. See Hayner, *Unspeakable Truths.*

59. TRC archival material SCO 0102, Pleno de Comisionados Memo, by Lisa Magarrrell, ICTJ June 6, 2002.

60. TRC archival material, Propuesta de Proyecto, "Incorporación de la perspectiva de género en la metodología de Investigación de la Comisión."

61. Ibid.

62. Julissa Mantilla's presentation at DEMUS.

63. TRC archival material, Elisabeth Acha, "De la exclusión al reconocimiento: Conflicto armado y diversidad de género," July 24, 2003. Núcleo de informe final consultoría, SCO 26908.

64. Mantilla, "Peruvian Case," 192.

65. TRC archival material, "Proposal for operational definitions of human rights violations, crimes and other juridical situations," prepared by the juridical team in May of 2002, p. 57.

66. TRC archival material, Mabel González Bustelo, "Sentencia histórica contra el uso de la violación como arma de guerra," available at http://www.lainsignia.org/2001/febrero/der_023.htm (accessed March 6, 2001).

67. TRC archival material, Documents by Julissa Mantilla: Violencia sexual contra la mujer, la violencia contra la mujer como una violación de los derecho humanos, aplicando la perspectiva de género al análisis de las violaciones a los derechos humanos: violencia sexual contra las mujeres (January 22, 2002), violencia sexual contra la mujer, la comisión de la verdad en el Perú: El inciso que faltaba.

68. Comentarios: Materiales de trabajo del equipo de apoyo metodológico. Julissa Mantilla, January 2002.

69. Conversation with Julissa Mantilla, USIP symposium, Washington, D.C., February 2013.

70. Diana Portal, Melissa Bustamante, Cecilia Reynoso, Carla Lecaro, and Julissa Mantilla.

71. TRC archival material. The document "Linea de género: Ampliación del presupuesto y del equipo de género" states that they analyzed 408 testimonies using ATLAS-T.

72. TRC archival material, Memorandum 240-2002-CVR/I Base de Datos 23 de Mayo 2002. From Julissa Mantilla to Juan Alberto Núñez, Methodology team.

73. TRC archival material, Memorandum 576-2002-CVR/I from Julissa Mantilla to José Burneo, the lawyers and interns of the Juridical Unit.

74. TRC archival material, Propuesta metodológica para el análisis de testimonios de la Comision de la Verdad y Reconciliación desde la perspectiva de género, November 2002, Patricia Ruiz Bravo and Tesania Velázquez, p. 3.

75. Meintjes, "Gender," 110.

76. TRC archival material, "Propuesta metodológica para el análisis de testimonios de la Comisión de la Verdad y Reconciliación desde la perspectiva de género," November 2002, Patricia Ruiz Bravo and Tesania Velázquez.

77. Comisioner Carlos Iván Degregori and consultants Patricia Ruiz Bravo, Tesania Velázquez, and Narda Henríquez, for example.

78. Mantilla, "Perspectiva," 434.

79. So the parameters laid out here would determine who would testify at the hearing.

80. Mantilla, "Peruvian Case," 192.

81. See Leiby, "Digging in the Archives."

82. TRC archival material, "Informe Final sobre la perspectiva de género en la oficina regional lima/N-O-S," January 30, 2003.

83. Interview with Carola Falconi, COMISEDH.

84. Kimberly Theidon made this point in her presentation at the conference "Violence and Reconciliation in Latin America: Human Rights, Memory, and Democracy"

conference, University of Oregon, January 31–February 1, 2008. Also discussed in Theidon, *Intimate Enemies*.

85. Meintjes, "Gender," 105.

86. Hays-Mitchell, "Who Are the Victims?" 202.

87. Coordinadora de Trabajo con Mujeres de Ayacucho.

88. Federación Departamental de Clubes de Madres de Ayacucho.

89. COMISEDH.

90. TRC archival material, Pautas para incorporar la perspectiva de género en la toma de testimonios.

91. Interview with Julissa Mantilla, 2005.

92. Ibid.

93. Interview Narda Henríquez April, 23, 2012. Lima, Peru.

94. TRC archival material SCO 0101, Pleno de Comisionados November 9, 2001. Visit from Frank LaRue, who worked on CEH, including a discussion of historical truth and interpretation of historical causes.

95. TRC archival material SCO 0101, Pleno de Comisionados September, 29, 2001.

96. TRC archival material, Pleno de Comisionados: Carlos Iván Degregori, "Sobre el diseño de la investigación," documento de discusión pendiente de aprobación por los comisionados, p. 11.

97. TRC archival material SCO 0103, Pleno de Comisionados, December 19, 2002.

98. TRC archival material, Pleno de Comisionados: Degregori, "Sobre el diseño de la investigación."

99. TRC archival material, Perspectiva de Género en el trabajo de la comisión de la verdad: Comentarios preliminares de Narda Henríquez, October 19, 2001.

100. Acha, "De la exclusión."

101. TRC archival material, Julissa Mantilla Falcón, Lima, October 2001, "Incorporación de la perspectiva de género al trabajo de la CVR: Propuesta desde el derecho international de los derechos humanos."

102. Another significant section of the PTRC final report is "Popular women's organizations," which is in volume 3, part 1, chapter 3. This section delves deeply into women's roles, their drive toward autonomy, and how Shining Path targeted women leaders, highlighting the righteous-mother role, and does important work to explain the difficult context in which women organized for survival and in search of their family members.

103. Julissa Mantilla Falcón, May 31, 2013. Washington D.C., as well as Rocío Silva Santiesteban, explained the details of this revision process in a personal communication. Julissa Mantilla and Cecilia Reynoso from the Juridical Unit wrote the first draft. Narda Henríquez revised and expanded it, as did Elizabeth Acha. Patricia Ruiz Bravo and Tesania Velázquez completed the final draft.

104. Interview with Narda Henríquez.

105. Conversation with Julissa Mantilla at the USIP symposium, Washington, D.C., February 2013.

106. PTRC chapter, "Violence and Gender Inequality," 45.

107. Ibid., 46.

108. Ibid., 47.

109. Ibid., 49.

110. Ibid., 47.

111. Ibid., 72.

112. Ibid., 74.

113. Ibid., 82.

114. Ibid., 82.

115. Julissa Mantilla Falcón, presentation, DEMUS.

116. Ní Aoláin, Haynes, and Cahn, *On the Frontlines*, 18.

117. Nagy, "Transitional Justice"

118. Mani, "Editorial Dilemmas," 256.

119. Laplante, "Transitional Justice," 341.

120. Laplante, "Transitional Justice," 342.

121. Valji, *A Window of Opportunity?*

122. Laplante, "Transitional Justice."

Chapter 3. National Reconciliation through Public Hearings

1. When the PTRC legally incorporated the public hearings, a Public Hearing and Victim Protection Unit was created and charged with coordinating the hearings. Reglamento de Audencias Públicas de la Comisión de la Verdad y Reconciliación, SCO 653 02.

2. I use the term *testimoniante* in Spanish; it translates to "testimony giver."

3. TRC archival material, "La Comisión de la Verdad y Reconciliación y la realización de audiencias públicas: Declaración de Principios," Lima, April 3, 2002. The other seven principles include: to recognize that "one of the most grave consequences of the violence suffered in Peru consists of the negation of the right to know our own history"; "to rescue the collective memory and national ethic, and affirm the inalienable dignity of human life as a supreme value of a democratic society"; "to give the victims of grave crimes and human rights violations the opportunity to express their version of what happened . . . to give voice to those without voice, contribute to their vindication and reaffirmation of their rights as citizens"; to organize different types of hearings; to affirm "the basis of informed consent of the participants and their right to not be discriminated against"; to consider "the testimonies . . . [as] illustrative of larger patterns of crimes and violations"; and to "respect . . . the dignity of all persons, including those [who] could be identified as possible perpetrators" SCO 653 02.

4. See Laplante and Phenicie, "Media, Trials and Truth Commissions."

5. Manrique, "Memoria y violencia."

6. PTRC appendix 10.

7. Manrique, "Memoria y violencia."

8. Ross, *Bearing Witness*, 163.

9. Sharma and Gupta, *Anthropology of the State*, 18.

10. Interview with Sofia Macher. The videos were subsequently digitalized with Ford Foundation funding at the University of Notre Dame Center for Civil and Human Rights (U.S.A.), in collaboration with the Legal Defense Institute (Peru) and the Center of Information for the Collective Memory and Human Rights (Peru).

11. This is the dominant approach for constructing public hearings. See Ross, *Bearing Witness;* and Agger and Jensen, "Testimony."

12. PTRC appendix 10.

13. TRC archival material, "Fórmulas protocolares: Relativas al título III del reglamento de audencias públicas de la Comisión de la Verdad y Reconciliación (De la formalidad de las audencias públicas)," SCO 653 02.

14. TRC archival material, Comisión de la Verdad y Reconciliación (CVR), Unidad de Audencias Públicas y Protección de Víctimas y Testigos, "Las audencias públicas: Principios normativos y operativos," SCO 653 01.

15. Paco de Onis, Peter Kinoy, and Pamela Yates, *State of Fear: The Truth about Terrorism*, documentary film (Skylight Pictures, 2002). Also see Burt, *Political Violence*.

16. Interview with Sofia Macher.

17. Interview with Miguel Rubio.

18. TRC archival material, "Propuesta para las audencias publicas y audencias públicas de la mujer," SCO 653 02.

19. TRC archival material, "Audencias públicas de mujer," SCO 416 06.

20. Another controversial issue was abortion rights in cases of rape. When this issue arose in preparatory meetings with civil-society groups, Macher "nodded but made clear that she was not the voice of the commissioners and that it would need to be discussed" (TRC archival material, "Reunión audencias y organizaciones de la sociedad civil," July 22, 2002, SCO 416 02). Feminist advocacy on the issue of abortion rights clashed with the more religious and socially conservative elements of the PTRC. Here, Macher continued to be the commissioner enabling debate and discussion on volatile issues. These issues were documented as important topics to be included in the public hearings as early as February 2002, in Julissa Mantilla's "Comentarios: Formato de Audencia Pública Temática de Mujer," SCO 416 02.

21. TRC archival material, "Audencias Públicas Temática de Mujer," SCO 416 06.

22. Comisión de Verdad y Reconciliación, *Rompiendo el silencio*, 15–16.

23. TRC archival material, "Audencia Pública Temática: Violencia contra la mujer en el contexto del conflicto armado,'" SCO 418 01.

24. Interview with Gubercinda Reynaga Farfán.

25. Ibid.

26. Schutte, "Cultural Alterity."

27. Mignolo and Schiwy, "Double Translation," 10.

28. Interview with Mercedes Crisóstomo.

29. The following is my translation from Spanish to English of selected portions of Maria Cecilia Malpartida's testimony.

30. This analysis has developed out of personal communications with Gina Dent and Anjali Arondekar.

31. McClintock, *Imperial Leather*.

32. Alexander, *Pedagogies of Crossing*.

33. TRC archival material, Actas de Pleno de Comisionados, October 19, 2002, SCO 0102.

34. Also former executive secretary of the National Human Rights Network.

35. Comisión de Verdad y Reconciliación, *Rompiendo el silencio*, 46.

36. TRC archival material, Memorandum 296-2002CVR/I, SCO 416 08.

37. TRC archival material, Rosario Salazar Segovia, "Enlace de Género, Sede Regional del Sur Andino Informe de Actividades" Dic, 2002, SCO 416 08.

38. *Nunca Mas*.

39. See works by Otto for more on representation of males and females within the human rights framework.

40. One case that breaks from this erasure is that of *Loayza Tamayo v. Peru*, Inter-American Court of Human Rights, Reparations, Judgment of November 27, 1998, series C, no. 42 (1998), 107–92. María Elena Loayza Tamayo was a victim of sexual violence. Because she was affiliated with a subversive group, no human rights lawyer would take the case at the national level. Loayza Tamayo won her case against Peru in the Inter-American Human Rights Court, but Peru has not fully implemented the sentence.

41. In 1981 Georgina Gamboa was raped at age sixteen by police, first in her house and then in the police department of Vilcashuamán (Ayacucho). She was held in prison for five years and three months under the charge of terrorism, during which time it became evident that she was pregnant. She identified the eleven police officers and one civilian who raped her, yet they were declared innocent, based on the idea that such claims by women against the forces of order were made to delegitimize the police.

42. Silva Santiesteban, *Factor asco*, 71.

43. Alexander, *Pedagogies of Crossing*, 250.

44. Silva Santiesteban, *Factor asco*, 90.

45. van der Merwe, Baxter, and Chapman, *Assessing the Impact of Transitional Justice*, 143.

46. "Impact of the Public Hearings on Participants," 6.

47. See Coxshall, "Peruvian Reconciliation Commission."

48. See Yezer, "Who Wants to Know?" for how an economy of memory plays out in Ayacucho.

49. The communication team was responsible for this audience, which included preparing the journalists covering the hearings on protocol and providing them with the necessary information and resources. Email communication with Sofia Macher, April 24, 2012.

50. A'Ness, "Resisting Amnesia"; and Taylor, "Adiós, Ayacucho."

51. See A'Ness, "Resisting Amnesia," for more history of Yuyachkani. The "fusion of local and global performance modes and symbolic languages gave birth to a syncretic and transcultural form of theatre that was ideal for representing a more coherent, critical, and representative idea of Peru" (399–400).

52. Rubio, *Cuerpo ausente*, 190.

53. See A'ness, "Resisting Amnesia," 399.

54. See the video *Alma Viva* that documents the work of *Yuyachkani* on April 8, 2002, in Huamanga, Ayacucho, and April 11, 2002, in Huanta, Ayacucho.

55. For the importance of public truth-telling spaces as related to a more democratic future based on justice, see Milton's work.

56. Interview with Sofia Macher.

57. Interview with Javier Torres.

58. Taylor, *Disappearing Acts*, 123.

59. Laplante and Phenicie, "Media, Trials and Truth Commissions," 217.

60. See Crosby and Lykes, "Mayan Women Survivors Speak," for a further discussion of this in the Guatemalan case.

61. Interview with Ana Correa.

62. TRC archival material, "Impact of the Public Hearings on Participants," 13.

63. See http://peru21.pe/politica/sofia-macher-me-opuse-llevar-militares -audiencias-cvr-2041549 (accessed November 10, 2014).

64. Interview with Javier Torres.

Chapter 4. Sexual Violence beyond Consent and Coercion

1. According to article 1 of the UN Convention against Torture, "torture means any act by which severe pain or suffering, whether physical or mental, is intentionally inflicted on a person for such purposes as obtaining from him or a third person information or a confession, punishing him for an act he or a third person has committed or is suspected of having committed, or intimidating or coercing him or a third person, or for any reason based on discrimination of any kind, when such pain or suffering is inflicted by or at the instigation of or with the consent or acquiescence of a public official or other person acting in an official capacity. It does not include pain or suffering arising only from, inherent in or incidental to lawful sanctions."

2. Also note that sexual violence can constitute grave breaches of the Geneva Convention and are also recognized as war crimes under article 8. See Rome Statute.

3. The other sexual violence case of Magdalena Monteza is emblematic of how sexual violence occurred in the urban context in police installations.

4. TRC final report, volume 6, chapter 1.5, 277.

5. Encuesta Nacional de Hogares sobre Condiciones de Vida y Pobreza (ENAHO), 2002, prepared by El Instituto Nacional de Estadística e Informática (INEI).

6. Of the Southern Security Zone based in Ayacucho.

7. PTRC legal case 2003, 11.

8. Cahn and Ní Aoláin, "Hirsch Lecture."

9. There are documented cases of sexual violence against men; PTRC final report. A full exploration of this issue is beyond the scope of this chapter.

10. This essay, "Mujeres y fuerzas armadas en un contexto de violencia política— Casos: Manta y Vilca en Huancavelica," was commissioned and funded by the program "Memoria y violencia política en el Peru, las perspectivas regionales" of the Network for the Development of Social Sciences in Peru.

11. On April 3, 2002, Julissa Mantilla, director of the Gender Unit, passed the information on to the head of the Regional Histories Unit, Elisabeth Acha, who incorporated the case into their investigations. TRC archival material, Memorandum 135-2002-CVR/I, SCO 416 08.

12. Interview with Mercedes Crisóstomo.

13. Interview with Diana Portal.

14. Alexander, *Pedagogies of Crossing*, 34

15. See Ní Aoláin, "Women, Security, and the Patriarchy of Internationalized Transitional Justice," on the role of international institutional patriarchies and masculine bias.

16. See Martinez-Salazar, "State Terror and Violence," for a parallel analysis of state expressions of masculinity.

17. Thanks to conversations with Sora Han for this insight.

18. Escribens et al., *Reconociendo otros saberes*.

19. Cárdenas et al., *Notas*.

20. "constituye una forma de sintetizar el carácter jerárquico de las relaciones sociales aún vigentes en la sociedad peruana." Ruiz Bravo and Neira, "Tiempo de mujeres," 403.

21. "The idea of the 'new' structured through the 'old' scrambled, palimpsestic character of time, both jettisons the truncated distance of linear time and dislodges the impulse for incommensurability, which the ideology of distance creates. It thus rescrambles the 'here and now,' and the 'then and there' to a 'here and there' and a 'then and now,' and makes visible what Payal Banerjee calls the ideological traffic between and among formations that are otherwise positioned as dissimilar." Alexander, *Pedagogies of Crossing*, 190.

22. Ibid., 190.

23. "Permite nombrar aquello que durante mucho tiempo molesta, pero que no es possible identificar. Nuestra hipótesis al respecto es que la metáfora-teoría del patrón permite politizar un discurso sobre situaciones ilegítimas que afectan emocionalmente—coaptan el deseo—e impiden la consolidación de la ciudadanía y la democracia." Ruiz Bravo, Neira, and Rosales, "El orden patronal y su subversión," 280–281.

24. Mohanty and Alexander, *Feminist Geneologies*, xxi.

25. "Esta figura, proponemos, tiene hoy un carácter de metáfora para referirse a un tipo de vínculo social marcado por el poder, la dominación y la colonialidad." Ruiz Bravo, Neira, and Rosales, "El orden patronal y su subversion," 260.

26. "El patrón se sentía el dueño y el amo no solo de las propiedades sino también de las personas que en estas vivían. En el caso de las mujeres, ellas eran obligadas a someterse a prácticas sexuales contra su voluntad y como forma de 'agradar' al dueño o al empleado del mayor rango." Ruiz Bravo, Neira, and Rosales, "El orden patronal y su subversion," 265.

27. PTRC Manta and Vilca legal case 2003, p. 7.

28. PTRC report, vol. 6, chapter 1.5.

29. Boesten, "Narrativas de sexo."

30. Crisóstomo, "Mujeres y fuerzas armadas," 25.

31. PTRC Manta and Vilca case 2003, p. 27–28.

32. Crisóstomo, "Mujeres y fuerzas armadas," 26–27.

33. Ruiz Bravo, Neira, and Rosales, "El orden patronal y su subversión," 270.

34. Kelly, "Wars against Women," 53.

35. Crisóstomo, "Mujeres y fuerzas armadas," 28.

36. Henríquez and Mantilla, *Contra viento y marea.*

37. *Nunca Mas.*

38. DEMUS draft version of Juridical Strategy document. The International Criminal Court for Rwanda (ICTR) addresses this issue. Wood, "Woman Scored," underscores how the ICTR acknowledged that sexual assaults did not require physical force and that coercion may be inherent in certain circumstances (1). This precedent is a critical component for the construction of a legal framework to address sexual violence during long-term military occupation.

39. COMISEDH, *Abusaruwanku*, 167.

40. Crisóstomo, "Mujeres y fuerzas armadas," 31.

41. Aurelio is the same pseudonym Boesten uses in "Marrying Your Rapist."

42. PTRC Manta and Vilca case, 2003, p. 29.

43. Boesten, "Marrying Your Rapist."

44. Henríquez and Mantilla Falcón, *Contra viento y marea.*

45. Barrig, "What is Justice?" 122.

46. While I conducted research with DEMUS (2006–2007) in Manta, one of their activities was a short story contest for high school students on the history of Manta. This excerpt comes from one of the student's short stories. . . . los comuneros se acostumbraron y hicieron la base militar y empezaron a trabajar en conjunto dias y dias y hicieron safar y los militares vivieron en el local que hicieron la comunidad y tambien ellos empezaron a burlarse de algunas señoritas y les hicieron embarasarse y no reconocieron sus hijos y se fueran del distrito de Manta y existen algunos niños, hoy jovenes y señoritas, que no conocen a su padre y eso se debe apuntar la justicia por que los senderistas se burlaron y llegaron los militares tambien empezaron a burlarse y eso es el peor que sin reconocer su hijo se van del pueblo y pobre niño o

niña no conoce a su padre. En la gente no hay confianza y buscamos la justicia para aquellos niños y niñas que no tienen padre. Asi culmina la historia de manta ahora estan traumado psicologicamente.

47. "La representación escolar puede ser vista como una alegoría que nos permite acceder a la subjetividad y al imaginario de mujeres y varones de una comunidad de los Andes del Sur." Ruiz Bravo and Neira, "Tiempo de mujeres," 394.

48. This research would be particularly challenging, given the guilt and shame surrounding the issue. See Theidon, *Intimate Enemies*, 137–40.

49. Boesten, "Marrying Your Rapist."

50. Barrig, "What is Justice?" 110.

51. "La relación patrón-siervo, marcado como una ortodoxia patriarchal conformada por una masculinidad dominante y una subordinada." Ruiz Bravo and Neira, "Tiempo de mujeres," 401.

52. As I will elaborate in chapter 5, I carried out ethnographic research in Manta in 2006 and 2007 with the feminist NGO DEMUS.

53. Theidon writes of this as "womanly narratives of heroism" in *Intimate Enemies*, 118, 128–31.

54. "En otros casos, las mujeres eran entregadas por sus propios parientes como una manera de evitar represalias y cobros por pérdidas del ganado. El cuerpo de la mujer era, así, un objeto de intercambio en el que también intervenían los varones de su propio grupo." Ruiz Bravo, Neira, and Rosales, "El orden patronal y su subversion," 265.

55. See Theidon's work for an account of how this worked in Ayacucho.

56. Poole, "Between Threat and Guarantee," 50.

57. Crisóstomo Meza and Cecconi Zambolo, "La violencia en las mujeres," 75.

58. Vargas, "Del silencio a la palabra."

59. Facio and Fries, *Género y Derecho.*

60. Alexander, *Pedagogies of Crossing*, 24.

61. Crisóstomo Meza and Cecconi Zambolo, "La violencia en las mujeres," 76.

62. PTRC vol. 6, chapter 1.5, p. 364.

63. As Wood asserts, "Witnesses want to document the story of their suffering and survival in their natural voice (229); whereas, prosecutors and defense counsel need testimony molded to the legal requirements of evidence (230). These disparate expectations produce frustration and reluctance to participate in the process."

64. Copelon, "Toward Accountability," 256. Wood, "Woman Scored," 274.

65. Crisóstomo, *Memorias de mujer*, 32.

66. Wood, "Sexual Violence during War."

67. PTRC vol. 6, chapter 1.5.

68. PTRC legal case, 2003, p. 12.

69. Salazar Luzula, "Género," 199.

70. Theidon, *Intimate Enemies*, 135.

71. PTRC vol. 6, chapter 1.5.

72. Cohen, "Explaining Rape during Civil War."
73. Gonzalez-Cueva, "Conscription and Violence in Peru."
74. Sjoberg, *Gendering Global Conflict*, 171.
75. Wood, "Sexual Violence during War," 343–44.
76. Instituto Defensa Legal, "Protocolo," 35.
77. Theidon, *Intimate Enemies*, 134.
78. See Boesten, "Narrativas de sexo": "Algunas mujeres estaban menos deshumanizadas que otras, que algunas mujeres merecían más respeto, y también que algunos soldados merecían 'mejores versions de la mujer' que otros" (201). Her main argument: "la violencia sexual perpetrada por estas instituciones estatales es una ampliación de la violencia institutionalizada y normativa existente contra la mujer, y reflejaba un viejo racismo y sexismo" (203).
79. Theidon, *Intimate Enemies*, 132.
80. Instituto Defensa Legal, "Protocolo," 129.
81. Miñolo, *Darker Side of Western Modernity*, 162.
82. Cahn and Ní Aoláin, "Hirsch Lecture," 4.
83. "Un elemento central que es preciso considerar es que se trata de una categoría que ha sido aprendida y transmitida mediante formas particulares que no son parte del proyecto hegemónico eurocéntrico. En efecto, no se trata de un conocimiento escrito y elaborado desde categorías racionales modernas. Se trata de un saber trasmitido oralmente y mediante representaciones. Es una forma de producir conocimiento que es parte de una estrategia de resistencia. Estaríamos, siguiendo a Quijano, frente a procesos de subversión de un orden. Esta compresión de la situación que los oprime no viene desde arriba . . . sino que ha sido elaborada a partir de una experiencia secular transmitida oralmente y que articula de manera central afectos y sentimientos. El patrón es odiado y rechazado; la construcción de la metáfora y del conocimiento incluye esta dimension subjectiva." Ruiz Bravo and Rosales, "El orden patronal y su subversión," 280.
84. Miñolo, *Darker Side of Western Modernity*, 174.
85. Copelon, "Toward Accountability," 422.
86. Alexander, *Pedagogies of Crossing*.

Chapter 5. Finding Each Other's Hearts

1. Estudio para la Defensa de los Derechos de la Mujer.
2. See http://www.demus.org.pe/pagina.php?id=31 (accessed January 3, 2014).
3. Interview with Javier Ciurlizza.
4. Interview with Cecilia Reynoso.
5. Tubino, "Interculturalismo Latinoamericano," 10.
6. In addition to DEMUS's work on sexual violence during internal armed conflict, DEMUS has been working on a legal case of forced sterilization of Andean women under the Fujimori administration in the 1990s. Forced sterilization is also recognized by article 7 of the Rome Statute as sexual violence.

7. While I do have a good amount of ethnographic data from interactions with Mantinas during my research with DEMUS, it does not satisfy what I would consider to be a full exploration of intercultural theorizing on the part of Mantinas.

8. I have shared the analysis contained here with the Manta fieldwork team and wish to express my deepest gratitude to María Ysabel Cedano, Tesania Velázquez, Diana Portal, Paula Escribens, Silvia Ruiz, Jessenia Casani, Nora Cárdenas, Eloy Neira, Vivian Valz-Gen, and Marisol Vega.

9. Interview with Cecilia Reynoso.

10. These consultants speak Quechua as their maternal language and have cultural continuity with the rural community of Manta. Cuzco is a neighboring department to Huancavelica.

11. Poole explains the two internal boundaries that shaped colonial Peru: "the 'Republic of the Spaniards' and the 'Republic of the Indians' and the 'geographical divide and distance that separated the Andes—and the even more remote Amazon jungle provinces—from the viceroyal capital of Lima on its central coast.'" Poole, "Between Threat and Guarantee," 39. Basarde coined the term *Perú profundo* to describe this mapping. Basadre, *Multitud*.

12. DEMUS 2007 internal document: Estrategia jurídica.

13. Velázquez, "Reconociendo y reconstuyendo subjetividades," 122–23.

14. Poole, "Between Threat and Guarantee," 61.

15. Henríquez Afín, "En nombre de la justicia," 24.

16. Theidon, *Entre Prójimos*, 193.

17. And any other additional sexual violence in violation of the Geneva Conventions as crimes of war (article 8).

18. DEMUS internal document: "Ayuda memoria: Adecuación de la legislación penal peruana al Estatuto de Roma de la Corte Penal International."

19. Interview with Miguel Huerta, lawyer at COMISEDH.

20. Carbovella, *Una mirada a la verdad*, 13.

21. The master's degree program in community psychology at the Pontifícia Universidad Católica de Peru includes the core courses, Exclusion, Discrimination and Violence in Peru and Human Rights, Gender, and Intercultural Relations, in addition to various elective courses on related issues. The director of this program, Tesania Velázquez, also directed the DEMUS Manta Project.

22. "(Nos)otr@s saberes 2006," DEMUS internal document. The Manta project staff and I submitted the proposal "(Nos)otr@s Saberes: Comprensiones diferentes sobre las nociones de reparación en el contexto post conflicto armado en el Perú," to the Latin American Studies Association "Otros Saberes" call for proposals in 2006, and it did not receive funding.

23. Escribens, Portal, Ruiz, Velázquez, *Reconociendo otros saberes*, 137.

24. Escribens et al., *Reconociendo otros saberes*, 137.

25. "(Nos)otr@s saberes, 2006."

26. Cárdenas, "¿Casas de espera o casas que desesperan?" 156.

27. See Taylor, "Staging Traumatic Memory." Comment during the discussion that followed the presentation of my research to DEMUS.

28. Quijano, "Coloniality of Power, Eurocentrism, and Latin America," 540.

29. Mignolo and Schiwy point out how "modern nation-states reproduced, within the territorial frontiers, the structure of power put in place by the colonial model. That is the way the coloniality of power is not a question related only to colonial 'periods,' here and there, but also to the entire modern/colonial world-system from its inception to its current form of global and transnational coloniality." Mignolo and Schiwy, "Double Translation," 20.

30. As de la Cadena asserts in "Women Are More Indian," while the process of "colonization assumed the feminization of indigenous populations as the basis for patriarchal structures, the inverse, the indianization of women is the presupposition that undergirds modern patriarchy" (202).

31. Lugones, "Heterosexualism."

32. Lugones, "Heterosexualism," 206.

33. Francke, "Género."

34. Schiwy, *Indianizing Film*, 275.

35. In 1989 the Intercultural Bilingual Education, and in 1991 the National Policy of Intercultural Education and Intercultural Bilingual Education. See Zúñiga and Gálvez, "Repensando." Also see Godenzzi, "Discourses of Diversity," for a discussion of the Plan for Intercultural Bilingual Education (1997–2000).

36. Fuller, *Interculturalidad y política*, 10.

37. The capacity to reorient their program in the way they did has everything to do with the flexible financial support they received from international funders.

38. Fuller, *Interculturalidad y política*, 11.

39. Escribens, Portal Farfán, Ruiz, and Velázquez, "Escuchando las voces," 1.

40. "(Nos)otr@s saberes, 2006."

41. Escribens et al., *Reconociendo otros saberes*, 117.

42. Lugones, "Toward a Decolonial Feminism," 753.

43. Escribens et al., *Reconociendo otros daberes*, 52.

44. "(Nos)otr@s saberes, 2006."

45. See Mantilla, "Peruvian Case."

46. Henríquez Ayín, "Códigos de género," paper delivered at the Latin American Studies Association Conference, Montreal, Canada, 2007, 17.

47. "(Nos)otr@s saberes, 2006."

48. Maese-Cohen, "Introduction," 19.

Conclusion

1. Ciurlizza and González, "Truth and Justice," 6.

2. Historian Paulo Drinot made this comment at the CVR+10 preconference to the Latin American Studies Association Congress, Washington, D.C., 2013.

3. McEvoy, "Beyond Legalism," 419.

4. Ciurlizza and González, "Truth and Justice," 6.

5. Interview with Ana Correa.

6. See Theidon and Phenicie, "Gender, Conflict and Peacebuilding," for how these lessons learned are relevant to broader transitional justice processes.

7. A loose translation of the following: Acuerdo Plenario N° 1–2011/CJ-116, page 4.

A. Reconocer las relaciones de poder que se dan entre los géneros, en general favorables a los varones [adultos] como grupo social, y discriminatorias para las mujeres [es de incluir niños y niñas].

B. Que dichas relaciones han sido constituidas social e históricamente y son constitutivas de las personas.

C. Que las mismas atraviesan todo el entramado social y se articulan con otras relaciones sociales, como las de clase, etnia, edad, preferencia sexual, etcétera [GAMBA, Susana: ¿Qué es la perspectiva de género y los estudios de género? Artículo publicado en el "Diccionario de estudios de Género y Feminismo." Editorial Biblos 2008. http://www.nodo50.org/mujeresred/spip.php?article1395. Consultado el 6 de noviembre de 2011].

La violencia de género, enraizada en pautas culturales, en razón a un patrón androcéntrico, común a las diferentes culturas y sociedades, abarca como postula Naciones Unidas: a) la violencia (física, sexual y psicológica) producida en la familia, incluyéndose aquí no sólo los malos tratos sino también la violencia relacionada con la dota, la mutilación genital femenina o la violencia relacionada con la explotación; b) la violencia (física, sexual y psicológica) perpetrada dentro de la comunidad en general, incluyéndose aquí las agresiones sexuales, el acoso o la intimidación sexual en el ámbito laboral, la trata de mujeres y la prostitución forzada: y, c) la violencia (física, sexual o psicológica) tolerada por el Estado—la más grave y la más difícil de solucionar- [OLGA FUENTES SORIANO: El ordenamiento jurídico español ante la violencia de género. http://rua.ua.es/dspace/bitstream/10045/5651/1/ALT_10_09 .pdf]. Consultado el 6 de noviembre de 2011.

8. Abeysekera, "Gendering Transitional Justice."

9. Rule 70: Principles of evidence in cases of sexual violence. This can also be found in "Caso Perú: El proceso de reparaciones a las mujeres víctimas de violencia sexual durante el conflicto interno en el Perú," in *Sin Tregua: Políticas de reparación para mujeres víctimas de violencia sexual durante dictaduras y conflictos armados* (Santiago: Humanas, 2008), 155.

10. Interview with Javier Torres.

11. Sigsworth and Valji, "Continuities of Violence," 127.

12. Ní Aoláin, Haynes, and Cahn, *On the Frontlines*, 2.

13. For more on taking the long view on human rights and gender, or "historical perspective," see Scully, "Gender, History and Human Rights," 17–31.

14. U.S. women of color and postcolonial feminists utilize double, multiple, and oppositional consciousness to address the multiple subjectivities and contradictory

selves that cannot be divided. See Anzaldua, *Borderlands/La Frontera*; Kapur, *Erotic Justice*; King, "Multiple Jeopardy, Multiple Consciousness"; Matsuda, "When the First Quail Calls," 7; Mohanty, Russo, and Torres, *Third World Women*; Romany, "Themes."

15. See work by Crenshaw; see also Collins, *Black Feminist Thought*, and Crooms, "Indivisible Rights."

16. Alexander, *Pedagogies of Crossing*; Incite! *Color of Violence*; Kapur, "Tragedy of Victimization Rhetoric"; Merry, *Human Rights and Gender Violence*; Visweswaran, *Fictions of Feminist Ethnography*; Wing, *Global Critical Race Feminism*.

17. Two examples include Organización Nacional de Mujeres Indígenas Andinas y Amazónicas del Perú (ONAMIAP) and La Federación Nacional de Mujeres Campesinas, Artesanas, Indígenas, Nativas y Asalariadas del Perú (FEMUCARINAP).

18. Personal communication with Eloy Neira.

19. These nineteen cases are by no means exhaustive of all the possible cases of sexual violence during internal armed conflict. Since the state does not produce a national report on the issue, there is a margin of error given that there are most likely cases in process of which the authors' were not aware. For example, Rossy Salazar mentioned a case represented by the Vicaría de Sicuani in Cusco that does not appear on the list. Furthermore, cases of sexual violence during the internal armed conflict perpetrated against people who were sentenced and remain imprisoned for the crime of terrorism are also not included.

20. Interview with Rossy Salazar.

21. Ibid.

22. Latin American and the Caribbean Committee for the Defense of Women's Rights (CLADEM) coordinated. "Shadow Report at Seventh and Eighth Periodic Report of the Peruvian State, for the 58th Session of the CEDAW Committee," Lima, June 2014, 4.

23. Committee on the Elimination of Discrimination against Women (CEDAW), "Concluding Observations on the Combined Seventh and Eighth Period Reports of Peru," July 24, 2014, 6–7.

24. Burt, "Transitional Justice in Post-Conflict Peru."

25. See http://www.rightsperu.net/index.php/human-rights-trials-in-peru-juicios -por-derechos-humanos/sentencias, accessed January 29, 2014.

26. Cano and Salazar, *Informe CEDAW*, 9.

27. Personal communication with attorney Víctor Álvarez, December 22, 2014.

28. DEMUS, "Hoja informativa Perú: Violencia sexual durante el conflicto armado interno," 2014, 2.

29. DEMUS, NotiDEMUS, "A 11 años de la entrega del informe final de la Commission de la Verdad y Reconciliación (CVR) las mujeres siguen esperando justicia," Lima, August 2014.

30. Cano and Salazar, *Informe CEDAW*, 4.

31. DEMUS, "Hoja informativa Perú: Violencia sexual durante el conflicto armado interno," 2014, 2.

32. "Las comisiones de la verdad no se diseñaron para sustituir a la justicia, sino para iniciar un proceso de movilización social que fortaleciera un duradero proceso de justicia. Sin embargo, la realidad empírica de las transiciones indica que, muchas veces, extinto el entusiasmo inicial de la restauración democrática, las recomendaciones de las comisiones quedan sin ser atendidas. Esta situación es muy dañina para las posibilidades de refundar sobre bases sólidas la democracia y el estado de derecho." PTRC Final Report Appendix 10, p.13.

33. Ceremonia por los cinco años de publicación del Informe Final, Palabras del ex presidente de la CVR. Salomón Lerner Febres, Lima, 28 de agosto del 2008.

Bibliography

Archival Materials

Defensoría del Pueblo. Peruvian Truth and Reconciliation Commission archive, Lima, Peru.

Estudio para la Defensa de los Derechos de la Mujer. The Study and Defense of Women's Rights (DEMUS) archive.

Mujeres por la Democracia. Women for Democracy (MUDE) archive.

Selected Interviews

Antezana, Ofelia. Lima, August 20, 2005.

Barrig, Maruja. Lima, February 2, 2007, and May 7, 2012.

Ciurlizza, Javier. Lima, March 7, 2007.

Coronel, José. Ayacucho, August 18, 2006.

Correa, Ana. Lima, April 2, 2012.

Crisóstomo, Mercedes. Lima, September 3, 2006.

Dent, Gina. Petaluma, California, May 5, 2008.

Falconi, Carola. Lima, July 19, 2006.

Henríquez, Narda. Lima, July 26, 2005, and April 23, 2012.

Huerta, Miguel. Lima, July 25, 2006, and May 2012.

Loli, Silvia. Lima, September 12, 2005.

Lora, Carmen. Lima, April 18, 2012.

Macher, Sofía. Lima, August 8, 2006, and March 28, 2012.

Manrique, Marie. Lima, July 30, 2006.

Mantilla, Julissa. Lima, August 29, 2005; Washington D.C., February 2013 and May 31, 2013.

Martinez, Patricia. Lima, August 12, 2005.

Panizo, Liliana. Lima, March 9, 2007.
Portal, Diana. Lima, March 1, 2007.
Reynaga Farfan, Gubercinda. Ayacucho, August 15, 2006.
Reynoso, Cecilia. Lima, July 26, 2006.
Rojas, Pablo. Lima, September 12, 2005.
Rubio, Miguel. Lima, April 23, 2012.
Salazar, Rossy Lima, March 27, 2012.
Soberón, Francisco. Lima, March 5, 2007.
Torres, Javier. Lima, May 3, 2012.
Vargas, Virginia. Lima, April 6, 2012.
Vásquez, Roxana. Lima, September 12, 2005.

Legal Cases

El Caso de Maria Magdalena Monteza Benavides. Comisión de la Verdad y la Reconciliación. 2003.
Loayza Tamayo v. Peru. Inter-American Court of Human Rights, Reparations. Judgment of November 27, 1998, (ser. C) no. 42, paras. 107–92. 1998.
Violencia Sexual en Huancavelica: Las Bases Militares de Manta y Vilca. Comisión de la Verdad y la Reconciliación. 2003.

Public Events

Mantilla, Julissa. "Programa de género de la Comisión de Verdad y Reconcilación Peruana." Taller de la Mesa de Trabajo Mujer y Conflicto Armado, Bogota. June 14–15, 2002.
Mantilla, Julissa. "Reflections on the Peruvian Truth and Reconciliation Commission Gender Analysis." DEMUS, Lima. June 5, 2006.
Nunca Mas panel presentation: Sofía Macher, Rocío Villanueva, and Tesania Velázquez. DEMUS, Lima. August 21, 2006.
Zarkov, Dubravka. "Beyond Sisterhood in Rape: Rethinking Feminist Theories and Strategies of War, Peace and Sexual Violence." University of California, Berkeley. March 18, 2008.

Works Cited

Abeysekera, Sunila. "Gendering Transitional Justice." In *Engendering Human Security: Feminist Perspectives*, edited by Thanh-Dam Truong, Saskia Wierginga, and Amirtra Chhachhi, 3–35. New York: Zed, 2006.
Acosta Vargas, Gladys. "Los derechos humanos y los derechos de las mujeres." In Henríquez and Alfaro, *Mujeres*, 135–67.
———. "Pacificación y humanismo." *VIVA!* 5, no. 18 (1990): 33–35.
Acuerdo Plenario Nº 1-2011/Cj-116. "Apreciación de la prueba en los delitos contra la libertad sexual." Corte Suprema de Justicia de la República. 7th Pleno Jurisdiccional de las Salas Penales Permanente y Transitoria.

"¿A donde va el feminismo?" *Mujer y Sociedad* 4, no. 8 (1984): 27–29.

Agger, Ingrid, and Soren Jensen. "Testimony as Ritual and Evidence in Psychotherapy for Political Refugees." *Journal of Traumatic Stress* 3 (1990): 115–30.

Albó, Xavier. "Ethnic Identity and Politics in the Central Andes." In *Politics in the Andes*, edited by Jo-Marie Burt and Philip Mauceri, 17–37. Pittsburgh: University of Pittsburgh Press, 2004.

Alcalde, M. Cristina. *The Woman in the Violence: Gender, Poverty, and Resistance in Peru.* Nashville: Vanderbilt University Press. 2010.

Alexander, M. Jacqui. *Pedagogies of Crossing.* Durham, N.C.: Duke University Press, 2005.

Alexander, M. Jacqui, and Chandra Talpade Mohanty, eds. *Feminist Genealogies, Colonial Legacies and Democratic Futures.* New York: Routledge, 1997.

"Alma Viva." *Acompañamiento de Yuyachkani a la Audiencia Pública de la Comisión de Verdad y Reconciliación del Perú.* April 2002. Video, 20 minutes.

Alvarez, Sonia. "Translating the Global." *Meridians* 1, no. 1 (2000): 29–67.

Alvarez, Sonia, Claudia de Lima Costa, Veronica Feliu, Rebecca Hester, Norma Klahn, and Millie Thayer, eds. *Translocalities/Translocalidades: Feminist Politics of Translation in the Latin/a Americás.* Durham, N.C.: Duke University Press, 2014.

Alvarez, Sonia, Evelina Dagnino, and Arturo Escobar. *Cultures of Politics, Politics of Cultures.* Boulder, Colo.: Westview, 1998.

Americas Watch Committee. *Abdicating Democratic Authority: Human Rights in Peru.* New York: Americas Watch Committee, 1984.

Ames Cobián, Rolando. "Los derechos humanos como cultura y practica: Opción y posibilidades." In *El Perú Frente al Siglo 21*, edited by Gonzalo Portocarrero and Marcel Valcárcel, 591–615. Lima: Pontificia Universidad Católica de Perú Fondo Editorial, 1995.

Ames, Patricia. "Educación e interculturalidad: Repensando mitos, identidades y proyectos." In Fuller, *Interculturalidad y Política*, 343–71.

Amoros, Celia. *Hacia una crítica de la razón patriarchal.* Madrid: Anthropos, 1985.

Andreas, Carol. "It's Right to Fight: Women Insurgents in Peru." In Dombrowski, *Women and War*, 232–44.

A'Ness, Francine Mary. "Resisting Amnesia: Yuyachkani, Performance, and the Postwar Reconstruction of Peru." *Theatre Journal* 56, no. 3 (2004): 395–414.

Anzaldua, Gloria. *Borderlands/La Frontera: The New Mestiza.* San Francisco: Spinsters Aunt Lute, 1987.

Arthur, Paige. "How 'Transitions' Reshaped Human Rights: A Conceptual History of Transitional Justice" *Human Rights Quarterly* 31, no. 2 (2009): 321–67.

Arya, Lakshmi. "Imagining Alternative Univeralisms: Intersectionality and the Limits of Liberal Discourse." In Emily Graban et al., *Intersectionality and Beyond*, 326–51.

Asociación Pro Derechos Humanos (APRODEH), ed. *Violencia contra la mujer durante el conflicto armado interno "Warmikuna Yuyariniku" lecciones para no repitir la historia, selección de textos del Informe Final del a Comisión de la Verdad y Reconciliación.* Lima: Asociación Pro Derechos Humanos. 2005.

Baden, Sally, and Anne Marie Goetz. "Who Needs [Sex] When you Can Have [Gender]? Conflicting Discourses on Gender at Beijing." *Feminist Review* 56 (1997): 3–25.

Balasco, Lauren. "The Transitions of Transitional Justice: Mapping the Waves from Promise to Practice." *Journal of Human Rights* 12, no. 2 (2013): 198–216.

Ballón, Alejandra eds. *Memorias del caso peruano de esteralización forzada.* Lima: Biblioteca Nacional del Perú, Fondo Editorial, 2014.

Barria, Lilian A., and Steven D. Roper, eds. *The Development of Institutions of Human Rights: A Comparative Study.* New York: Palgrave Macmillan, 2010.

Barrig, Maruja. "The Difficult Equilibrium between Bread and Roses: Women's Organizations and the Transition from Dictatorship to Democracy in Peru." In *The Women's Movement in Latin America,* edited by Jane S. Jaquette, 151–76. Boston: Unwin Hyman, 1989.

———. "La persistencia de la memoria. Feminismo y estado en el Perú de los 90." In *Sociedad civil, esfera pública y democratización en América Latina: Andes y Cono Sur,* edited by Aldo Panfichi, 578–609. Lima: Pontificia Universidad Católica del Perú, 2002.

———. "Latin American Feminism: Gains, Losses and Hard Times." *NACLA Report on the Americas* 34, no. 5 (2001): 29–35.

———. "What is Justice? Indigenous Women in Andean Development Projects." In *Women and Gender Equity in Development Theory and Practice: Institutions, Resources and Mobilization,* edited by Jane S. Jaquette and Gale Summerfield, 107–33. Durham, N.C.: Duke University Press, 2006.

Basadre, Jorge. *La multitud, la ciudad y el campo en la historia del Perú.* Lima: Huascaran, 1947.

Basombrío, Carlos. "Sendero Luminoso and Human Rights: A Perverse Logic that Captured the Country." In Stern, *Shining and Other Paths,* 425–46.

Basu, Amrita. "Globalization of the Local/Localization of the Global: Mapping Transnational Women's Movements." *Meridians* 1, no. 1 (2000): 68–84.

Bebbington, Anthony, Marin Scurrah, and Claudia Bielich, eds. *Los movimientos sociales y la política de la pobreza en el Perú.* Lima: Instituto de Estudios Peruanos, Centro Peruano de Estudios Sociales, Grupo Propuesta Ciudadana, 2011.

Bell, Christine, and Catherine O'Rourke. "Does Feminism Need a Theory of Transitional Justice? An Introductory Essay." *International Journal of Transitional Justice* 1, no. 1 (2007): 23–44.

Beltrán Pedriera, Elena. "Público y privado (Sobre feministas y liberales: argumentos en un debate acerca de los límites de lo politico)." In *Ciudadanía y Feminismo,* edited by Marta Lamas, 299–319. México D.F.: Métis, 2001.

Benhabib, Seyla, and Drucilla Cornell, eds. *Feminism as Critique: on the Politics of Gender.* Minneapolis: University of Minnesota Press, 1987.

Bermúdez Valdivia, Violeta. "Intervención de la representante del Movimiento Manuela Ramos." Lima: Movimiento Manuela Ramos, 1993.

Bermúdez Valdivia, Violeta. "Los logros de las mujeres en Viena y la Plataforma de Accion Mundial." Lima: n.p., 1995.

Binion, Gayle. "Human Rights: A Feminist Perspective." In Lockwood, *Women's Rights*, 70–86.

Blondet, Cecilia. "The 'Devil's Deal': Women's Political Participation and Authoritarianism in Peru." In *Gender Justice, Development and Rights*, edited by Maxine Molyneux and Shahra Razavi, 277–305. Oxford: Oxford University Press, 2002.

Boesten, Jelke. "Analyzing Rape Regimes at the Interface of War in Peace in Peru." *International Journal of Transitional Justice* 4, no. 1 (2010): 110–29.

———. "Free Choice or Poverty Alleviation? Population Politics in Peru under Alberto Fujimori." *European Journal of Latin American and Caribbean Studies* 82 (2007): 3–20.

———. *Intersecting Inequalities: Women and Social Policy in Peru, 1990–2000*. University Park: Pennsylvania State University Press, 2010.

———. "Marrying Your Rapist: Domesticated War Crimes in Peru." In *Gendered Peace: Women's Struggles for Post-War Justice and Reconciliation*, edited by Donna Pankhurst, 205–27. New York: Routledge, 2008.

———. "Narrativas de sexo, violencia y disponibilidad: Raza, género y jerarquías de la violación en Perú." In *Raza, etnicidad y sexualidades: Ciuidadanía y multiculturalismo en América Latina*, edited by Peter Wade, Fernando Urrea Giraldo, and Mara Viveros Vigoya, 199–220. Bogotá: Universidad Nacional de Colombia, 2008.

———. *Sexual Violence during War and Peace: Gender, Power, and Post-Conflict Justice in Peru*. London: Macmillan, 2014.

Boesten, Jelke, and Melissa Fisher. "Sexual Violence and Justice in Postconflict Peru." United States Institute for Peace (USIP) Special Report. Washington D.C.: USIP, 2012.

Bourque, Susan C., and Kay B. Warren. "Democracy without Peace: The Cultural Politics of Terror in Peru." *Latin American Research Review* 24, no. 1 (1989): 7–34.

Braidotti, Rosi. "The Way We Were: Some Post-Structural Memoirs." *Women's Studies International Forum* 23, no. 6 (2000): 715–28.

Brems, Eva. "Enemies or Allies? Feminism and Cultural Relativism as Dissident Voices in Human Rights Discourse." *Human Rights Quarterly* 19, no. 1 (1997): 136–64.

Brems, Eva. "Globalisation and Social Rights." In *Constantin Meunier: A Dialogue with Allan Sekula*, edited by Hilde van Gelder, 113–19. Leuven, Belgium: Leuven University Press, 2005.

———. "Protecting the Human Rights of Women." In *International Human Rights in the 21st Century*, edited by Gene M. Lyons and James Mayall, 100–138. Lanham, Md.: Rowman and Littlefield, 2003.

Brown, Wendy. "Suffering Rights as Paradoxes." *Constellations* 7, no. 2 (2000): 208–29.

Brysk, Alison. "Turning Weakness into Strength: The Internationalization of Indian Rights." *Latin American Perspectives* 23, no. 2 (1996): 38–57.

Buckley-Zistel, Susanne, and Ruth Stanley. "Introduction." In Buckley-Zistel and Stanley, *Gender in Transitional Justice*, 264–83.

Bueno, Antero. *Voces e Imagenes*. Berkeley: Centro de Estudios Literarios "Antonio Cornejo Polar," 2001.

Bueno-Hansen, Pascha. "Engendering Transitional Justice: Reflections on the Case of Peru." *Journal of Peacebuilding and Development* 5, no. 3 (2010): 61–74.

———. "Finding Each Other's Hearts: Intercultural Relations and the Drive to Prosecute Sexual Violence during the Internal Armed Conflict in Peru." In "New Directions in Feminism and Human Rights," special issue, *International Feminist Journal of Politics* 12, nos. 3–4 (2010): 319–40.

Burt, Jo-Marie. "Transitional Justice in Post-Conflict Peru: Progress and Setbacks in Accountability Efforts," *Aportes DPLf* 18, no. 6 (2013): 49–54.

———. *Political Violence and the Authoritarian State in Peru: Silencing Civil Society*. New York: Palgrave Macmillan, 2007.

———. "'Quien habla es terrorista': The Political Use of Fear in Fujimori's Peru." *Latin American Research Review* 41, no. 3 (2006): 32–62.

———. "Sterilization and Its Discontents." *NACLA Report on the Americas* 31, no. 5 (1998): 5.

Buss, Doris. "Performing Legal Order: Some Feminist Thoughts on International Criminal Law." *International Criminal Law Review* 11 (2011): 409–23.

———. "Robes, Relics and Rights: The Vatican and the Beijing Conference on Women." *Social Legal Studies* 7 (1998): 339–63.

Buss, Doris, and Ambreena S. Manji, eds. *International Law: Modern Feminist Approaches*. Oxford: Hart, 2005.

Caceres, Carlos, Marcos Cueto, and Nancy Palomino. "Sexual and Reproductive Rights Policies in Peru: Unveiling False Paradoxes." In *Sexpolitics: Reports from the Front Lines*, edited by Richard Parker, Rosalind Petchesky, and Robert Sember, 127–66. N.p.: Sexuality Policy Watch, 2006.

Cahn, Naomi, and Fionnuala Ní Aolain. "Hirsch Lecture: Gender, Masculinities, and Transition in Conflicted Societies." *New England Law Review* 44, no. 1 (2009): 1–23.

Canessa, Andrew. "Introduction." In *Natives Making Nation: Gender, Indigeneity, and the State in the Andes*, edited by Andrew Canessa, 3–31. Tucson: University of Arizona Press, 2005.

Cano, Gloria, and Karim Ninasquipe. "The Role of Civil Society in Demanding and Promoting Justice." In *The Legacy of Truth: Criminal Justice in the Peruvian Transition*, edited by Lisa Magarrell, and Leonardo Filippini, 39–50. New York: International Center for Transitional Justice, 2006.

Cano, Gloria, and Rossy Salazar. "Informe CEDAW, violencia contra las mujeres en conflicto armado interno." Report submitted to CEDAW, December 2011.

Carbovella, Mary. *Una mirada a la verdad: Percepciones de la población de Huancavelica sobre la Comisión de la Verdad y Reconciliación*. Lima: Consejería en Proyectos, 2002.

Cárdenas, Nora. "¿Casas de espera o casas que desesperan?" In *Fronteras interiores: Identidad, diferencia y protagonismos de las mujeres*, edited by Maruja Barrig, 141–58. Lima: Instituto de Estudios Peruanos, 2007.

———. *Políticas de salud en el Perú: Hacia la construcción de políticas de salud para todos y todas los peruanos y las peruanas*. Lima: Consorcio de Investigación Económica y Social (CIES), 2006.

Cárdenas, Nora, Mercedes Crisóstomo, Eloy Neira, Diana Portal, Silvia Ruiz, and Tesania Velázquez. *Notas, remesas y recados de Manta Huancavelica*. Lima: DEMUS, 2005.

Carrión, Julio. *The Fujimori Legacy: The Rise of Electoral Authoritarianism in Peru*. University Park: Pennsylvania State University Press, 2006.

"Caso Perú: El proceso de reparaciones a las mujeres víctimas de violencia sexual durante el conflicto interno en el Perú." In *Sin tregua: Políticas de reparación para mujeres víctimas de violencia sexual durante dictaduras y conflictos armados*. Santiago de Chile: Humanas, 2008.

Cecconi Zambolo, Arianna, and Mercedes Crisóstomo Meza. "La violencia en las mujeres: Entre la realidad y los sueños." *Páginas* 206 (2007): 70–83.

Centro de Estudios y Promoción de Desarrollo (DESCO), ed. *Tiempos de ira y amor: Nuevos actores para viejos problemas*. Lima: DESCO, 1990.

Centro de la Mujer Peruana Flora Tristan. *25 Años de feminismo en el Perú*. Lima: Centro de la Mujer Peruana Flora Tristan, 2004.

Centro de promoción y desarrollo poblacional (CEPRODEP). "Las mujeres en la Guerra: Impacto y respuestas" Lima: CEPRODEP, 2002.

Charlesworth, Hilary. "Not Waving but Drowning: Gender Mainstreaming and Human Rights in the United Nations." *Harvard Human Rights Journal* 18 (2005): 1–18.

———. "Symposium on Method in International Law: Feminist Methods in International Law." *American Journal of International Law* 93 (1999): 379–94.

Charlesworth, Hilary, and Christine Chinkin. *The Boundaries of International Law: A Feminist Analysis*. Manchester: Manchester University Press, 2000.

———. "The Gender of Jus Cogens." In Lockwood, *Women's Rights*, 87–100.

Chinkin, Christine, Shelley Wright, and Hilary Charlesworth. "Feminist Approaches to International Law: Reflections from Another Century." In Buss and Manji, *International Law*, 17–45.

Cho, Sumi, Kimberlé Crenshaw, and Leslie McCall. "Toward a Field of Intersectional Studies: Theory, Applications and Praxis." *Signs* 38, no. 4 (2013): 785–810.

Ciurlizza, Javier, and Eduardo González, "Truth and Justice from the Perspective of the Truth and Reconciliation Commission." In *The Legacy of Truth Criminal Justice in the Peruvian Transition*, edited by Lisa Magarrell and Leonardo Filippini, 5–14. New York: International Center for Transitional Justice, 2006.

CLADEM's Declaration at the World Conference on Human Rights. Vienna: CLADEM, 1993.

Coe, Anna-Britt. "From Anti-Natalist to Ultra-Conservative: Restricting Reproductive Choice in Peru." *Reproductive Health Matters* 12, no. 24 (2004): 56–69.

Cohen, Dara. "Explaining Rape during Civil War." *American Political Science Review* 107, no. 3 (2013): 461–77.

Collins, Patricia Hill. *Black Feminist Thought: Knowledge, Consciousness, and the Politics of Empowerment.* Boston: Unwin Hyman, 1990.

Comité de América Latina y el Caribe por la defensa de los derechos de la mujer (CLADEM). *Silencio y complicidad: Violencia contra las mujeres en los servicios públicos de salud en el Perú.* Lima: CLADEM, 1998.

———. *Nada personal: Reporte de derechos humanos sobre la aplicación de la anticonceptión quirurgica en el Perú.* Lima: CLADEM, 1999.

Comisión de Derechos Humanos (COMISEDH). *Memoria para los ausentes desaparecidos en el Perú (1982–1996).* Lima: COMISEDH, 2001.

———. *Abusaruwanku.* Lima: COMISEDH y Movimiento Manuela Ramos, 2003.

———. "El movimiento de derechos humanos en el Perú: 30 años de compromiso con la democracia y los derechos humanos informe sobre el Foro realizado en Lima el el 1,2 y 3 de diciembre de 2009." Lima: COMISEDH, 2010.

Comisión de la Verdad y la Reconciliación. *Rompiendo el silencio: Las voces de las mujeres en la búsqueda de la verdad.* Rompiendo el Silencio, Lima: Comisión de la Verdad y la Reconciliación, 2002.

———. *De la negación al reconocimiento: Seminario internacional, procesos post comisiones de la verdad, memoria.* Lima: Centro de Estudios y Publicaciones, 2003.

———. *Informacion Final de la Comisión de la Verdad y la Reconciliación.* Lima: Comisión de la Verdad y la Reconciliación, 2003.

———. "La violencia sexual contra la mujer." Vol. 6, chap. 1, sect. 1.5. Lima: Comisión de la Verdad y la Reconciliación. 2003.

———. "Violencia y desigualdad de género." Vol. 8, chap. 2, sect. 2.1. Lima: Comisión de la Verdad y la Reconciliación, 2003.

———. "El impacto de las audencias públicas en los participantes." Available at http://www.cverdad.org.pe/apublicas/audiencias/impacto.php (accessed December 30, 2014).

Comisión Episcopal de Acción Social. "El caminar de la iglesia catolica en la promocion y defensa de los derechos humanos en la contexto de la violencia politica 1980–2000." Informe preliminar. Conferencia Episcopal Peruana, 2002.

Committee on the Elimination of Discrimination against Women (CEDAW). "Concluding Observations on the Combined Seventh and Eighth Period Reports of Peru," July 24, 2014.

Coordinadora Nacional de Derechos Humanos (CNDDHH). *Análisis de la practica de la tortura en el Perú.* Section 2.9, "Tortura mediante abuso sexual," 38–46. Lima, 1999.

Cook, Rebecca, ed. *Human Rights of Women: National and International Perspectives.* Philadelphia: University of Pennsylvania Press, 1994.

Coomaraswamy, Radhika. "To Bellow Like a Cow: Women, Ethnicity, and the Discourse of Rights." In Cook, *Human Rights of Women*, 39–57.

Cooper, Andrew F., and Thomas Legler. "The OAS in Peru: A Model for the Future?" *Journal of Democracy* 12 no. 4 (2001): 123–36.

Copelon, Rhonda. "Surfacing Gender: Reengraving Crimes against Women in Humanitarian Law." In Dombrowski, *Women and War*, 245–266.

———. "Toward Accountability for Violence against Women in War: Progress and Challenges." In *Sexual Violence in Conflict Zones: From the Ancient World to the Era of Human Rights*, edited by Elizabeth D. Heinaman, 232–56. Philadelphia: University of Pennsylvania Press, 2011.

Coral-Cordero, Isabel. "Women in War: Impact and Responses." In Stern, *Shining and Other Paths*, 345–374.

Coronil, Fernando. "Beyond Occidentalism: Toward Nonimperial Geohistorical Categories." *Cultural Anthropology* 11:1 (1996): 52–87.

Coxshall, Wendy. "From the Peruvian Reconciliation Commission to Ethnography: Narrative, Relatedness and Silence." *Political and Legal Anthropology Review* 28:2 (2005): 203–222.

Crenshaw, Kimberly. "Mapping the Margins: Intersectionality, Identity Politics, and Violence Against Women of Color." *Stanford Law Review* 43 (1991): 1241–1299.

Crisóstomo, Mercedes. "Mujeres y fuerzas armadas en un contexto de violencia política. Casos: Manta y Vilca Huancavelica." Lima, La Red de Desarrollo de las Ciencias Sociales de Perú, 2002.

Crisóstomo, Mercedes. "Las mujeres y la violencia sexual en el conflicto armado interno." In APRODEH, *Violencia*, 11–29.

———. *Memorias de mujer (en el conflicto armado interno).* Lima: Consejería en Proyectos, 2004.

Crisóstomo Meza, Mercedes, and Arianna Cecconi Zambolo. "La violencia en las mujeres: Entre la realidad y los sueños." *Páginas* 206 (2007): 70–83.

Crooms, Lisa A. "Indivisible Rights and Intersectional Identities; or, 'What Do Women's Human Rights Have to Do with the Race Convention?'" *Howard Law Journal* 40 (1997): 619–40.

Crosby, Alison, and M. Brinton Lykes. "Mayan Women Survivors Speak: The Gendered Relations of Truth Telling in Postwar Guatemala." *International Journal of Transitional Justice* 5 (2011): 456–76.

Dal Secco, Alessandra. "Truth and Reconciliation Commissions and Gender Justice." In Pankhurst, *Gendered Peace*, 65–105.

Degregori, Carlos Iván. "Desiguadades persistentes y construcción de un pais pluricultural." 2002. Available at http://red.pucp.edu.pe/ridei/libros/desigualdades

-persistentes-y-construccion-de-un-pais-pluricultural-reflexiones-a-partir-del -trabajo-de-la-cvr (accessed December 30, 2014).

———. "Heridas abiertas, derechos esquivos: reflexiones sobre la Comisión de la Verdad y Reconciliación." In *Memorias en conflicto: Aspectos de la violencia política contemporánea*, edited by Raynald Belay, Jorge Bracamonte, Carlos Iván Degregori, and Jean Joinville Vacher, 75–85. Lima: Instituto de Estudios Peruanos, 2004.

———. "Identidad étnica, movimientos sociales y participación en el Perú." In *Estados nacionales, etnicidad y democraria en América Latina*, edited by Y. Mutsuo and C. I. Degregori, 161–78. Osaka: JCAS, National Museum of Ethnology, 2002.

———. *Qué difícil es ser dios: El partido comunista del Perú—Sendero Luminoso y el conflicto armado*. Lima: IEP, 2011.

Degregori, Carlos Iván, Elizabeth Jelin, Ponciano del Pino, Pablo Sandoval, Ana Maria Tamayo and Leslie Villapolo, eds. *Jamás tan cerca arremetió lo lejos: Memoria y violencia política en el Perú*. Lima: IEP/SSRC, 2003.

de la Cadena, Marisol. "Alternative Indigeneities: Conceptual Proposals." *Latin American and Caribbean Ethnic Studies* 3, no. 3 (2008): 341–49.

———. "Are Mestizos Hybrids? The Conceptual Politics of Andean Identities." *Journal of Latin American Studies* 37 (2005): 257–84.

———. "Discriminación etnica." *Cuestion del Estado* 32 (2003): 1–9.

———. *Indigenous Mestizos*. Durham. N.C.: Duke University Press, 2000.

———. "The Racial Moral Politics of Place: Mestizas and Intellectuals in Turn-of-the-Century Peru." In *Gender's Place: Feminist Anthropologies of Latin America*, edited by Rosario Montoya, Lessie Jo Frazier, and Janise Hurtig, 155–75. New York: Palgrave Macmillan, 2002.

———. "Reconstructing Race: Racism, Culture and Mestizaje in Latin America." *North American Congress on Latin America (NACLA) Report on the Americas* 34, no. 6 (2001): 16–23.

———. "Silent Racism and Intellectual Superiority in Peru." *Bulletin of Latin American Research* 17, no. 2 (1998): 143–64.

———. "Women are More Indian: Gender and Ethnicity in a Community in Cuzco." In *Ethnicity, Markets and Migration in the Andes*, edited by Brooke Larson, Olivia Harris, and Enrique Tandeter, 329–48. Durham, N.C.: Duke University Press, 1995.

de Lima Costa, Claudia. "Being Here, Writing There: Gender and the Politics of Translation in a Brazilian Landscape." *Signs* 25, no. 3 (2000): 727–60.

———. "Lost (and Found?) in Translation: Feminisms in Hemispheric Dialogue." *Latino Studies* 4 (2006): 1–2.

Dhawan, Nikita. "Transitions to Justice." In Buckley-Zistel and Stanley, *Gender in Transitional Justice* 264–283.

Dixon, Rosalind. "Rape as a Crime in International Humanitarian Law: Where to from Here?" *European Journal of International Law* 13, no. 3 (2002): 697–719.

"Documento elaborado por mujeres peruanas denunciando la violacion de sus derechos humanos y exigiendo el cumplimiento de los mismos." N.p.: Lima, 1992.

Dombrowski, Nicole Ann, ed. *Women and War in the Twentieth Century*. New York: Garland, 1999.

Dorf, Julie, and Glora Careaga Pérez. "Discrimination and the Tolerance of Difference: International Lesbian Human Rights." In Peters and Wolper, *Women's Rights Human Rights*, 324–34.

Drinot, Paulo. *The Allure of Labor: Workers, Race, and the Making of the Peruvian State*. Durham, N.C.: Duke University Press, 2011.

Drzewieniecki, Johanna. "Coordinadora Nacional de Derechos Humanos: Un estudio de caso." In *Sociedad civil, esfera pública, y democratización en América Latina*, edited by Aldo Panfichi. Lima: Pontificia Universidad Católica del Perú, 2002.

Eckstein, Susan Eva, and Timothy P. Wickham-Crowley. *What Justice? Whose Justice?* Berkeley: University of California Press, 2003.

"El Fusil y las Flores." *VIVA!* 2, no. 5 (1985): 4–5.

Enloe, Cynthia. *Maneuvers*. Berkeley: University of California Press, 2000.

Escalante, Carmen. "Warmi Kay (Ser Mujer)." *Mujer y Sociedad* 7, no. 12 (1987): 18–19.

Escobar, Arturo. *Encountering Development*. Princeton, N.J.: Princeton University Press, 1995.

———. "Latin America at a Crossroads." *Cultural Studies* 24, no. 1 (2010): 1–65.

———. "Mundos y conocimientos de otro modo. El program de investigación de modernidad/colonialidad Latinoamericano." *Tabula Rasa* 1 (2003): 51–86.

Escribens, Paula, Diana C. Portal Farfán, Silvia Ruiz, and Tesania Velázquez. "Escuchando las voces de la comunidad de Manta—Huancavelica: Construyendo/recogiendo/reconociendo nociones de salud mental, justicia y reparación." Lima: DEMUS, 2007.

Escribens, Paula, Diana Portal, Silva Ruiz, and Tesania Velázquez, *Reconociendo Otros Saberes: Salud mental comunitaria, justicia y reparación*. Lima: DEMUS, 2008.

Escribens, Paula, and Silvia Ruiz. "La experiencia de manta: Intersubjectividad e interculturalidad." Paper delivered at the 16th Latin American Psychoanalysis Conference (FEPAL), October 5–8, 2006.

Estudio para la Defensa de los Derechos de la Mujer (DEMUS). "Violencia sexual durante el conflico armado interno peruano." Lima: DEMUS, 2005.

Ewig, Christine. *Second-Wave Neoliberalism: Gender, Race and Health Sector Reform in Peru*. University Park: Penn State University Press, 2010.

Ewig, Christine. "Hijacking Global Feminism: Feminists, the Catholic Church, and the Family Planning Debacle in Peru." *Feminist Studies* 32, no. 3 (2006): 632–59.

Facio, Alda. "From Basic Needs to Basic Rights." In *Women and Rights*, edited by Caroline Sweetman, 16–22. Oxford: OXFAM, 1995.

Facio, Alda, and Lorena Fries, eds. *Género y Derecho*. Chile: LOM, 1999.

"Feminismo y Mujeres de Sectores Populares." *Mujer y Sociedad* 6, no. 10 (1986): 4–6.

Francke, Marfil. "Género, clase y etnía: La trenza de la dominación." In *Tiempos de ira y amor: Nuevos actores para viejos problemas*, edited by Carlos Iván Degregori et al., 79–103. Lima: DESCO, 1990.

Franco, Jean. "The Crisis of Liberalism and the Case for Subalternity." *A Contracorriente: Una revista de historia social y literatura de América Latina* 7, no. 1 (2009).

Franke, Katherine. "Gendered Subjects of Transitional Justice." *Columbia Journal of Gender and the Law* 15, no. 3 (2006): 813–28.

Fregoso, Rosa Linda. "We Want Them Alive! The Politics and Culture of Human Rights." *Social Identities* 12, no. 2 (2006): 109–38.

Friedman, Elisabeth. "Women's Human Rights: The Emergence of a Movement." In Peters Wolper, *Women's Rights Human Rights*, 18–35.

Fuller, Norma, ed. *Jerarquías en jaque: Estudios de género en el area Andina.* Lima: Red para el Desarrollo de las Ciencias Sociales en el Perú CLASCO, 2004.

———, ed. *Interculturalidad y política: Desafíos y posibilidades.* Lima: Red para el Desarrollo de las Ciencias Sociales en el Peru, 2005.

García, María Elena. "Introduction: Indigenous Encounters in Contemporary Peru." *Latin American and Caribbean Ethnic Studies* 3, no. 3 (2008): 217–26.

———. *Making Indigenous Citizens: Identity, Development and Multicultrual Activism in Peru.* Stanford: Stanford University Press, 2005.

———. "The Politics of Community: Education, Indigenous Rights, and Ethnic Mobilization in Peru." *Latin American Perspectives* 30, no.1 (2003): 70–95.

Garcia, María Elena, and Antonio Lucero. "¿Un País Sin Indígenas? Rethinking Indigenous Politics in Peru." In *The Struggle for Indian Rights in Latin America*, edited by Nancy Grey Postero and Leon Zamsc, 158–88. Brighton: Sussex Academic, 2004.

Garcia, María Elena, and José Antonio Lucero. "Authenticating Indians and Movements: Interrogating Indigenous Authenticity, Social Movements, and Fieldwork in Contemporary Peru." In *Histories of Race and Racism: The Andes and Mesoamerica from Colonial Times to the Present*, edited by Laura Gotkowitz, 278–98. Durham, N.C.: Duke University Press, 2011.

———. "Sobre indígenas y movimientos: Reflexiones sobre la autenticidad indígena, los movimientos sociales y el trabajo de campo en el Perú contemporáneo." In *Formaciones de indianidad: Articulaciones raciales, mestizaje y nación en América Latina*, edited by Marisol de la Cadena, 327–53. Bogota-Lima: Envión, 2007.

Gardam, Judith, and Hilary Charlesworth. "Protection of Women in Armed Conflict." *Human Rights Quarterly* 22 (2000): 148–66.

Gardam, Judith, and Michelle J. Jarvis. *Women, Armed Conflict and International Law.* The Hague: Kluwer Law International, 2001.

Getgen, Jocylyn E. "Untold Truths: The Exclusion of Enforced Sterilizations from the Peruvian Truth Commission's Final Report." *Boston College Third World Law Journal* 29, no. 1 (2009): 1–34.

Giles, Wenona, Malathi de Alwis, Edith Klein, and Neluka Silva. *Feminists under Fire: Exchanges Across War Zones.* Toronto: Between the Lines, 2003.

Giles, Wenona, and Jennifer Hyndman. *Sites of Violence: Gender and Conflict Zones.* Berkeley: University of California Press, 2004.

Godenzzi, Juan Carlos. "The Discourses of Diversity: Language, Ethnicity and Interculturality in Latin America." In *Cultural Agency in the Americas*, edited by Doris Sommer, 146–66. Durham, N.C.: Duke University Press. 2006.

Gonzalez-Cueva, Eduardo. "Conscription and Violence in Peru." In "Violence, Coercion, and Rights in the Americas," special issue, *Latin American Perspectives* 27, no. 3 (2000): 88–102.

Goodale, Mark. "Legal Ethnography in an Era of Globalization: The Arrival of Western Human Rights Discourse to Rural Bolivia." In Starr and Goodale, *Practicing Ethnography in Law*, 50–71.

Goodale, Mark, and Sally Engle Merry, eds. *The Practice of Human Rights*. Cambridge: Cambridge University Press, 2007.

Gorriti, Gustavo. *The Shining Path: A History of the Millenarian War in Peru*. Chapel Hill: University of North Carolina Press, 1999.

Grabham, Emily, Davina Cooper, Jane Krishnadas, and Didi Herman. *Intersectionality and Beyond: Law, Power and the Politics of Location*. New York: Routledge-Cavendish, 2009.

Grandin, Greg. "The Instruction of Great Catastrophe: Truth Commissions, National History and State Formation in Argentina, Chile and Guatemala." *American Historical Review* 110, no. 1 (2007): 46–67.

Gready, Paul. *The Era of Transitional Justice: The Aftermath of the Truth and Reconciliation Commission in South Africa and Beyond*. New York: Routledge, 2011.

Greene, Shane. "Getting over the Andes: The Geo-Eco-Politics of Indigenous Movements in Peru's Twenty-First-Century Inca Empire." *Journal of Latin American Studies* 38, no. 2 (2006): 327–54.

———. *Customizing Indigeneity*. Stanford: Stanford University Press, 2009.

Grewal, Inderpal. "'Women's Rights as Human Rights': Feminist Practices, Global Feminism, and Human Rights Regimes in Transnationality." *Citizenship Studies* 3, no. 3 (1999): 337–54.

Grewal, Inderpal, and Caren Kaplan, ed. *Scattered Hegemonies*. Minneapolis: University of Minnesota Press, 1994.

Guillerot, Julie. "Linking Gender and Reparations in Peru: A Failed Opportunity." In Rubio-Marín, *What Happened to the Women?* 136–93.

Guillerot, Julie, and Lisa Magrrell. *Memorias de un proceso inacabado*. Lima: APRODEH, 2006.

Harris, Angela P. "Race and Essentialism in Feminist Legal Theory." *Stanford Law Review* 42, no. 3 (1990): 581–616.

Haworth, Nigel. "Radicalization and the Left in Peru, 1976–1991." In *The Latin American Left from the Fall of Allende to Perestroika*, edited by Barry Carr and Steve Ellner, 41–59. Boulder, Colo.: Westview, 1993.

Hayner, Priscilla. *Unspeakable Truths: Facing the Challenge of Truth Commissions*. New York: Routledge, 2011.

Hays-Mitchell, Maureen. "Who Are the Victims? Where Is the Violence? The Spatial Dialectics of Andean Violence as Revealed by the Truth and Reconciliation Commission of Peru." In *War, Citizenship, Territory*, edited by Deborah Cowen and Emily Gilberts, 199–218. New York: Routledge, 2007.

———. "Women's Struggles for Sustainable Peace in Post-Conflict Peru: A Feminist Analysis of Violence and Change." In *A Companion to Feminist Geography*, edited by Lise Nelson and Joni Seager, 590–606. Malden, Mass.: Blackwell, 2005.

Henríquez Ayín, Narda. Z. "Códigos de género y vida cotidiana en el conflicto armado en el Perú." Paper delivered at the Latin American Studies Association Conference, Montreal, Canada, 2007.

———. *Cuestiones de género y poder en el conflicto armado en el Perú.* Lima: CONCYTEC, 2006.

———. "En nombre de la justicia y del buen gobierno." *Coyuntura: Análisis económico y social de actualidad* 2, no. 6 (2006): 24–29.

———. "Movimientos sociales en la encrucijada: Ensayos y crónicas sobre el movimiento de mujeres, de los 70 a los 90." N.p.: Lima. 1993.

Henríquez Ayín, Narda Z., and Rosa María Alfaro, eds. *Mujeres, violencia y derechos humanos.* Madrid: IEPALA, 1991.

Henríquez Ayín, Narda Z., and Julissa Mantilla Falcón. *Contra viento y marea: Cuestiones de género y poder en la memoria colectiva.* Lima: Comisión de Verdad y Reconciliación, 2003.

Hinojosa, Iván. "On Poor Relations and the Nouveau Riche: Shining Path and the Radical Left." In Stern, *Shining Path and Other Paths*, 60–83.

Hirsch, Susan. "Feminist Participatory Research on Legal Consciousness." In Starr and Goodale, *Practicing Ethnography in Law*, 13–33. New York: Palgrave Macmillan, 2002.

Incite! Women of Color against Violence. *Color of Violence.* Cambridge: South End, 2006.

———, ed. *The Revolution Will Not Be Funded.* Cambridge: South End, 2007.

Instituto Defensa Legal. "Protocolo para la investigación de casos de violación sexual en el conflicto armado interno." Lima: Instituto Defensa Legal. 2010.

Jelin, Elizabeth. "Women, Gender and Human Rights." In Jelin and Hershberg, *Constructing Democracy*, 177–96.

Jelin, Elizabeth, and Eric Hershberg, eds. *Constructing Democracy: Human Rights, Citizenship and Society in Latin America.* Boulder, Colo.: Westview, 1996.

Kapur, Ratna. "The Tragedy of Victimization Rhetoric: Resurrecting the "Native" Subject in International/Post-Colonial Feminist Legal Politics." *Harvard Human Rights Journal* 15 (2002): 1–38.

———. *Erotic Justice: Law and the New Politics of Postcolonialism.* London: Glasshouse, 2005.

Keck, Margaret, and Kathryn Sikkink. *Activists beyond Borders.* Ithaca, N.Y.: Cornell University Press, 1998.

Kelly, Liz. "Wars against Women: Sexual Violence, Sexual Politics and the Militarized State." In *States of Conflict: Gender, Violence and Resistance*, edited by Susie Jacobs, Ruth Jacobson, and Jennifer Marchbank, 45–65. New York: Zed, 2000.

King, Deborah. K. "Multiple Jeopardy, Multiple Consciousness: The Context of a Black Feminist Ideology." *Signs* 14, no. 1 (1988): 42–72.

Krauss, Clifford. "Peru Congress Says Fujimori Is 'Unfit' and Picks Successor." *New York Times*, November 22, 2000.

Kristeva, Julia. *Powers of Horror: An Essay on Abjection*. New York: Columbia University Press, 1982.

Lagarde y de los Ríos, Marcela. "Preface: Feminist Keys for Understanding Feminicide: Theoretical, Political and Legal Construction." In *Terrorizing Women: Feminicide in the Americas*, edited by Rosa Linda Fregoso and Cynthia Bejarano, xi–xxv. Durham, N.C.: Duke University Press, 2010.

Laplante, Lisa. J. "On the Indivisibility of Rights: Truth Commissions, Reparations, and the Rights to Development." *Yale Human Rights and Development Law Journal* 10 (2007): 141–77.

———. "Transitional Justice and Peace Building: Diagnosing and Addressing the Socioeconomic Roots of Violence through a Human Rights Framework." *International Journal of Transitional Justice* 2 (2008): 331–55.

Laplante, Lisa J., and Kelly Phenicie. "Media, Trials and Truth Commissions: 'Mediating' Reconciliation in Peru's Transitional Justice Process." *International Journal of Transitional Justice* 4 (2010): 207–29.

Latin American and the Caribbean Committee for the Defense of Women's Rights (CLADEM). "Shadow Report at Seventh and Eighth Periodic Report of the Peruvian State, for the 58th Session of the CEDAW Committee." Lima: June 2014.

Lazreg, Marnia. "The Triumphant Discourse of Global Feminism: Should Other Women Be Known?" In *Going Global: The Transnational Reception of Third World Women Writers*, edited by Amal Amireh and Lisa Suhair Majaj, 29–38. New York: Garland, 2000.

Leebaw, Bronwyn Anne. "The Irreconcilable Goals of Transitional Justice." *Human Rights Quarterly* 30, no. 1 (2008): 95–118.

Leiby, Michele. "Digging in the Archives: The Promise and Perils of Primary Documents." *Politics Society* 37 (2009): 75–99.

Lindsey-Curtet, Charlotte. *Women Facing War: ICRC Report on the Impact of Armed Conflict on Women*. Geneva: ICRC, 2001.

Lockwood, Bert B., ed. *Women Rights: A Human Rights Quarterly Reader*. Baltimore, Md.: Johns Hopkins University Press, 2006.

López Jiménez, Sinesio. "Estado, regimen político e institucionalidad en el Perú (1950–1994)." In *El Perú Frente al Siglo 21*, edited by Gonzalo Portocarrero and Marcel Valcéarcel, 543–85. Lima: Pontificia Universidad Católica del Perú Fondo Editorial, 1995.

Lorentzen, Lois Ann, and Jennifer Turpin. *The Woman and War Reader.* New York: New York University Press, 1998.

Lugones, Maria. "Heterosexualism and the Colonial/Modern Gender System." *Hypatia* 22, no. 1 (2007): 186–209.

———. "Toward a Decolonial Feminism." *Hypatia* 25, no. 1 (2010): 742–59.

Lutz, Helma, Maria Teresa Herrera Viva, and Linda Supik. *Framing Intersectionality: Debates on a Multi-Faceted Concept in Gender Studies.* Burlington, Vt.: Ashgate, 2011.

Maese-Cohen, Marcelle. "Introduction: Toward Planetary Decolonial Feminisms." *Qui Parle* 18, no. 2 (2010): 3–27.

Mahmood, Saba. "Feminist Theory, Embodiment, and the Docile Agent: Some Reflections on the Egyptian Islamic Revival." *Cultural Anthropology* 16, no. 2 (2001): 202–36.

Mani, Rama. "Editorial Dilemmas of Expanding Transitional Justice; or, Fording the Nexus between Transitional Justice and Development." *International Journal of Transitional Justice* 2 (2008): 253–65.

Manrique, Nelson. *El tiempo del miedo: La violencia política en el Perú 1980–1996.* Lima: Fondo Editorial del Congreso del Perú, 2002.

———. "Memoria y violencia: La nación y el silencio." In *Batallas por la memoria: Antagonismos de la promesa peruana*, edited by Santiago López Maguiña, Gonzalo Portocarrero, and Víctor Vich, 421–33. Lima: Red para el desarrollo de las ciencias sociales en el Perú, 2003.

Mantilla, Julissa. *Gender, Justice and Truth Commissions.* Washington D.C.: World Bank, 2006.

———. "La Perspectiva de género en la búsqueda de la verdad, la justicia y la reconciliación: El caso del Perú." In *Más Allá de la Justicia: Justicia y Género en América Latina*, edited by Luisa Cabal and Cristina Motta, 415–44. Bogotá: Siglo del Hombre, 2006.

———. "The Peruvian Case: gender and transitional justice." In Yarwood, *Women and Transitional Justice*, 184–97.

Mantilla Falcón, Julissa. "Gender and Human Rights: Lessons from the Peruvian Truth and Reconciliation Commission." In *Feminist Agendas and Democracy in Latin America*, edited by Jane S. Jaquette, 129–41. Durham, N.C.: Duke University Press, 2009.

Martinez Salazar, Elga. *Global Coloniality of Power in Guatemala: Racism, Genocide, Citizenship.* Lanham, Md.: Lexington, 2012.

———. "State Terror and Violence as a Process of Lifelong Teaching-Learning: the Case of Guatemala." *International Journal of Lifelong Education* 27, no. 2 (2008): 201–16.

Matsuda, Mari J. "When the First Quail Calls: Multiple Consciousness as Jurisprudential Method." *Women's Rights Law Reporter* 7, no. 9 (1989): 7.

McClintock, Anne. *Imperial Leather.* New York: Routledge, 1995.

McClintock, Cynthia. "Peru's Sendero Luminoso Rebellion: Origins and Trajectory."
In *Power and Popular Protest: Latin American Social Movements*, edited by Susan
E. Eckstein et al., 61–101. Berkeley: University of California Press, 2001.

———. *Revolutionary Movements in Latin America: El Salvador's FMLN and Peru's
Shining Path*. Washington D.C.: United States Institute for Peace, 1998.

McEvoy, Kieran. "Beyond Legalism: Towards a Thicker Understanding of Transitional
Justice." *Journal of Law And Society* 34, no. 4 (2007): 411–40.

Meertus, Julie A. *War's Offensive on Women: The Humanitarian Challenge in Bosnia,
Kosovo and Afghanistan*. Bloomfield: Kumarian, 2000.

Meintjes, Sheila. "Gender and Truth and Reconciliation Commissions: Comparative
Reflections." In Sriram and Pillay, *Peace versus Justice?* 96–112.

Meintjes, Sheila, Anu Pilay, and Meredeth Turshen, eds. *The Aftermath: Women in
Post-Conflict Transformation*. London: Zed, 2001.

Menjívar, Cecilia. *Enduring Violence: Ladina Women's Lives in Guatemala*. Berkeley;
University of California Press, 2011.

Merry, Sally E. *Human Rights and Gender Violence*. Chicago: University of Chicago
Press, 2006.

Mignolo, Walter. *The Darker Side of Western Modernity: Global Futures, Decolonial
Options*. Durham, N.C.: Duke University Press, 2011.

———. "Epistemic Disobedience, Independent Thought and Decolonial Freedom."
Theory Culture Society 26, nos. 7–8 (2009): 159–181.

———. *Local Histories/Global Designs*. Princeton, N.J.: Princeton University Press, 2000.

Mignolo, Walter, and Freya Schiwy. "Double Translation: Transculturation and the
Colonial Difference." In *Translations and Ethnography: The Anthropological Challenge of Intercultural Understanding*, edited by Tullio Maranhãs and Bernard Streck,
3–29. Tucson: University of Arizona Press, 2003.

Milton, Cynthia E. "At the Edge of the Peruvian Truth Commission: Alternative Paths
to Recounting the Past." *Radical History Review* 98 (2007): 3–33.

———. "Public Spaces for the Discussion of Peru's Recent Past." *Antípoda* 5 (2007):
143–68.

Minow, Martha. *Between Vengeance and Forgiveness: Facing History after Genocide
and Mass Violence*. Boston: Beacon, 1998.

Mohanty, Chandra T., and Jacqui Alexander. *Feminist Geneologies, Colonial Legacies
and Democratic Futures*. New York: Routledge, 1997.

Mohanty, Chandra T., Ann Russo, and Lourdes Torres, eds. *Third World Women and
the Politics of Feminism*. Bloomington: Indiana University Press, 1991.

Montoya, Rodrigo. "¿Por qué no hay en Perú un movimiento político indígena como
en Ecuador y Bolivia?" In *Movimiento Indígena en América Latina: Resistencia y
proyecto alternativo—Volumen 2*, edited by Raquel Gutiérrez and Fabiola Escar-
zada, 237—41. Puebla: Universidad Autónoma de Puebla, 2006.

Moorehead, Caroline. "Hostage to a Male Agenda." *Index on Censorship* 24, no. 4
(1995): 64–69.

Moser, Annalise. "Happy Heterogeneity? Feminism, Development, and the Grass-roots Women's Movement in Peru," *Feminist Studies* 30, no. 1 (2004): 211–37.

Moser, Caroline, and Fiona Clark. *Victims, Perpetrators or Actors? Gender, Armed Conflict and Political Violence.* London: Zed, 2001.

Municipalidad Distrital de Anco y Asociación Servicios Educativos Rurales (SER): *Anco, Haciendo Memoria.* Lima: SER, 2007.

Muvingi, Ismael. "Sitting on Powder Kegs: Socioeconomic Rights in Transitional Societies." *International Journal of Transitional Justice* 3, no. 2 (2009): 163–82.

Nagy, Rosemary. "Transitional Justice as Global Project: Critical Reflections." *Third World Quarterly* 29, no. 2 (2008): 275–89.

Nash, Jennifer. "Re-thinking Intersectionality," *Feminist Review* 89 (2008): 1–15.

Naveda Felix, Igidio. "The Reconstitution of Indigenous Peoples in the Peruvian Andes." *Latin American and Caribbean Ethnic Studies* 3, no. 3 (2008): 309–17

Neira, Eloy, and Patricia Ruiz Bravo. "Enfrentados al patrón: Masculinidades rurales en el medio rural peruano." In *Estudios Culturales: Discursos, poderes, pulsiones,* edited by López Maguiña, 211–31. Lima: Red para el Desarrollo del las Ciencias Sociales en el Perú, 2001.

Nesiah, Vasuki. "Discussion Lines on Gender and Transitional Justice: An Introductory Essay Reflecting on the ICTJ Bellagio Workshop on Gender and Transitional Justice." *Columbia Journal of Gender and the Law* 15, no. 3 (2006): 799–813.

———. "Truth Commissions and Gender: Principles, Policies and Procedures." International Center for Transitional Justice, Gender Justice Series. New York. 2006.

Ní Aoláin, Fionnuala. "Advancing Feminist Positioning in the Field of Transitional Justice." *International Journal of Transitional Justice* 6, no. 2 (2012): 205–28.

———. "Women, Security, and the Patriarchy of Internationalized Transitional Justice." *Human Rights Quarterly* 31, no. 4 (2009): 1055–85.

Ní Aoláin, Fionnuala, and Michael Hamilton. "Rule of Law Symposium: Gender and the Rule of Law in Transitional Societies." *Minnesota Journal of International Law* 18 (2009): 380–402.

Ní Aoláin, Fionnuala, Dina Francesca Haynes, and Naomi Cahn, eds. *On the Frontlines: Gender, War, and the Post-Conflict Process.* New York: Oxford University Press, 2012.

Ní Aoláin, Fionnuala, and Eilish Rooney. "Underenforcement and Intersectionality: Gender Aspects of Transition for Women." *International Journal of Transitional Justice* 1 (2007): 338–54.

Oliart, Patricia. "Indigenous Women's Organizations and the Political Discourses of Indigenous Rights and Gender Equity in Peru." *Latin American and Caribbean Ethnic Studies* 3, no. 3 (2008): 291–308.

Oosterveld, Valerie. "The Definition of 'Gender' in the Rome Statute of the International Criminal Court: A Step Forward or Back for International Criminal Justice?" *Harvard Human Rights Journal* 18 (2005): 55–84.

Orford, Anne. "Commissioning the Truth." *Columbia Journal of Gender and Law* 15, no. 3 (2006): 851–83.

Otto, Diane. "The Exile of Inclusion: Reflections on Gender Issues in International Law over the Last Decade." *Melbourne Journal of International Law* 10 (2009): 11–26.

———. "Lost in Translation: Re-Scripting the Sexed Subjects of International Human Rights Law." In *International Law and Its Others*, edited by Anne Orford, 318–56. Cambridge: Cambridge University Press, 2006.

Pankhurst, Donna, ed. *Gendered Peace: Women's Struggles for Post-War Justice and Reconciliation.* New York: Routledge, 2008.

———. "Post-War Backlash Violence against Women: What Can 'Masculinity' Explain?" in Parkhurst, *Gendered Peace*, 293–320.

Pateman, Carole. "Feminist Critiques of the Public/Private Dichotomy." In *Public and Private in Social Life*, edited by S. I. Benn and Gerald F. Gauss, 281–303. London: Marin, 1983.

Pateman, Carole, and Charles W. Mills. *Contract and Domination.* Cambridge: Polity, 2007.

Peters, J. S., and Andrea Wolper. *Women's Rights Human Rights: International Feminist Perspectives.* New York: Routledge, 1995.

Pieper Mooney, Jadwiga E. "Re-Visiting Histories of Modernization, Progress, and (Unequal) Citizenship Rights: Coerced Sterilization in Peru and in the United States." *History Compass* 8, no. 9 (2010): 1036–54.

Pistor, Katharina, Antara Halday, and Amrit Amirapu. "Social Norms, Rule of Law, and Gender Reality." Paper prepared for World Justice Forum, Vienna, July 2–5, 2008.

Poole, Deborah. "Between Threat and Guarantee: Justice and Community in the Margins of the Peruvian State." In *Anthropology in the Margins of the State*, edited by Veena Das and Deborah Poole, 35–65. Santa Fe: School of American Research Press, 2004.

Poole, Deborah, and Gerardo Renique. "Popular Movements, the Legacy of the Left and the Fall of Fujimori." *Socialism and Democracy* 14, no. 2 (2000): 53–74.

Portal, Diana. "Plan integral de reparaciones, una mirada de género." DEMUS, 2006.

Portal, Diana, and Flor de Maria Valdez. *Reflexiones sobre el marco jurídico de la violencia sexual antes, durante y después del conflicto armado interno peruano.* Lima: DEMUS, 2006.

Protocolo para la investigación de casos de violación sexual en el conflicto armado interno. Lima: Instituto Defensa Legal (IDL), 2010.

Quijano, Aníbal. "Coloniality of Power, Eurocentrism, and Latin America." *Napantla: Views from the South* 1, no. 3 (2000): 533–80.

Radcliffe, Sarah. "Indigenous Women, Rights and the Nation-state in the Andes." In *Gender and the Politics of Rights and Democracy in Latin America*, edited by Niki Craske and Maxine Molyneux, 149–72. New York: Palgrave, 2002.

Rehn, Elisabeth, and Ellen Johnson Sirleaf. *Women, War, Peace: The Independent Expert's Assessment on the Impact of Amred Conflict on Women and Women's Role in Peacebuilding.* New York: UNIFEM, 2002.

Reilly, Niamh. "Cosmopolitan Feminism and Human Rights." *Hypatia* 22, no. 4 (2007): 180–98.

Reynaga Farfán, Gumercinda. "Cambios en las relaciones familiares campesinas a partir de la volencia política y el nuevo rol de la mujer." Documento de trabajo 75, serie talleres 3. Proyecto "II Taller de Investigación con profesores universitarios." Fundación Ford. Lima: Instituto de Estudios Peruanos. 1996.

Rimmer, Susan Harris. *Gender and Transitional Justice: The Women of East Timor.* New York: Routledge, 2010.

Rodriguez Beruff, Jorge. "The Right-Wing Offensive in Peru and the General Strike of July 1977." *Social Scientist* 6, no. 10 (1978): 69–73.

Roht-Arriaza, Naomi, Hugo Van Der Merwe, Victoria Baxter, and Audrey R. Chapman, eds. *Assessing the Impact of Transitional Justice: Challenges for Empirical Research.* Washington D.C.: United States Institute for Peace, 2009.

Romany, Celia. "Themes for a Conversation on Race and Gender in International Human Rights Law." In Wing, *Global Critical Race Feminism,* 53–66.

Root, Rebecca K. "Through the Window of Opportunity: The Transitional Justice Network in Peru." *Human Rights Quarterly* 31, no. (2009): 452–73.

———. *Transitional Justice in Peru.* New York: Palgrave Macmillan, 2012.

Ross, Fiona C. *Bearing Witness: Women and the Truth and Reconciliation Commission in South Africa.* London: Pluto, 2003.

———. "The South African Truth and Reconciliation Commission on Having Voice and Being Heard: Some After-Effects of Testifying Before." *Anthropological Theory* 3, no. 3 (2003): 325–41.

Rousseau, Stéphanie. "Populism from Above, Populism from Below." In *Gender Populism in Latin America: Passionate Politics,* edited by Karen Kampwirth, 140–61. University Park: Pennsylvania State University Press, 2010.

Rousseau, Stéphanie. *Women's Citizenship in Peru: The Paradoxes of Neopopulism in Latin America.* New York: Palgrave Macmillan, 2009.

Rubio, Miguel Zapata. 2008. *El cuerpo ausente.* Lima: Grupo Cultural Yuyachkani.

Rubio-Marín, Ruth ed. *What Happened to the Women?* New York: Social Science Research Council, 2006.

Rubio-Marín, Ruth, and Pablo de Greiff. "Women and Reparations." *International Journal of Transitional Justice* 1 (2007): 318–37.

Rubio-Marín, Ruth, Claudia Paz y Paz, and Julie Guillerot. "Indigenous Peoples and Claims for Reparation: Tentative Steps in Peru and Guatemala." In *Identities in Transition: Challenges for Transitional Justice,* edited by Paige Arthur, 17–53. New York: Cambridge University Press, 2011.

Ruiz Bravo, Patricia. "Andinas y criollas: Identidades femeninas en el medio rural peruano." In Fuller, *Jerarquías en jaque,* 283–320.

Ruiz Bravo, Patricia, and Eloy Neira. "Enfrentados al patron: Una aproximación al estudio de las masculinidades en el medio rural peruano." In *Estudios culturales*, edited by S. López Maguiña, Gonzalo Portocarrero, and Víctor Vich, 211–31. Lima: PUCP, 2001.

Ruiz Bravo, Patricia, and Eloy Neira. "Tiempo de mujeres: Del caos al orden venidero; Memoria, género e identidad en una comunidad andina." In *Batallas por la memoria: Antagonismos de la promesa peruana*, edited by Marita Hamann, Santiago López Maguiña, Gonzalo Portocarrero, and Víctor Vich, 393–419. Lima: Red para el desarrollo de las ciencias sociales en el Perú, 2003.

Ruiz Bravo, Patricia, Eloy Neira, and José Luis Rosales. "El orden patronal y su subversion." In *Clases sociales en el Peru: Visions y trayectorias*, edited by Orlando Plaza, 259–82. Lima: PUCP/CISEPA, 2007.

Ruiz Bravo, Patricia, and Tesania Velázquez. "La violencia política y su impacto en las mujeres." Lima: Comisión de la Verdad y la Reconciliación, 2003.

Salazar Luzula, Katia. "Género, violencia sexual y derecho penal en el período posterior al conflicto en el Perú." In *El legado de la verdad: La justicia penal en la transición peruana*, edited by Lisa Magrrell and Leonardo Filippini, 185–209. Lima: ICTJ-IDEHPUCP, 2006.

Santa Cruz Feminist of Color Collaborative. "Building on the Edges of Each Other's Battles." In "Interstices: Women of Color Feminist Philosophy," special issue, *Hypatia* 29, no. 1 (2014): 23–40.

Schiwy, Freya. *Indianizing Film: Decolonizing, the Andes, and the Question of Technology*. New Brunswick, N.J.: Rutgers University Press, 2009.

Schmidt, Gregory. "All the President's Women: Fujimori and Gender Equity in Peruvian Politics." In *The Fujimori Legacy: The Rise of Electoral Authoritarianism In Peru*, edited by Julio Carrión, 150–77. University Park: Pennsylvania State University Press, 2006.

Schutte, Ofelia. "Cultural Alterity: Cross-Cultural Communication and Feminist Theory in North-South Contexts." *Hypatia* 13, no. 2 (1998): 53–72.

———. "Engaging Latin American Feminisms Today: Method, Theory, Practice." *Hypatia* 26, no. 4 (2011): 783–803.

Scully, Pamela. "Gender, History and Human Rights." In *Gender and Culture at the Limits of Rights*, edited by Dorothy L. Hodgson, 17–31. Philadelphia: University of Pennsylvania Press, 2011.

Sharma, Arandhana, and Akhil Gupta, eds. *The Anthropology of the State: A Reader*. Malden, Mass.: Blackwell, 2006.

Sigsworth, Romi, and Nahla Valji. "Continuities of Violence against Women and the Limitations of Transitional Justice: The Case of South Africa." In Buckley-Zistel and Stanley, *Gender and Transitional Justice*, 115–35. New York: Palgrave Macmillan, 2012.

Sikkink, Katherine. "The Emergence, Evolution and Effectiveness of the Latin American Human Rights Network." In Jelin and Hershberg, *Constructing Democracy*, 59–84.

Silva Santiesteban, Rocío. *El factor asco: Basurización simbólica y discursos autoritarios en el Perú contemporáneo*. Lima: Red para el Desarrollo de las Ciencias Sociales en el Perú, 2009.

Sjoberg, Laura. *Gendering Global Conflict: Toward a Feminist Theory of War*. New York: Columbia University Press. 2013.

Spade, Dean. "Intersectional Resistance and Law Reform." *Signs* 38, no. 4. (2013): 1031–55.

Sriram, Chandra Lekha. "Introduction: Transitional Justice and Peacebuilding." In Sriram and Lekha, *Peace versus Justice?* 1–17.

Sriram, Chandra Lekha, Olga Martin-Ortega, and Johanna Herman. *War, Conflict and Rights: Theory and Practice*. New York: Routledge. 2010.

Sriram, Lekha, and Suren Pillay. *Peace versus Justice? The Dilemma of Transitional Justice in Africa*. Suffolk: Currey, 2010.

Starn, Orin, Carlos Iván Degregori, and Robin Kirk, eds. *The Peru Reader: History, Culture and Politics*. Durham, N.C.: Duke University Press, 1995.

Starr, June, and Mark Goodale. "Introduction Legal Ethnography: New Dialogues, Enduring Methods." In Starr and Goodale, *Practicing Ethnography in Law*, 1–10.

Starr, June, and Mark Goodale. *Practicing Ethnography in Law: New Dialogues, Enduring Methods*. New York: Palgrave Macmillan, 2002.

Stern, Steve. J. *Shining and Other Paths: War and Society in Peru, 1980–1995*. Durham, N.C.: Duke University Press, 1998.

Sullivan, Donna J. "The Public/Private Distinction in International Human Rights Law." In Peters and Wolper, *Women's Rights Human Rights*, 126–34. New York: Routledge, 1995.

———. "Women's Human Rights and the 1993 World Conference on Human Rights." *American Journal of International Law* 88, no. 1 (1994): 152–67.

Tamayo, Ana María. "ANFASEP y la lucha por la memoria de sus desaparecidos (1983–2000)." In Degregori et al., *Jamás tan cerca arremetió lo lejos*, 95–134.

Tanaka, Martín. *Los espejos y espejismos de la democracia y el colapso de un sistema de partidos en el Perú*. Lima: FLASCO, 1997.

Taylor, Diana. "Adiós Ayacucho." in *Stages of Conflict: A Critical Anthology of Latin American Theater and Performance*, edited by Diana Taylor and Sarah J. Townsend, 291–95. Ann Arbor: University of Michigan Press. 2008.

———. *Disappearing Acts: Spectacles of Gender and Nationalism in Argentina's "Dirty War."* Durham, N.C.: Duke University Press, 1997.

———. "Staging Traumatic Memory: Yuyachkani." In *The Archive and the Repertoire: Performing Cultural Memory in the Americas*, edited by Diana Taylor, 190–210. Durham, N.C.: Duke University Press, 2003.

Teitel, Ruti G. *Transitional Justice*. New York: Oxford University Press, 2000.

———. "Transitional Justice Genealogy." *Harvard Human Rights Journal* 16 (2003): 69–94.

Thayer, Mille. "Transnational Feminism: Reading Joan Scott in the Brazilian Sertão." *Ethnography* 2, no. 2 (2001): 243–71.

———. "Traveling Feminisms." In *Global Ethnography: Forces, Connections and Imaginations in a Postmodern World*, edited by Michael Burawoy, 203–34. Berkeley: University of California Press, 2000.

Theidon, Kimberly. *Entre prójimos: El conflicto armado interno y la política de la reconciliación en el Perú*. Lima: Instituto de Estudios Peruanos, 2004.

———. "Gender in Transition: Common Sense, Women, and War." *Journal of Human Rights* 6, no. 4 (2007): 453–78.

———. "Género en transición: Sentido común, mujeres y guerra." Paper delivered at the Latin American Studies Association Conference, Montreál, 2007.

———. *Intimate Enemies*. Philadelphia: Pennsylvania University Press, 2013.

———. "Reconstructing Masculinities: The Disarmament, Demobilization and Reintegration of Former Combatants in Colombia." *Human Rights Quarterly* 31, no. 1 (2009): 1–34.

Theidon, Kimberly, and Kelly Phenicie. With Elizabeth Muray. "Gender, Conflict and Peacebuilding: State of the Field and Lessons Learned from USIP Grantmaking." Washington D.C.: United States Institute for Peace. 2011.

Thorton, Margaret, ed. *Public and Private: Feminist Legal Debates*. Oxford: Oxford University Press, 1995.

Tlostanova, M. V., and Mignolo, Walter. *Learning to Unlearn: Decolonial Reflections from Eurasia and the Americas*. Columbus: Ohio State University Press, 2012.

"Tortura mediante abuso sexual." Coordinadora National de Derechos Humanos. Section 2.9. In *Análisis de la práctica de la tortura en el Perú*, 38–46, Lima, 1999.

Tsing, Anna. "Transitions as Translations." In *Transitions, Environments, Translations: Feminisms in International Politics*, edited by Joan Scott, Cora Kaplan, and Debra Keates. 253–72. New York: Routledge, 1997.

Tubino, Fidel. "El interculturalismo latinoamericano y los estados nationales." Paper delivered at the Latinamerican Forum on Interculturality, Citizenship and Education (FLAPE), November 2004.

Turshen, Meredeth, and Clotilde Twagiramariya, ed. *What Women Do in Wartime*. London: Zed, 1998.

"Un clamor de justicia." *Mujer y Sociedad* 7, no. 16 (1988): 4–5.

UN Women. 2011–2012 Progress of the World's Women. In Pursuit of Justice, Available at http://progress.unwomen.org (accessed November 15, 2014).

Valji, Nahla. *A Window of Opportunity? Making Transitional Justice Work for Women*. UNIFEM, 2010.

van der Merwe, Hugo, Victoria Baxter, and Audrey Chapman, *Assessing the Impact of Transitional Justice*. Washington, D.C.: United States Institute of Peace, 2009.

Vargas, Virginia. "Apuntes para una reflexión feminista sobre el movimiento de mujeres." In *Género, clase y raza en America Latina*, edited by L. Luna, 195–204. Barcelona: Promociones y Publicaciones Universitarias, 1991.

———. "Del silencio a la palabra." Paper presented at "De la Negación al Recono-cimiento," seminario de la Comisión de la Verdad, Lima, 2003.

———. *El movimiento feminista en el horizonte democrático peruano (décadas 1980–1990)*. Lima: Centro de la Mujer Peruana Flora Tristan, 2006.

———. "Mujeres por la democracia: Los conjuros contra la tentación de la igualdad en clave," *Cuestión de Estado*, September 2000.

Vásquez Sotelo, Roxana. "Los un@s y las otr@s: Feminisimos y derechos humanos." *Pensamiento Propio* 23 (2006): 171–204.

———. *Vientos del sur: Huellas de las mujeres en la conferencia de Viena*. Lima: CLA-DEM, 1993.

Velázquez, Tesania. "Reconociendo y Reconstuyendo Subjetividades: El Encuentro con Manta." In *Fronteras interiores: Identidad, diferencia y protagonismos de las mujeres*, edited by Maruja Barrig, 121–40. Lima: Instituto de Estudios Peruanos, 2007.

———. *Vivencias diferentes: La indocumentación entre las mujeres rurales del Perú*. Lima: DEMUS-OXFAM-DFID, 2004.

"Violencia sexual durante el conflico armado interno peruano." GACETADEMUS. Lima: DEMUS, 2006.

Visweswaran, Kamala. *Fictions of Feminist Ethnography*. Minneapolis: University of Minnesota Press, 1994.

Walsh, Catherine, Walter Migñolo, and Álvaro García Linera, eds. *Interculturalidad, descolonización del estado y del conocimiento*. Buenos Aires: Ediciones del Signo, 2006.

Wilson, Richard. A. *The Politics of Truth and Reconciliation in South Africa: Legiti-mizing the Post-Apartheid State*. Cambridge: Cambridge University Press, 2001.

Winants, Oliver. "The Interplay of Ethnicity, Gender and Sexual Violence During Wartime and in Coercive Interrogation: What Role for Human Dignity?" *Jura Falconis* 5 (2006–2007). DOI:www.law.kuleuven.be/jura/43n1/winants.html.

Wing, Adrien Katherine, ed. *Global Critical Race Feminism*. New York: New York University, 2000.

Wood, Elisabeth Jean, "Sexual Violence during War: Toward an Understanding of Variation." In *Order, Conflict and Violence*, edited by Stathis N. Kalyvus, Ian Sha-piro, and Tarek Masoud, 321–51. Cambridge: Cambridge University Press. 2008.

Wood, Stephanie. "A Woman Scored for the 'Least Condemned' War Crime: Prec-edent and Problems with Prosecuting Rape as a Serious War Crime in the Inter-national Criminal Tribunal for Rwanda." *Columbia Journal of Gender and Law* 13, no. 2 (2004): 274.

Yarwood, Lisa eds. *Women and Transitional Justice: The Experience of Women as Participants*. New York: Routledge. 2013.

Yashar, Deborah. "Contesting Citizenship: Indigenous Movements and Democracy in Latin America." *Comparative Politics* 31, no. 1 (1998): 23–42.

———. *Contesting Citizenship in Latin America: The Rise of Indigenous Movements and the Postliberal Challenge.* Cambridge: Cambridge University Press, 2005.

———. "Democracy, Indigenous Movements, and the Postliberal Challenge in Latin America." *World Politics* 52, no. 1 (1999): 76–104.

Yezer, Caroline. "Who Wants to Know? Rumors, Suspicions, and Opposition to Truth-Telling in Ayacucho." *Latin American and Caribbean Ethnic Studies* 3, no. 3 (2008): 271–89.

Youngers, Coletta. *Violencia Política y Sociedad Civil en el Perú.* Lima: Instituto de Estudios Peruanos, 2003.

Yuval-Davis, Nira. "Intersectionality and Feminist Politics." *European Journal of Women's Studies* 13, no. 3 (2006): 193–209.

Zinsstag, Estelle. "Sexual Violence against Women in Armed Conflicts: Standard Response and New Ideas." *Social Policy and Society* 5, no. 1 (2005): 137–48.

Zúñiga, Madeleine, and Modesto Gálvez. "Repensando la educación bilingüe intercultural en el Perú: Bases para una propuesta política." In Fuller, *Interculturalidad y política,* 309–27.

Index

Alcalde, Cristina, 14–15
Alexander, M. Jacqui, 114–15
ANFASEP. *See* National Association of
   Families of the Kidnapped, Detained, and
   Disappeared of Peru
Antezana, Ofelia, 26, 34
APRODEH. *See* Pro-Human Rights
   Association
armed forces, Peruvian, 23, 106, 117, 124–25
Arthur, Paige, 51–52
Ayacucho, department of, 4–6, 23, 38, 69,
   160–61

Barrig, Maruja, xi, 35, 47, 59, 120
binary logic, 56, 68, 79, 97, 158
Boesten, Jelke, 15

campesinas, 3, 23–24, 50, 115, 139
Carbovella, Mary, 139
Cárdenas, Nora, xi, 143, 187n8
CEAS. *See* Episcopal Commission of Social
   Action
CEDAW. *See* Convention for the
   Elimination of all forms of
   Discrimination against Women
Centro del la Mujer Peruana "Flora Tristan,"
   35, 174n26, 175n30
citizenship, 8, 49, 114, 136, 144–46
Ciurlizza, Javier, 44

CLADEM. *See* Latin American
   Committee for the Defense of Women's
   Rights
COFADER. *See* Committee of Family
   Members of the Disappeared
Cohen, Dara, 125
Coll, Pilar, 41, 93
colonialism, legacy of, 4, 7–8, 19–21, 69, 131
coloniality, 114–15, 143–51, 154, 168n74,
   188n29. *See also* modernity/coloniality
COMISEDH. *See* Commission on Human
   Rights
Commission on Human Rights, 38, 73, 139,
   159–60
Committee of Family Members of the
   Disappeared, 26, 34, 41–42
conceptual myopia regarding sexual
   violence, 9–11, 54, 66, 111, 127–28
Convention for the Elimination of all forms
   of Discrimination against Women, 11, 29,
   159–61, 167n29
convivencia, 133–34, 140, 143, 146, 148
Crisóstomo Meza, Mercedes, xi, 111–12, 116,
   118, 123

decolonial feminisms, 3, 7, 18, 21, 114, 158
Degregori, Carlos Iván, 41, 75, 80, 104,
   176n56
De la Cadena, Marisol, 7, 27

PASCHA BUENO-HANSEN is an assistant professor of women and gender studies and is affiliated with the Political Science and International Relations Department and the Latin American Studies Program at the University of Delaware.

The University of Illinois Press
is a founding member of the
Association of American University Presses.

Composed in 10.5/13 Minion Pro
by Kirsten Dennison
at the University of Illinois Press
Manufactured by Cushing-Malloy, Inc.

University of Illinois Press
1325 South Oak Street
Champaign, IL 61820–6903
www.press.uillinois.edu